SHADOWS IN A PHANTOM EYE

ATTRACTIONS & ABERRATIONS IN THE MOVING IMAGE

VOLUME EIGHT : 1928-1929

"At the same time, in every city of the world, a crowd exits the cinema and spills into the street like black blood. Like a powerful beast, it extends its thousand tentacles and, with a tiny effort, crushes palace and prison."

—Blaise Cendrars

"All film is equal"

—The Nocturne Group

SHADOWS IN A PHANTOM EYE
VOLUME EIGHT : 1928-1929

Conceived & Originated by — Black Gas Entertainment
Written, Researched, Translated & Edited by — The Nocturne Group
Designed & Typeset by — Broken Fang Cryptography
Additional Photographic Research by — Red-Hot Ryder
Published in 2024 by — Black Gas Books
By courtesy of — Bonefyre World Emporium
Copyright © 2024 by — The Nocturne Group
Rights — Worldwide
ISBN — 978-1-917285-07-0
https://black-gas.org

FOREWORD

ABOUT THE SERIES

Shadows In A Phantom Eye is a multi-volume publication investigating and documenting attractions and aberrations in the moving image from 1872 onwards. Attractions and aberrations are defined as filmed images and themes which exert a vicarious or even morbid fascination over the viewer; in early cinema, these included images of magic tricks, Satan and Hell, human freaks and anomalies, accidental deaths or executions, explosions and natural disasters, human zoos and ethnic stereotyping, drug abuse and alcoholism, voyeurism and nudity, science fiction and horror, walking skeletons, ghosts and seances, war and atrocities, surgical operations, disease admonitories, xenomorphic organisms, hypnosis, absurdist decapitations and destruction of the human body, crime and murder, animal cruelty and hunting, plane wrecks, train wrecks and car wrecks, daredevil stunts and chases, time-lapse cinematography and microcinematography, phantom rides, and other thrill-based visual phenomena. At the heart of these mediations was metamorphosis – the transmutation of matter, or reality itself, before the naked eye.

Shadows In A Phantom Eye includes information on thousands of films, many of them never before documented in the English language (including many from Japan and pre-revolutionary Russia, for example); within the book's text readers can trace histories of not only narrative cinema but also documentary, newsreel, science and medical, animation, and many other worldwide forms and genres of moving image, plus histories of exhibition modes, film technologies, censorship, special effects, art direction, and many other peripheral issues and disciplines.

The text also demonstrates how the history of film is directly intertwined with human history itself, and how early film was continually shaped by historical events such as war, scandal and crime, politics, art movements (such as Futurism and Surrealism), prohibitions, and other social forces.

In summary, **Shadows In A Phantom Eye** presents an unprecedented resource for all students of early cinema, with information on thousands of films from the silent era and beyond, and thousands of rare and often never-seen-before images.

ABOUT THE FORMAT

Each volume is arranged chronologically, by year. Within each year a selection of relevant films are alphabetically listed and discussed; each listing may also reference a number of other films, some dating from beyond the parameters of the volume. A complete index of film titles is also provided. This format means that the book can be used as an encyclopedia with easily referenced entries; however, the authors recommend that each volume also be read from cover to cover like a regular history book, since this is the only way that the ongoing history of attractions and aberrations in the moving image can be fully comprehended.

ABOUT THE ENTRIES

A large percentage – some say at least 90% – of all silent films are lost. This is due to various factors, including the ephemeral nature of early film stock, recycling, accidents, war, and simple neglect. Where films referenced in this book were not available to view, descriptions of them were constructed by cross-referencing a variety of surviving sources, including synopses, advertising materials, reviews, shooting scripts, censor records, posters, production and publicity photographs, news stories, memoirs, press releases, and all other relevant documentation. The book covers films from all countries of the world; all films are listed by their original titles, and translations into English by the book's authors are provided where necessary. The film director, production year and country are all clearly listed at the top of each entry, below the title; where a director is unknown, the film's production company is listed instead.

ABOUT THE ILLUSTRATIONS

The production photographs and other illustrations reproduced in this book and subsequent volumes were sourced both from the authors' private collections and from a large number of international film archives. Many of these images have never been previously published, or widely seen. The film archives visited in person include: MOMA, New York/Hamlin; Margaret Herrick Library, Los Angeles; UCLA, Los Angeles; USC, Los Angeles; Eastman House, Rochester; Library of Congress, Washington DC; BFI, London; Cineteca Nacional, Mexico City; UNAM, Mexico City; China Film Archives, Beijing; National Film Archive of Japan, Tokyo; Kawakita Memorial Library, Tokyo; Cinémathèque Française, Paris; Deutsche Kinemathek, Berlin; Národní Filmový Archiv, Praha; Nemzeti Filmintézet, Budapest; Filmoteca Española, Madrid; Cineteca Nazionale, Roma; Film Museum, Wien; and Theater Museum, Wien. Images were also sourced from: Deutsche Film Institut, Wiesbaden; Archivio Fotografico, Milano; and DFI, Copenhagen.

Wherever possible, images were scanned in high resolution from original, high quality photographs but, owing to the scarcity of visual materials from the early years of cinema, a relatively small percentage of images had to be derived from secondary sources such as frame enlargements, photograms, pre-printed lobby cards and postcards, or even magazines. The authors and publishers wish to apologize in advance for any discernible drop in quality in images taken from these secondary sources.

ABOUT THE INDEX

The book's index lists all film titles referenced in the text, including original foreign-language titles, translated release titles, alternative titles, and titles of unfilmed projects. A page number in bold type indicates an illustrated reference.

ABOUT THIS VOLUME

Volume Eight of **Shadows In A Phantom Eye** covers the period 1928-1929, when revolutions in sound, colour and widescreen technology gave rise to a new era in cinema's history. This volume references approximately 900 films, and contains around 250 photographic illustrations from film productions and also from relevant documentary sources.

ABOUT THE AUTHORS

The Nocturne Group is a cine-coven of thirteen film historians, all dedicated to researching and documenting the history of the moving image, and also to film restoration and preservation. They are also the proprietors of Black Gas Entertainment, a film blog.

SHADOWS IN A PHANTOM EYE

VOLUME EIGHT

THE FINISHING TOUCH (HAL ROACH, 1928) – PRODUCTION PHOTOGRAPH.

1928

BE MY KING – PRODUCTION PHOTOGRAPH.

BE MY KING
(Lupino Lane, 1928: USA)

Even as the decade drew towards its close, cannibal comedies were still on the movie-goer's menu; **Be My King** is another classic example, in which Lupino Lane, like many ship-wrecked sailors before him, ends up in the cooking-pot after rejecting the sexual advances of a grotesque female savage. Another, longer example of the sub-genre was **Why Sailors Go Wrong** (also 1928), an island picture with cannibals, wild beasts, and a notoriously rabid Jewish stereotype for good measure. Cannibal comedies were not only produced in the US, as **Hallo! Afrika Forude!** ("Ahoy! Africa Ahead!"), a 1929 film from Denmark illustrates. **Hallo! Afrika Forude!** was one of many movie farces made by Danish comedy duo Fyrtårnet and Bivognen, played by actors Carl Schenstrøm and Harald Madsen (a semi-midget). The duo began in 1921 and became renowned in many countries, primarily Germany where they were known as Pat and Patachon. **Hallo! Afrika Forude!** – released in German as **Pat Und Patachon Als Kannibalen** ("Pat And Patachon Go Cannibal") – was a feature-length adventure in which the pair end up on a ship bound for the dark continent, where they inevitably fall foul of the natives. A pair of white-girl stowaways add to the predictable antics, and the film also contains topless female nudity, something which would not be accepted in US comedies of the same period. Live-action cannibal comedies largely died out in the early days of sound; notable exceptions include Hal Roach's **Wild Babies** (1932), a typical white-men-in-cooking-pot farce, and Roach's **The Kid From Borneo** (1933), an **Our Gang** short in which the kids mistake a sideshow wild man for a genuine cannibal savage.

WHY SAILORS GO WRONG – PRODUCTION PHOTOGRAPH (*OPPOSITE TOP*); HALLO! AFRIKA FORUDE! – PRODUCTION PHOTOGRAPH (*OPPOSITE BOTTOM*).

WILD BABIES – PRODUCTION PHOTOGRAPH (*OVERLEAF*).

The BIRTH OF WHITE AUSTRALIA
(Phil K. Walsh, 1928: Australia)

Presumably an attempt by American Walsh to emulate the phenomenal success of D.W. Griffith's **Birth Of A Nation** for Australian audiences, **The Birth Of White Australia** features on two racially-oriented, historic cultural clashes; first, the initial murderous conflict between white settlers and native aboriginals, and second the Lambing Flat race riots of 1860-61, in which white and Chinese mine-workers clashed in the gold fields. These violent protests lasted for several months, with the Chinese repeatedly being driven away and subjected to physical assaults, and resulting in numerous arrests. By all accounts well-produced but flawed as narrative cinema, **The Birth Of White Australia** was not the hoped-for success, but remains a prime example of "white supremacist" propaganda film.

CHIKEMURI TAKADANOBABA
("Blood-Bath At Takadanobaba"; Daisuke Ito, 1928: Japan)

Ito, a key *chambara* director of the 1920s, presents the famous story of the *ronin* Nakayama Yasube (played by *kabuki*-trained action star Okochi Denhiro), who in 1694 slaughtered a vast number of swordsmen in a whirlwind of blood and death as they attacked his uncle. Only 6 minutes of this classic Nikkatsu swordplay film are known to survive; Ito's 1926 film **Chokon** ("The Grudge") is in a similar state; its 12 surviving minutes show wild camerawork, angles and editing bordering on experimental cinema. The story of Yasube at Takadanobaba was filmed numerous times, but his character is even better known as one of the 47 *ronin* featured in the *Chusingura*. Okochi Denjiro also starred in the Nikkatsu production **Chikemuri Kojinyama** ("Blood-Bath At Kojinyama", 1929), directed by Kichiro Tsuji. Denjiro's partnership with director Ito (and innovative cinematographer Karasawa Hiromitsu), established in the 3-part 1927 film **Chuji Tabi Nikki** ("Diary Of Chuji's Wanderings"), was instrumental in breaking the *chambara* genre to a wider audience.

CHOKON – PRODUCTION PHOTOGRAPH (*BELOW*).
CHIKEMURI KOJINYAMA – PRODUCTION PHOTOGRAPH (*OPPOSITE TOP*); CHUJI TABI NIKKI – PRODUCTION PHOTOGRAPH (*OPPOSITE BOTTOM*).

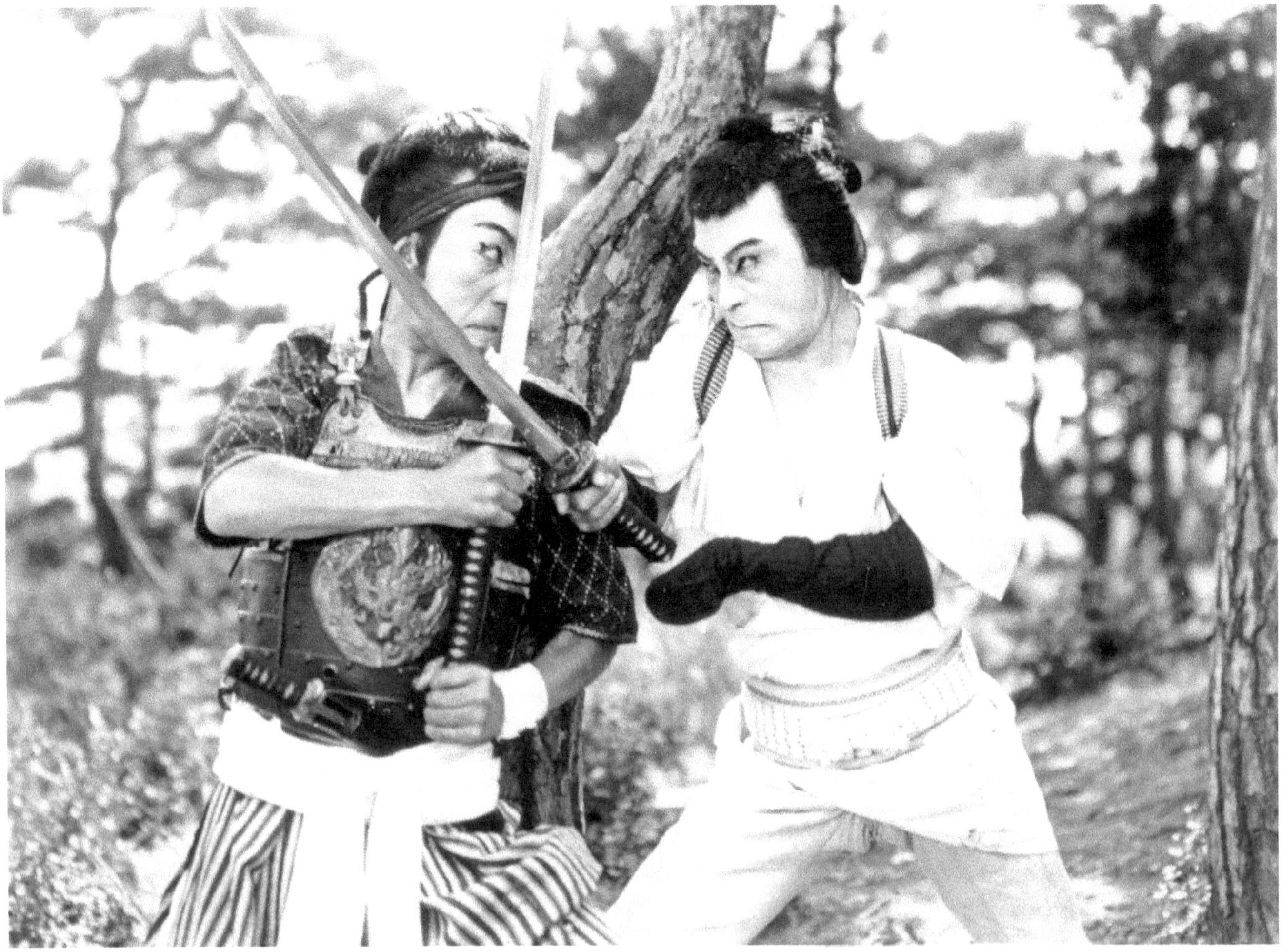

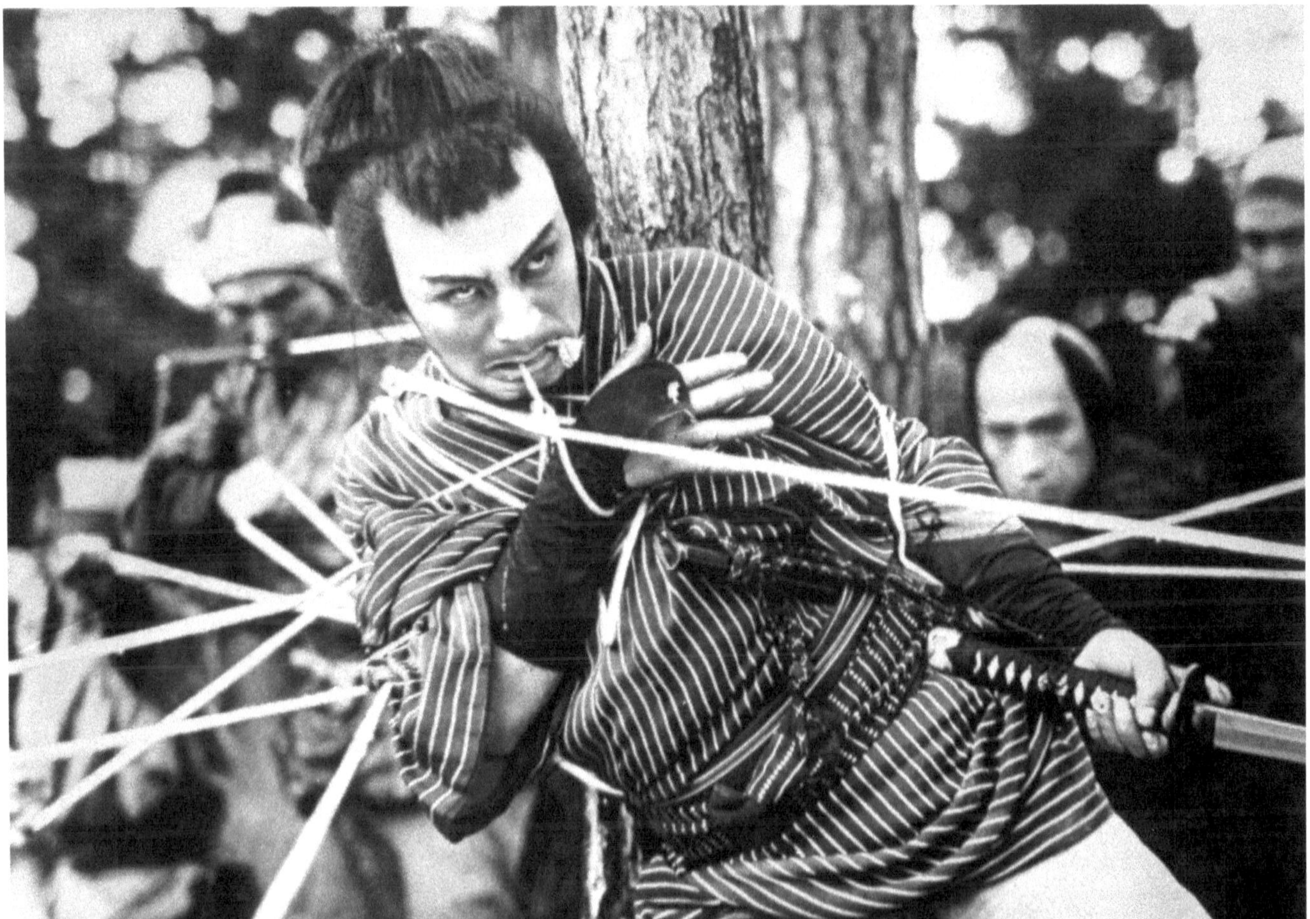

SHINPAN OOKA SEIDAN (TOA) – DAN TOKUMARO AS TANGE SAZEN; PRODUCTION PHOTOGRAPHS (*ABOVE & OPPOSITE PAGE*).

SHINPAN OOKA SEIDAN (MAKINO) – ARASHI KANJURO AS TANGE SAZEN; PRODUCTION PHOTOGRAPHS (*RIGHT*).

He was also renowned for multiple portrayals of Tange Sazen, the misogynistic, brutal, drunk, disfigured, one-armed, one-eyed *samurai* created in a comic strip by Fubou Hayashi in 1927. The first of these, Ito's 3-part **Shinpan Ooka Seidan** ("The Trial Of Ooka: New Edition", Nikkatsu 1928), was notorious for its brutal stance of rebellion and nihilism, and its challenging scenes of horrific violence. It also showcased actress Fushimi Naoe in a ground-breaking "bad girl" role, as a tattooed, pistol-wielding bandit slut. Tange Sazen – who was portrayed in ten films by various directors in 1928 alone – figured in at least another ten in the following pre-war years, culminating with a 4-part series from Toho that commenced with Kunio Watanabe's **Shinpen Tange Sazen: Yoto-Hen** ("New Tange Sazen: Demon Blade") in 1938. **Chikemuri Takadanobaba** was remade by Masahiro Makino in 1937.

1. **Shinpan Ooka Seidan** (Makino, 2 parts); **Shinpan Ooka Seidan** (Toa, 3 parts); **Shinpan Ooka Seidan** (Nikkatsu, 3 parts); **Ooka Seidan Suzukawa Genjuro** ("The Trial Of Ooka: Suzukawa Genjuro", Teikine); and **Ooka Seidan Suzukawa Genjuro** ("The Trial Of Ooka: Suzukawa Genjuro", Kawai Eiga). This followed the 1927 publication of the serial novel in the *Tokyo Nichinichi Shinbun*.

THE CHINATOWN MYSTERY – PRODUCTION PHOTOGRAPH.

The CHINATOWN MYSTERY
(J.P. MacGowan, 1928: USA)

MacGowan's 10-chapter yellow peril serial **The Chinatown Mystery** starred Joe Bonomo in perhaps his best strong-arm role as a Secret Service agent battling a nefarious Oriental villain, the Sphinx (played by Francis Ford), for possession of a formula for artificial diamonds. The serial's 10 chapters were: **The Chinatown Mystery; The Clutching Claw; The Devil's Dice; The Mysterious Thirteen; Galloping Fury; The Depth Of Danger; The Invisible Hand; The Wreck; Broken Jade;** and **The Thirteenth Hour**. The serial also featured many other silent serial stalwarts, including Sheldon Lewis, Paul Panzer, Duke Worne, Grace Cunard, and Helen Holmes, and showed that the mythic Chinatown was still a viable zone of cinematic thrills and mystery. Another Chinese villain was the Cobra, who in the sensationalistic American production **China Slaver** (1929) commanded an empire of drug trafficking and white slavery from a secluded island. The Cobra was played by Sojin Kamiyama, perhaps the leading Japanese actor known for such roles in the US; Kamiyama also featured in Pathé's 10-chapter serial **The Man Without A Face** (1928), directed by Spencer Gordon Bennet and starring Allene Ray.[1] Pathé's 10-chapter **The Tiger's Shadow**, also 1928, featured regular villain Frank Lacteen as Dr. Sandro, another exotic evil mastermind.[2] The first yellow peril movie shot with sound was William Wellman's **Chinatown Nights** (1929), started as a silent project and based on the story "Tong War" by Samuel Orbitz; it features Warner Oland in one of his many Oriental roles,

THE MAN WITHOUT A FACE – PRODUCTION PHOTOGRAPH.

THE TIGER'S SHADOW – PRODUCTION PHOTOGRAPH (*ABOVE*).

THE HAWK'S NEST – PRODUCTION PHOTOGRAPH (*OPPOSITE TOP*); THE HATCHET MAN – ACTORS IN YELLOWFACE; PRODUCTION PHOTOGRAPH (*OPPOSITE BOTTOM*).

as Chinese gangster Boston Charley. Wellman went on to shoot **The Hatchet Man** (1932), the story of a Tong assassin, with elements of drug abuse, adultery, and brutal killings (Tong assassins were known as "hatchet men" due to their propensity for hacking their victims into bloody pieces). The film is notable for boasting a complete cast of Chinese characters played by white actors, with names such as Wong Low Get, Bing Foo, and Lip Hop Fat. Not all Chinese in films were evil, however; in the underground American porno film **Chinese Love Life** (c.1925), a lucky man has explicit three-way sex with two horny Oriental hookers – a rare example of "mixed race" copulation in 1920s stag cinema.

1. The ten chapters of **The Man Without A Face** were: **A Perilous Mission**; **The Barrage**; **The Death Shell**; **The Abduction**; **The Mark Of Crime**; **The Road Of Peril**; **The Master Strikes**; **The Crime Craft**; **A Mysterious Visitor**; and **Unmasked**. It was set in Japan, and based on a story by A.M. Williamson. Sojin also appeared in C.C. Burr's **Chinatown Charlie** (1928), a yellow peril spoof which featured scenes of opium smoking and Anna May Wong in a typical role as a Chinese concubine, and in Benjamin Christensen's **The Hawk's Nest** (also 1928), which mixed yellow peril elements with the emergent gangster genre.

2. The ten chapters of **The Tiger's Shadow** were: **The Storm Breaks**; **The Tiger's Mark**; **The Secret Mission**; **The Danger Trail**; **The Gas Chamber**; **Behind The Clock**; **The Tiger's Claw**; **Prisoners In The Sky**; **A Desperate Chance**; and **The Sky Clears**. It was directed by Spencer Gordon Bennet.

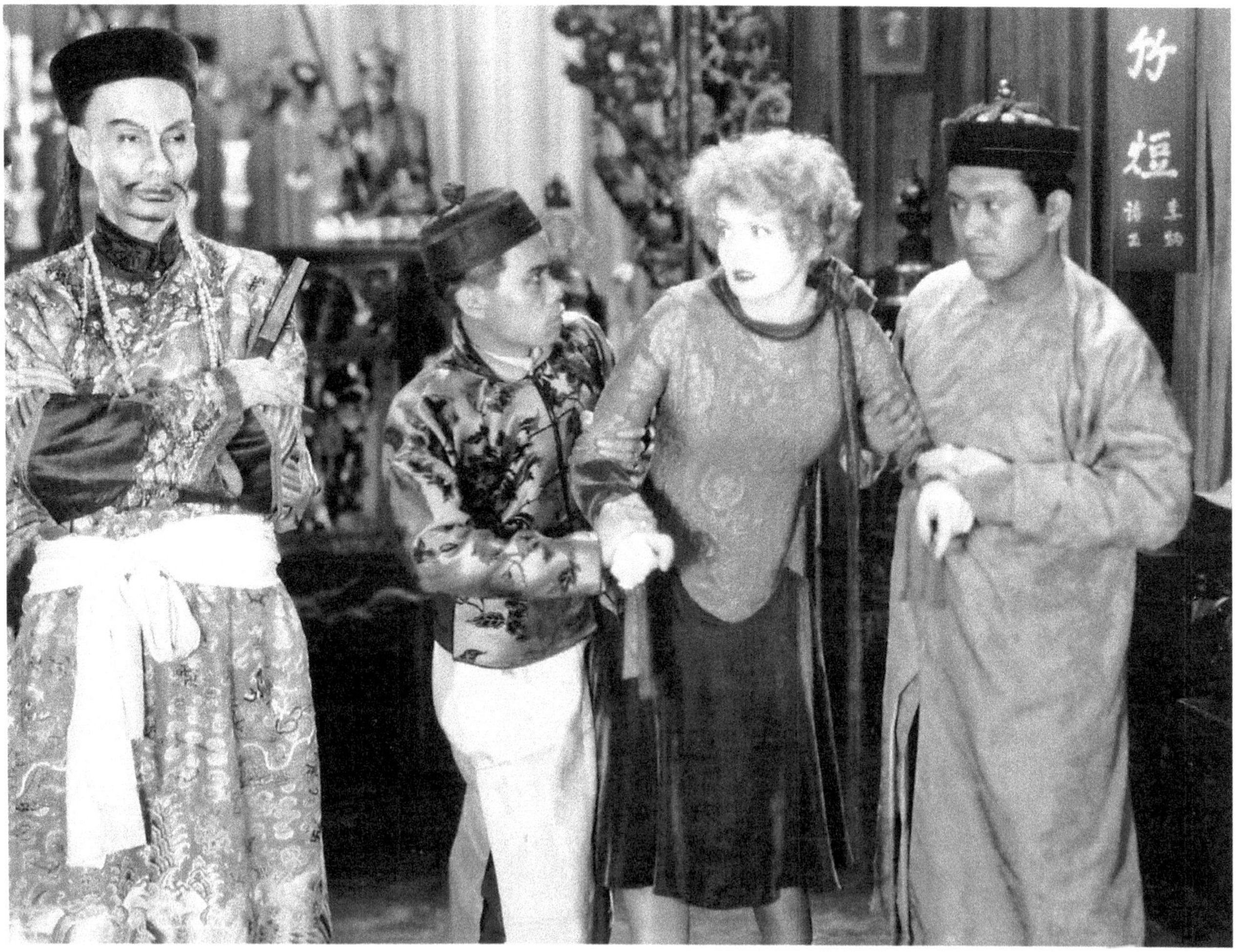

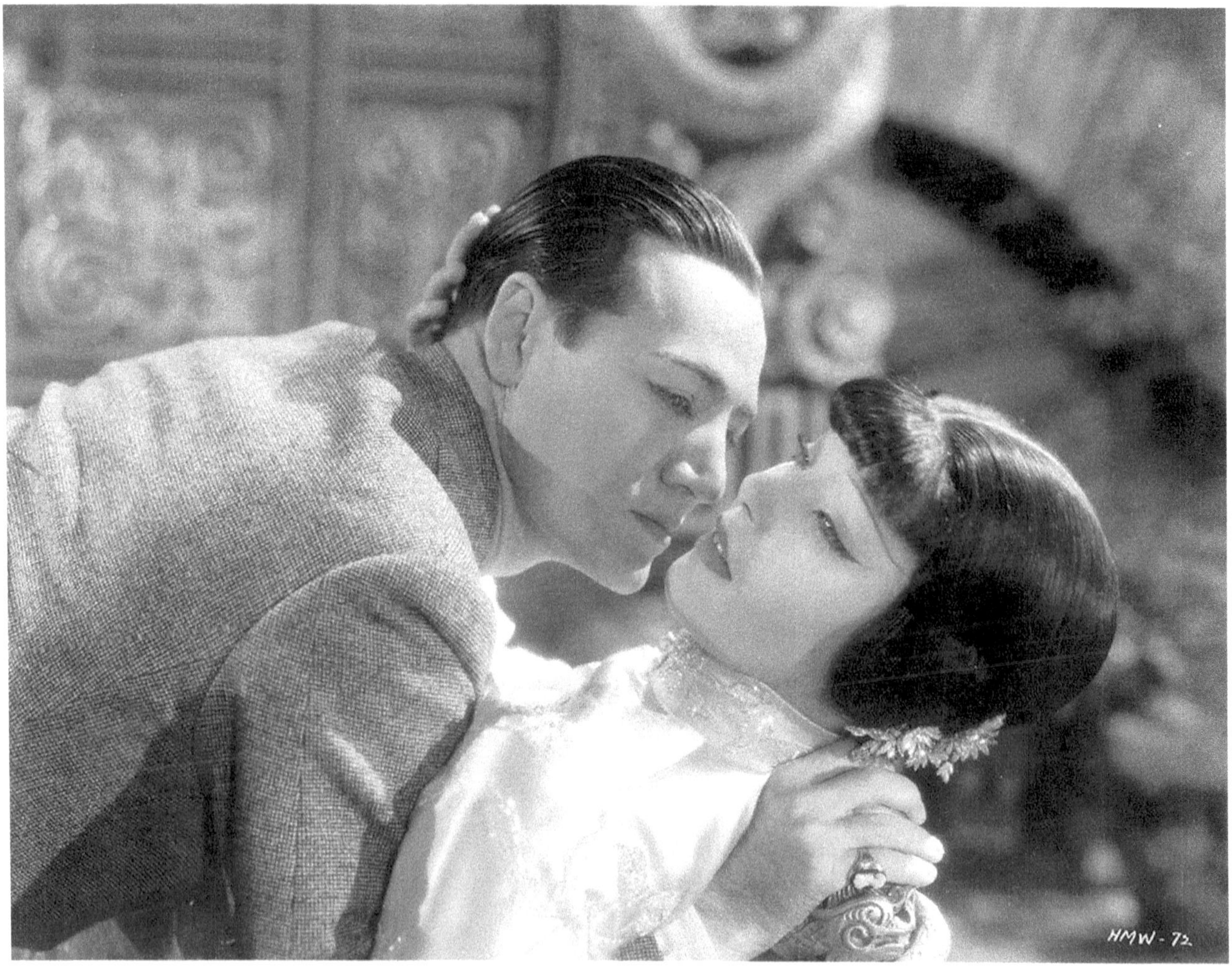
HMW - 72

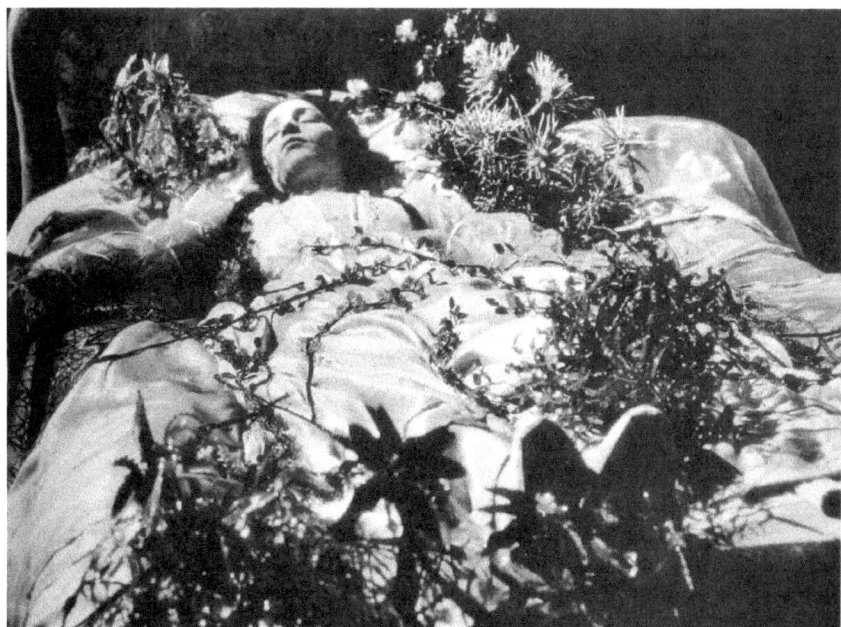

LA CHUTE DE LA MAISON USHER – PRODUCTION PHOTOGRAPHS (*OPPOSITE PAGE, ABOVE RIGHT & BELOW*); "LADY USHER" – PRODUCTION PAINTING BY THE FILM'S ART DIRECTOR PIERRE KEFER (*ABOVE*).

MOR VRAN – PHOTOGRAM (*BELOW RIGHT*).

La CHUTE DE LA MAISON USHER
("The Fall Of The House Of Usher"; Jean Epstein, 1928: France)

Assisted as second director by a young Luis Buñuel, Epstein produced a film of Poe which must be deemed impressionistic in its use of editing techniques and staging to represent the subjective mental and perceptual state of its characters. Taking elements from two "vampiric" Poe stories, "The Fall Of The House Of Usher" (1839) and "The Oval Portrait" (1850),[1] the film is marked by its mist-shrouded gothic atmosphere, complex lighting, deviant camera angles, and various experimental techniques, all employed to evoke a supernatural netherworld just within the limits of human vision. After this, Epstein turned to a form of poetic, quasi-documentary film-making with **Finis Terrae** ("Earth's End", 1929), the first in a Breton trilogy which continued with **Mor Vran** ("Sea Of Ravens", 1930) and **L'Or Des Mers** ("Gold Of The Seas", 1931).

1. Both first translated into French by Charles Baudelaire, and published in the 24-story anthology *Nouvelles Histoires Extraordinaires* ("New Extraordinary Tales", 1857).

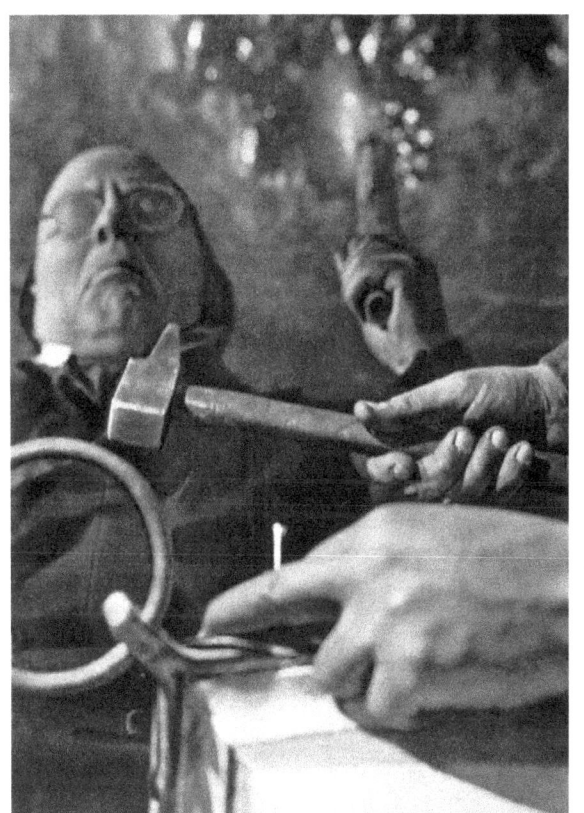

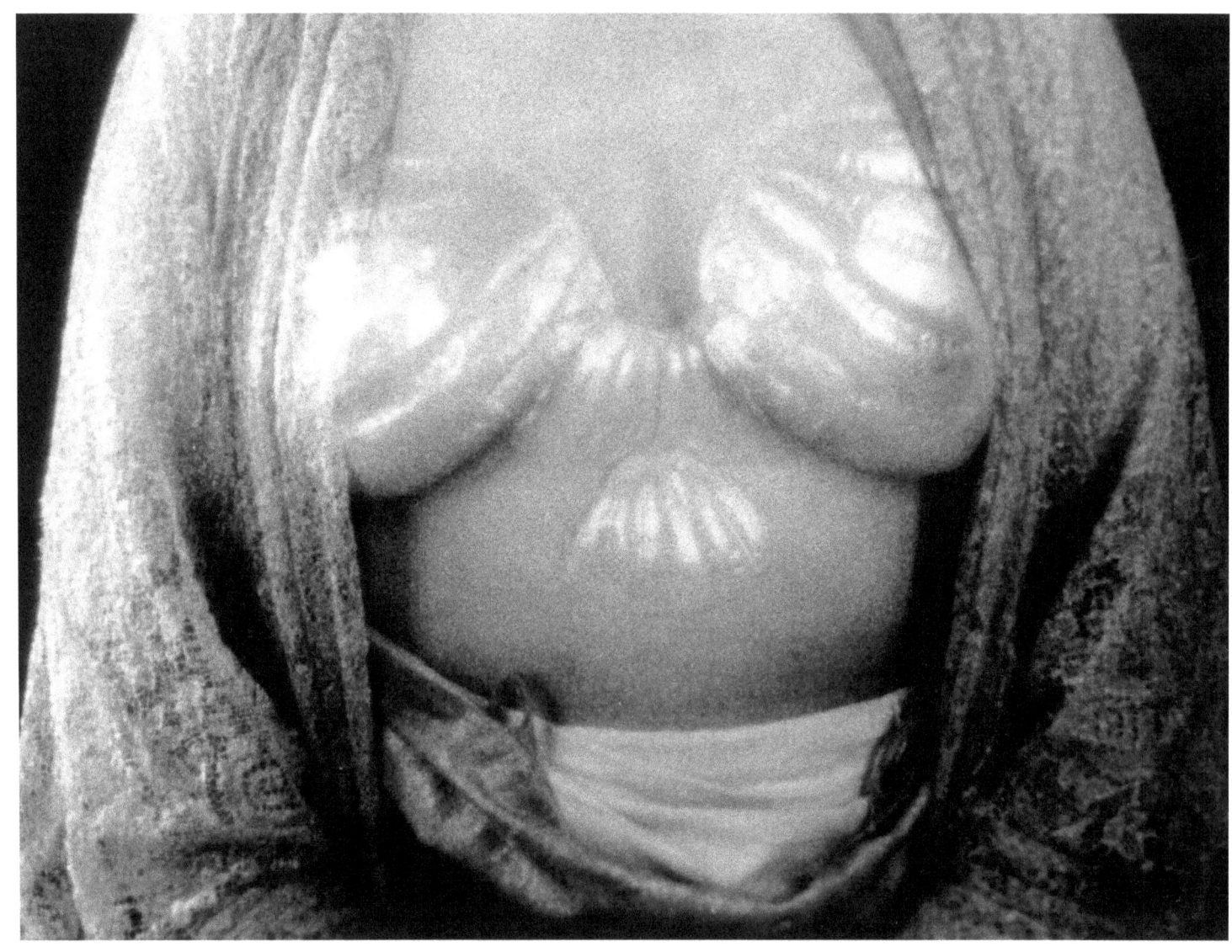

LA COQUILLE ET LE CLERGYMAN – PHOTOGRAM.

La COQUILLE ET LE CLERGYMAN
("The Seashell And The Clergyman"; Germaine Dulac, 1928: France)

One of only a handful of films which might reasonably be described as "Surrealist", **La Coquille Et Le Clergyman** was filmed from a scenario scripted by Antonin Artaud. In Artaud's original scenario, a clergyman undertakes a sequence of violent and obsessive actions. The fragmented narrative propels the clergyman through a perpetually shifting space of long corridors, crystalline landscapes and narrow city streets. He is sexually tormented in a confessional box by a beautiful woman with white hair, and vents his fury upon the figure of a lecherous military officer. The clergyman's identity collides with that of the officer, and he is constantly surrounded by shattering glass and flowing liquids. His multiple confrontations with the beautiful woman end with her suffering grotesque physical and facial distortions, her tongue "stretching out to infinity". Director Germaine Dulac filmed the images of the scenario with scrupulousness, but, for Artaud, neutralized their virulence by treating them as being simply the representation of a dream. However Dulac, who was – for that period – a technologically highly advanced director able to execute complex superimpositions, had used every technical means at her disposal to find cinematic equivalents for Artaud's written images in his scenario, which often gave no indication of the ways in which they should be transposed into cinematic images. When the film was screened for the first time, at the Ursulines cinema in Paris on 9 February 1928, Artaud announced that his scenario had suffered unacceptable distortion by Dulac, who, he claimed, had "butchered" it. Despite his forcible severance from the Surrealist movement, Artaud managed to gain the alliance of a number of Surrealists (and fellow expelled Surrealists) in his protests against the director; the Surrealists viewed Dulac as an opportunistic interloper on their preoccupations. The Ursulines screening descended into a cultural riot of the kind which the Surrealists habitually staged throughout the 1920s. At the screening, the writer Robert Desnos initiated a volley of invective and screams directed at Dulac, and the film projection was abandoned in chaos. Predictably, **La Coquille Et Le Clergyman** was prohibited from exhibition in England by the British Board of Film Censors, who used the classic justification: "The film is so cryptic as to be meaningless. If there is a meaning, it is doubtless objectionable", a pronouncement which neatly summed up their complete lack of intelligence and sophistication. *La Coquille Et Le Clergyman* was the only one of Artaud's numerous film scenarios, which he wrote between 1924 and 1935, to be realized. The most extraordinary of these unfilmed provocations was *La Révolte Du Boucher* ("The Butcher's Revolt") written early in 1930 at the crucial point of crossover between the end of silent cinema and the innovation of sound. The scenario possesses a far more cohesive narrative than *La Coquille Et Le Clergyman*; it even takes place in a specific location, around the Place de l'Alma in Paris. The principal figure in the scenario, introduced with irony by Artaud as "the madman", is in a dangerously obsessive state. While waiting to meet a woman in the street, he watches a carcass of meat fall from a speeding butcher's truck and becomes fascinated by the rapport between the texture of the meat and that of human flesh. He immediately provokes a brawl in a nearby café, and then takes part in a sequence of headlong chases (recalling those from Hollywood silent slapstick films) which culminate in his arrival at a slaughterhouse and his humiliation there at the hands of the police. As in *La Coquille Et Le Clergyman*, the identity of the protagonist is volatile, and he experiences extremes of sensation, from joy to paralysing despair. The action of *La Révolte Du Boucher* is powered by sudden transformations of space, punctuated by occasional outbursts of words, screams and noises, its imagery a perjorative conflation of eroticism, cruelty, the taste for blood, the search for violence, obsession with the horrible, dissolution of moral values, social hypocrisy, lies, false witness, sadism, and perversity. Had it been filmed, there is little doubt that this work would have constituted a revolutionary intersection of slapstick, Surrealism and the cinema of butchers.

L'ÉTOILE DE MER
("The Star-Fish"; Man Ray, 1928: France)

An experimental film made in collaboration with Surrealist writer Robert Desnos, this was the closest Ray got to producing an authentic work of Surrealist cinema (although it was ultimately rejected as such by André Breton). Running for around 20 minutes, and marked by acute visual distortion through gelatin filters, **Étoile De Mer** features Ray's muse, the model Kiki De Montparnesse, in a variety of scenarios (including nudity and eye-painted eyelids). The poet André de la Rivière is seen in drag. The starfish is the central recurring image, at one point being menaced with a superimposed knife, and other occult symbols appear seemingly at random. The enigmatic intertitles, presumably by Desnos, include such proclamations as *Il faut battre les morts quand ils sont froids* ("You must strike the dead when they are cold") and *Le soleil, un pied à l'étrier, niche un rossignol dans une voile de crêpe* ("The sun, one foot in the stirrups, nests a nightingale in a veil of crêpe"). The meaning, if any, of the film remains unclear, but would seem to centre around the concept of an incorporation of the feminine ideal through transmutation. Ray's next (and penultimate) completed experimental film was **Les Mystères Du Château De Dé** ("Mysteries Of The Chateau Of Dice", 1929), a fantastic Surrealist title for what sadly amounts to little more than a home movie showing friends such as Georges Auric and Le Vicomte de Noailles swimming and playing dice, with a few cryptic inserts and mannequin shots.[1] During 1929 Man Ray also filmed a short documentary on bull-fighting, **Corrida**, shot at Pamplona. This is not surprising, given the intense interest in certain Surrealist circles with tauromachy, and also its roots in the taurobolium (a blood sacrifice of the castration cult of Cybele, alluded to in **L'Étoile De Mer**). A bloody bullfight, resulting in the blinding of the toreador, features in Georges Bataille's 1928 novella *L'Histoire De L'Oeil* ("The Story Of The

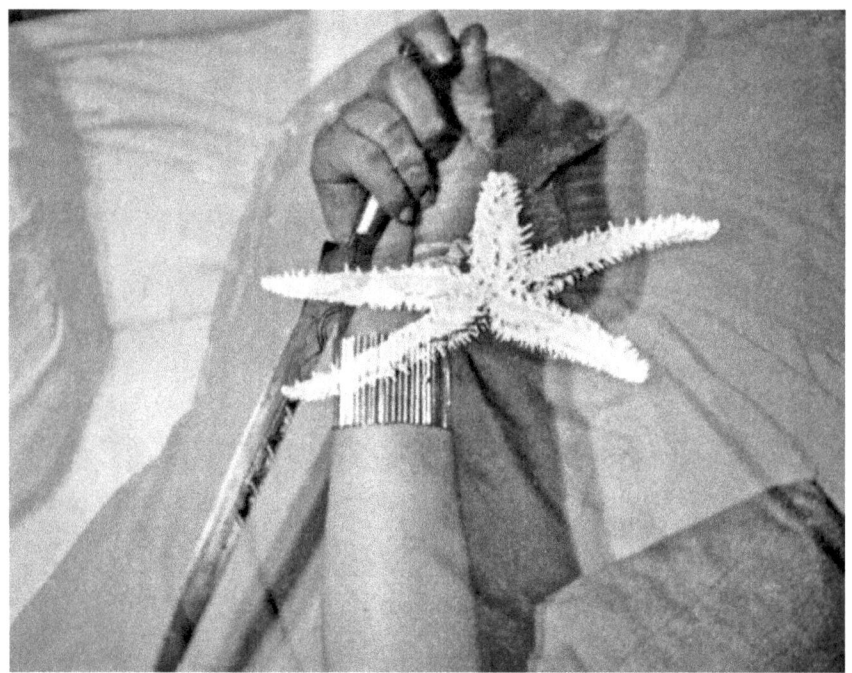
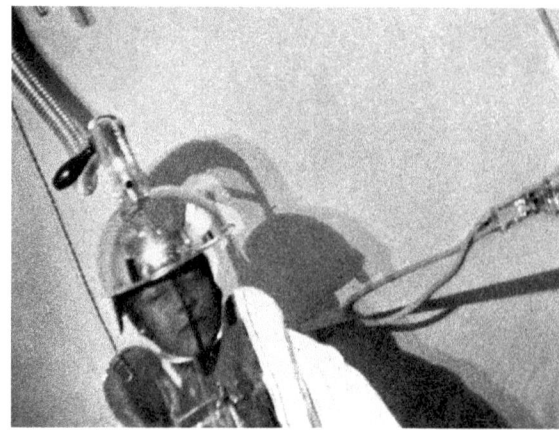

L'ÉTOILE DE MER – PHOTOGRAMS (*ABOVE & LEFT*).
LES MYSTÈRES DU CHÂTEAU DE DÉ – PHOTOGRAM (*BELOW*).

Eye"), whilst the artist André Masson – no doubt inspired by Picasso – painted a series of works depicting the myth of the Minotaur (it was Masson and Bataille who came up with the name, *Le Minotaure*, for Albert Skira's glossy Surrealist revue of 1933). Ray also filmed **Course Landaise** (1937), whose title refers to a bloodless form of bullfighting. Before that, he completed his last truly experimental film, **Autoportrait ou Ce Qui Manque À Nous Tous** ("Self-Portrait, or What We All Lack", 1930), a visual document of the properties and form of smoke, which also includes shots of Ray and his model, collaborator and muse Lee Miller.

1. The Villa Noailles was also filmed that year by Jacques Manuel, whose home movie **Biceps Et Bijoux** ("Biceps And Jewelry") shows the Noailles retinue relaxing in striped swimwear.

The EXPERIMENT
(F.N. Andrews, 1928: UK)
The Amateur Cinematographers Association, based in London and founded in 1927, produced a number of interesting film-makers including Andrews, whose **The Experiment** was a sub-Frankenstein depiction of the scientific quest to create human life. An existing scene photograph shows the apparent influence of German Expressionist decor, and a bandaged figure on an operating-table, both prefiguring the James Whale classic of two years later. During the same period, amateur cine-clubs in the US also gave rise to many short films of fantasy and terror, for example W.R. Poulson's **The Sign Of The Vampire**, said to feature a homicidal maniac; Poulson also directed a dinosaur fantasy, **The Quest For The Stegosaur**. H.S. Shagren's **The Crooked House**, also made in 1928, was reportedly a dark house horror mystery with trick effects. Another renowned amateur film made in the UK was **Terrors** (1930), directed by Erle O. Smith, concerning a tunnel through the earth's core and encounters with dinosaurs.

The FALL OF THE HOUSE OF USHER
(James Sibley Watson & Melville Webber, 1928: USA)
A 12-minute treatment of the story by Edgar Allan Poe, made the same year as the feature-length French adaptation by Jean Epstein and Luis Buñuel. Largely eschewing narrative in favour of morbid distortions, heretical shadows and claustrophobic psychogeometries, this wordless fugue of the insane is one of the key films from the early American avant-garde. With set design evidently influenced by German films like **Das Cabinet Der Dr. Caligari**, Watson and Webber's experimental horror also introduces elements of abstract cinema in its evocation of premature burial and

resurrection. Watson and Webber – who were regarded as "amateur" film-makers – went on to create the biblical trance-orgy **Lot In Sodom**.

FEED 'EM AND WEEP – PRODUCTION PHOTOGRAPH.

FEED 'EM AND WEEP
(Fred Guiol, 1928: USA)

The first of three short Hal Roach comedies in which showgirl and bit-part player Marion "Peanuts" Byron was paired with Anita Garvin in a female comedy duo (one of several such pairings made by Roach). The other two films were **Going Ga-Ga** (1928) and **A Pair Of Tights** (1929). **Feed 'Em And Weep** is set mainly in a train station diner (one customer is obese favourite Frank "Fatty" Alexander), and also has scenes on the road (the girls are itinerants). Byron could later be seen (uncredited) in sound films such **Hips, Hips, Hooray!** (1933), but her career came to an end before the end of that decade (and Garvin's, equally obscure, not long thereafter).

GESCHLECHT IN FESSELN - PRODUCTION PHOTOGRAPH.

GESCHLECHT IN FESSELN. DIE SEXUALNOT DER STRAFGEFANGENEN
("Sex In Chains: The Erotic Desires Of Prisoners"; Wilhelm Dieterle, 1928: Germany)
A daring film dealing with aspects of homosexuality,[1] based on Franz Hollering and Karl Plättner's text *Eros Im Zuchthaus* ("Jailhouse Eros"), an evocation of sexual frustration and same-sex temptation in prisons. The downbeat film, a catalogue of confusion, anguish and betrayal caused purely by the over-riding compulsions of human sexuality, ends bleakly in a double suicide.

1. This was an era when Weimar homo-sex magazines such as *Freundschaft* ("Friendship", for males) and *Die Freundin* ("Girlfriend", for lesbians) were prosecuted as Schmatz und Schund ("filth and trash").

The GODLESS GIRL
(Cecil B. DeMille, 1928-29: USA)
Pathé's production of **The Godless Girl** is generally considered to be the first in the "reform school for girls" genre. The remarkable plot involves a young girl who is imprisoned and subjected to torturous abuse after forming an atheist society, a provocation which precipitates a Christian riot during which another girl is killed. Released in both silent and sound versions, DeMille's original movie is a brutal, sadistic but moralistic quasi-religious melodrama, notable for setting the scene for a movie genre that would blossom into exploitation greatness in the 50s, 60s and 70s. In 1929 the film's female lead, Lina Basquette – who appears in a visually obscure nude bathing scene – received a particularly rabid fan letter from Austria, whose author proclaimed her his favourite Hollywood actress; the letter was from Adolf

THE GODLESS GIRL - PRODUCTION PHOTOGRAPH (*OPPOSITE*).

THE GODLESS GIRL – PRODUCTION PHOTOGRAPH (*LEFT*).
PAID – PRODUCTION PHOTOGRAPH (*BELOW*).

Hitler. The American WIP genre moved into the sound era with full-blown female prison scenes in the likes of **Paid** (1930), with notoriously "daring" and censored shower scenes.

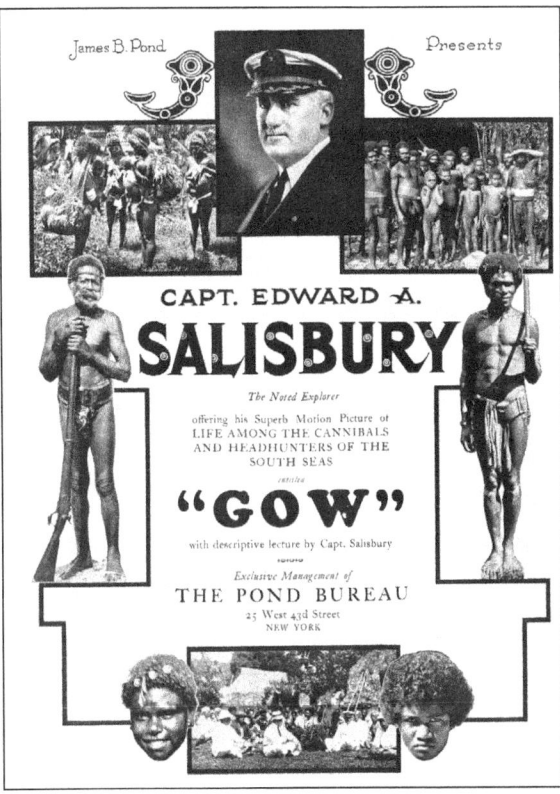

GOW – SALES BROCHURE (*ABOVE*); PRODUCTION PHOTOGRAPHS (*RIGHT & OVERLEAF VERSO*).
BLACK SHADOWS – PRODUCTION PHOTOGRAPH (*OVERLEAF RECTO*).

GOW THE HEAD-HUNTER
(Edward A. Salisbury, 1928: USA)

Exploitational travelogue film supposedly showing "savage orgies of man-eating humans" and "what actually happens at a cannibal sacrifice ceremony". Filmed in various parts of the South Pacific, the film shows pygmies, bare-breasted native women wearing the skulls of their dead husbands as necklaces, and finally a section with cannibals and head-hunters; Salisbury also includes staged sequences and stock footage, notably the shot of a roasting human arm from Frank Hurley's earlier **Pearls And Savages**. **Gow The Head-Hunter** was re-released in 1933, with an added voice-over, under the new title **Gow The Killer**; and **Gow The Killer** was later re-edited into a new film, **Cannibal Island** (1956) by one David F. Friedman, then a budding exploitation producer working at roadshow company Modern. Much of the footage in **Gow The Head-Hunter** was shot during an oceanic expedition to the South Seas led by Salisbury in 1921, in which he was accompanied by cinematographer Thomas Middleton and also Ernest B. Schoedsack and Merian C. Cooper, future creators of **King Kong**. The film-makers ended up in the Solomon Islands, shooting over 10,000 feet of raw footage documenting the rituals and warcraft of cannibals and head-hunters. The first edited ethnographic film to emerge from this mass of often disturbing scenes was **Black Shadows**, released in 1923, a "first contact" documentary which climaxes with gruesome images of a hunting-party displaying their war trophies, an array of freshly-severed heads. Another film from the same trip, but also including footage shot in Ceylon and Arabia, was **In Quest Of The Golden Prince** (1924), retitled **The Lost Empire** in 1929. It also appears that Antipodean rights to the Solomon Islands footage were somehow assigned to

Reginald Nicholson, a Methodist missionary, who in 1924 oversaw the production of **The Transformed Isle**. Sub-titled **Barbarism To Christianity**, this film replaced Salisbury's ethnographic concerns with ecclesiastic dogma, a demonstration of the world's wildest man-eating savages being tamed by "civilized" religion. A vivid written account by Salisbury of his trip and film-making methods, entitled "18 Months On The Trail Of Cannibals", was published in the *Atlanta Constitution* in 1922.

The GREAT ARCTIC SEAL HUNT
(Varick Frissell, 1928: Newfoundland)

In a line of hunting documentaries dating back to such films as American Mutoscope's **Moose Hunting In Newfoundland** (1905), Edison's **Stalking And Shooting Caribou In Newfoundland** (1907), and the British & Colonial Kinematograph Company's **Seal Hunting in Newfoundland** (1912), Varick Frissell's 39-minute violent death-report from the ice wastes north of Canada was both the most beautiful and most bloody. Filmed from aboard the SS Beothic, **The Great Arctic Seal Hunt** simultaneously celebrates the world's most stunning and pristine landscapes, and revels in scenes of skull-smashing, blood-spurting butchery and evisceration. Inspired by his experiences, Frissell returned two years later to film **The Viking** (1930), a fictional narrative about two rivals hunting each other across the vast frozen wilderness, the first sound feature shot in what is now Canadian territory. After a preview screening in Newfoundland's original cinema, the Nickel, Frissell decided he needed more footage of the ice floes; whilst obtaining these additional shots, the director and twenty-six crew were blasted to death when the ship's boiler-room exploded. Their corpses were never recovered.

THE VIKING – PRODUCTION PHOTOGRAPH.

HABEAS CORPUS - PRODUCTION PHOTOGRAPH.

HABEAS CORPUS
(James Parrott & Leo McCarey, 1928: USA)

Comic duo Laurel and Hardy's first "macabre" comedy, in which the pair are hired by a deranged surgeon to dig up a corpse, with grave results.[1] Stan Laurel and Oliver Hardy were first "officially" paired in Hal Roach's short farce **Putting Pants On Philip** (1927), before which both were established performers in their own right – Laurel in short comedies such as the parodic **Dr. Pyckle And Mr. Pryde** (1925), Hardy as the "heavy" in the likes of Larry Semon's frenetic orgy of destruction **Kid Speed** (1924) – and had shared screen time in several 2-reelers such as **Sugar Daddies** (1927) and, definitively, **The Second Hundred Years** (1927),[2] both of which also featured "straight man" James Finlayson.

1. The film is based on the earlier Roach comedy **Moonlight And Noses** (1925), co-directed by Stan Laurel. Laurel's engagement with "mad scientist" comedy also extended to scripting **Scared Stiff** (1925), and appearing in **Dirty Work** (1933), in which Hardy regresses to a chimpanzee after falling in a doctor's vat of rejuvenation fluid.

2. The first film in which the pair operated in tandem, **The Second Hundred Years** is renowned for its scene of Laurel absent-mindedly white-washing a flapper's tight-skirted buttocks, an example of his apparent fetish for the on-screen physical besmirchment of women; another example can be seen in **The Finishing Touch** (1928), also notable as the first in a line of comedies in which the duo played accident-prone builders inexorably heading towards a climax of utter destruction.

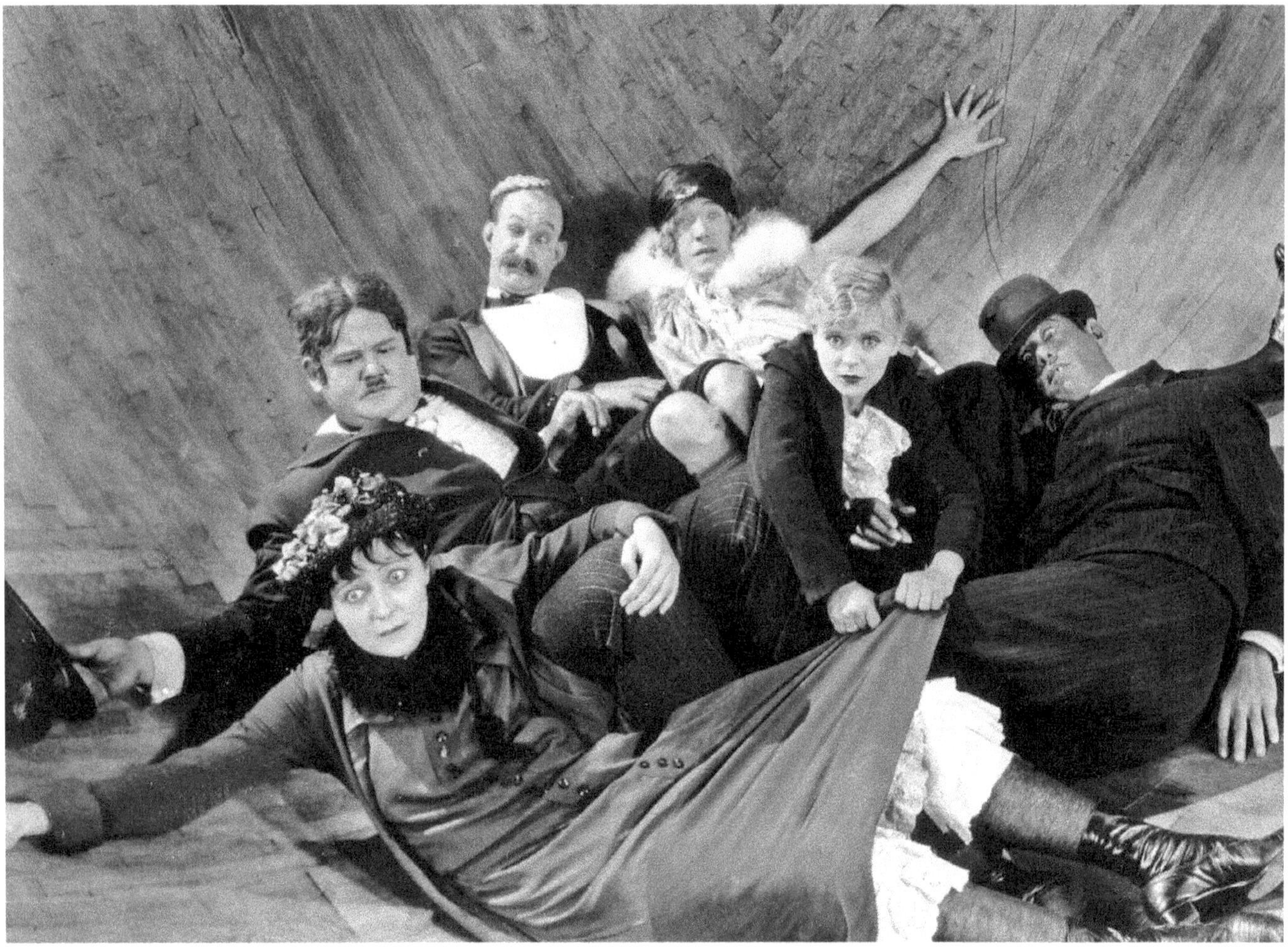

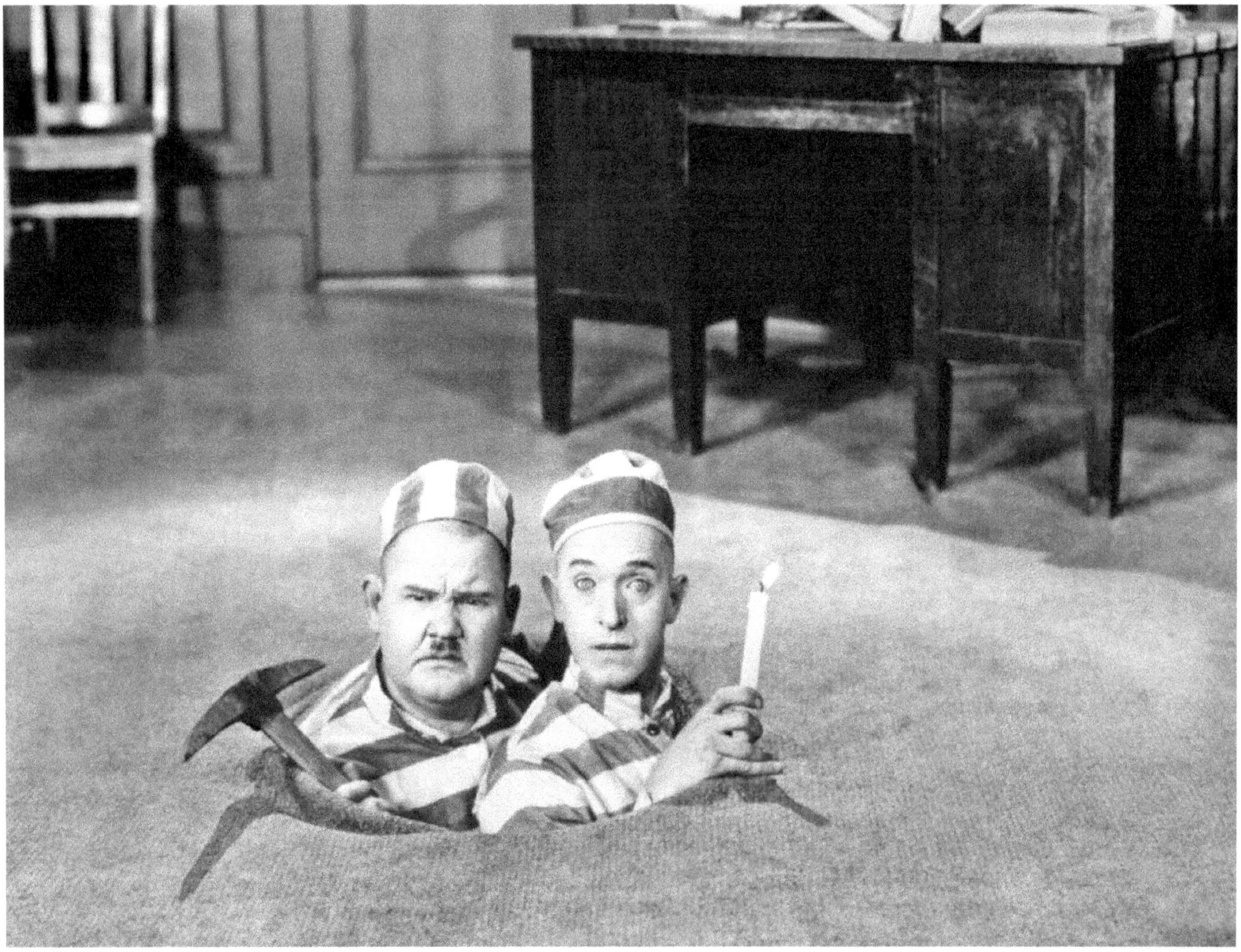

SUGAR DADDIES – FUNHOUSE SCENE, WITH LAUREL IN DRAG; PRODUCTION PHOTOGRAPH (*OPPOSITE TOP*).
THE SECOND HUNDRED YEARS – PRODUCTION PHOTOGRAPHS (*OPPOSITE BOTTOM & THIS PAGE TOP RIGHT*).
PUTTING PANTS ON PHILIP – PRODUCTION PHOTOGRAPH (*THIS PAGE CENTRE RIGHT*).
DR. PYCKLE AND MR. PRYDE – LOBBY CARD (*THIS PAGE BOTTOM RIGHT*).

THE HAUNTED HOUSE – LOBBY CARD (ABOVE);
PRODUCTION PHOTOGRAPHS (OPPOSITE TOP, OVERLEAF).
HOUSE OF HORROR – PRODUCTION PHOTOGRAPH
(OPPOSITE BOTTOM).

The HAUNTED HOUSE
(Benjamin Christensen, 1928: USA)

The first in a trio of weird mystery films directed virtually back-to-back by Christensen for First National and released with partial sound between November 1928 and April 1929; actress Thelma Todd and actor William V. Mong appear in all three films, supported by varying casts. **The Haunted House** follows a standard "mystery mansion" plotline – a dying, rich eccentric assembles his prospective heirs, giving each a key and a letter with directions on how to find hidden riches in an old dark house. Their efforts are predictably hindered by a range of sinister figures, including Montagu Love as a deranged doctor; a spectral, somnambulistic girl also wanders through the proceedings. Like Warner Brothers' **The Terror**, released two months before, **The Haunted House** was accompanied by a Vitaphone soundtrack of music and spooky sound effects. Christensen's **The House Of Horror** follows a similar plotline, with a pair of siblings summoned to their uncle's mansion which is populated with eccentrics and grotesques, as well as a masked prowler bent on stealing a valuable diamond. **The Haunted House** and **The House Of Horror** are both designated as "lost" films, with only a set of Vitaphone fright-soundtrack discs surviving from **The House Of Horror**; fortunately, much footage still survives from the third and crowning film of Christensen's trilogy, **Seven Footprints To Satan**, in which his grotesque and macabre visions were finally given full sway.

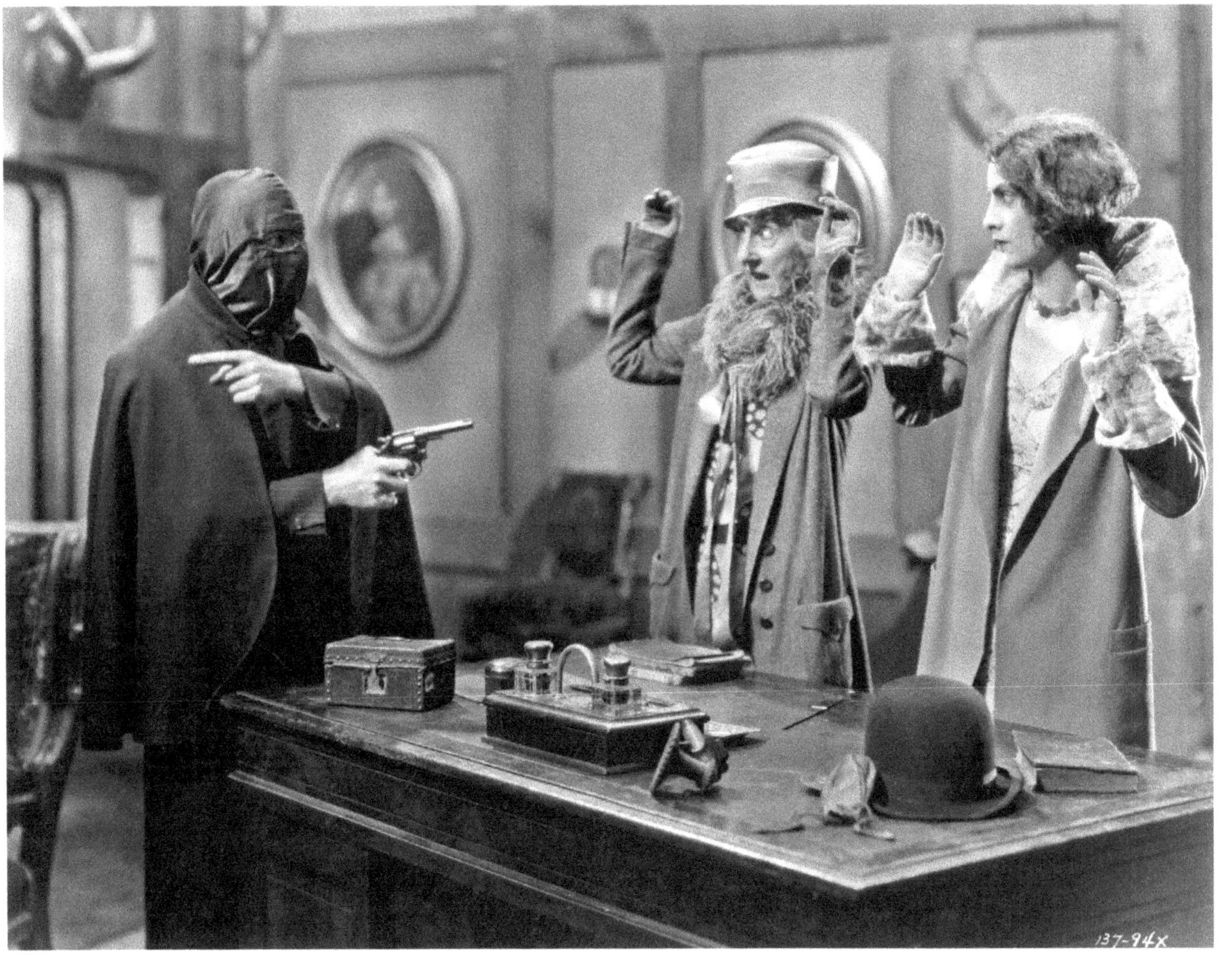
137-94X

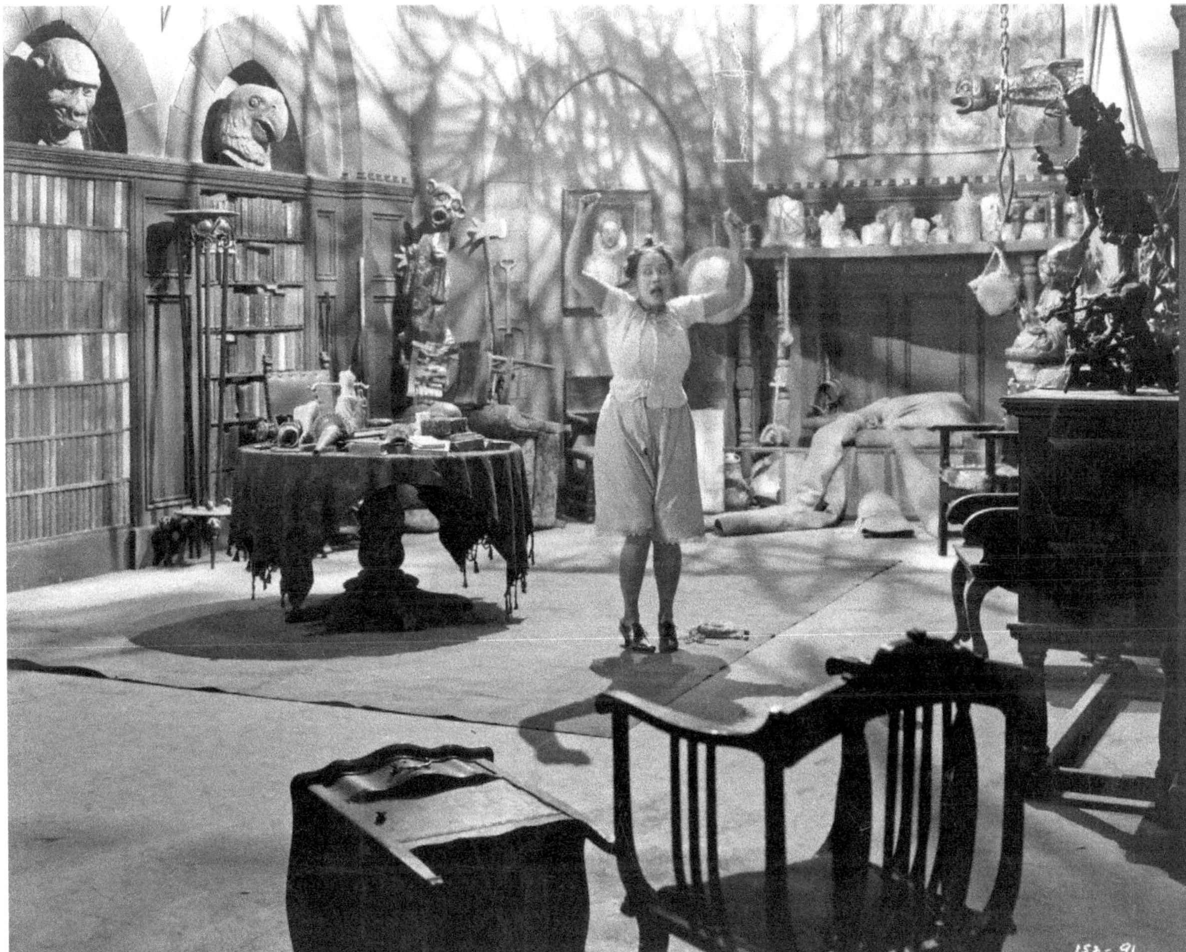
152-91

Het HEKSENLIED
("The Witch-Song"; Jan van Dommeln, 1928: NL)
A Dutch film of the 17th century witch persecutions, based on *Das Hexenlied*, a German narrative poem written in 1890 by Ernst von Wildenbruch, and designed by director/producer Dommeln to be screened with accompanying live narration and musical accompaniment. In a secluded monastery an ancient monk lies raving, seemingly possessed by Satan. In fact, he is reliving a dreadful experience from his youth, when he was sexually tempted by a girl accused of witchcraft. The next day the girl was burned alive at the stake, and he was compelled to watch in powerless horror. As she burned, the witch unleashed an accursed death-song, which has haunted him to his final days. After confessing all, the old monk falls back dead. Wildenbruch's poem was also the inspiration for Franz Porten's earlier German production **Hexenlied** (1909). **Das Hexenlied**, directed by Eugen Burg in 1919, is said to be based on *Die Elixiere Des Teufels* by E.T.A. Hoffmann; it features scenes of torture, witch-burning and self-immolation.

HICKMAN THE FOX
(Melba Films, 1928: USA)
Banned by all local authorities for glorifying criminality, **Hickman The Fox** was a so-called "sex and crime exposé" detailing the then-current case of William Edward Hickman, perpetrator of one of the most heinous kidnapping/murders in American history. Hickman had kidnapped a young Los Angeles girl, 12-year-old Marion Parker, in December 1927 and demanded a ransom by notes variously signed "Fate", "Death", and "The Fox". When Marion's father delivered the ransom, he was rewarded with his daughter's violated corpse – she had been raped, killed, drained of blood, disembowelled and butchered, her limbs scattered by the roadside, and her eyelids stitched open to give the grotesque semblance of life. **Hickman The Fox**, assembled mainly from still photographs and newsreel clips (the Hickman case had been the subject of two separate newsreels), was hastily produced in order to cash in on this atrocity, but was thwarted by the intervention of the law – a typical case of an offensive exploitation film being simply closed down by direct action (it was reported that in Oklahoma, a wax figure of Hickman used to promote the film was "thrown in the creek"). Hickman was hanged on October 19, 1928. William Hickman was not, however, the only child-killer at large in America; on February 11, 1927, a 4-year-old-boy named Billy Gaffney was abducted and never seen again, and on May 5, 1928, a similar fate met 10-year-old Grace Budd. Several years later, a sexually abnormal psychotic named Albert Fish was arrested after confessing to the cannibal-killing of Budd to her family in a letter.[1] Fish – a sado-masochist whose perineum was found to contain numerous needles which he had inserted himself – also confessed to killing and eating Billy Gaffney, as well as another child victim, Francis McDonnell, killed in 1924. Suspected in at least six other child-killings, Fish was executed by electric chair in January 1936, just two months before the release of Warner Brothers' electro-execution-resurrection horror phantasy **The Walking Dead**. Although a rumour was circulated that it took two attempts for Fish to fry – the needles in his groin short-circuiting the chair's voltage – he definitely did not return from the dead. Even more horrors were perpetrated in 1928 by Gordon Stewart Northcott, a farmer living near Wineville, California; police investigating a succession of missing pre-adolescent boys uncovered bones and body parts which betrayed a rampage of sodomistic rape, torture and decapitation committed by Northcott, who had claimed at least twenty victims. He was hanged in October 1930. The Northcott case also spawned a notorious side-bar, in which one of the murdered boys, Walter Collins (aged 9) was impersonated by a teenage runaway. The police handed him "back" to Collins' mother, who informed them that he was clearly not her son; in order to save face, they had her locked up in a lunatic asylum. Although the atrocities committed by Hickman, Fish and Northcott were simply too grim to ever be recreated for entertainment, 1928 did see the release of another film which claimed to be based on "actual police records" – **The Ape**, directed by B.C. Rule, about which little is confirmed save that it was a low-budget, low-quality effort, dealing with crimes by an apparently non-human killer.

1. The letter read in part: *"...I took her to an empty house in Westchester I had already picked out. When we got there, I told her to remain outside. She picked wild flowers. I went upstairs and stripped all my clothes off. I knew if I did not I would get her blood on them. When all was ready I went to the window and called her. Then I hid in a closet until she was in the room. When she saw me all naked she began to cry and tried to run down stairs. I grabbed her and she said she would tell her mama. First I stripped her naked. How she did kick – bite and scratch. I choked her to death then cut her in small pieces so I could take my meat to my rooms, cook and eat it. How sweet and tender her little ass was roasted in the oven. It took me 9 days to eat her entire body. I did not fuck her tho I could of had I wished. She died a virgin."* Unlike the macabre antics of later cannibal-killer Ed Gein, Fish's crimes have never been evoked on film, no doubt due to the taboo of child-murder – although this did not stop Austrian director Fritz Lang from producing M, an account of a child-killer in Berlin, just three years before Fish's capture.

HOLLYWOOD SAND WITCHES
(Cine-Art Productions, c.1928: USA)

Two young flappers cavort naked on the beach, rolling in the sand, but are forced to protect their modesty with a parasol when a young voyeur approaches them. **Hollywood Sand Witches** also packs a xenophobic sting in the tail – the man next comes across a sun-bathing negress, and flees into the sea in horror. This short 16mm film of upper front and rear female nudity was one of the first productions from Cine-Art, a California company making movies for the "home projection" market, which at that time was just starting to take off, largely thanks to the technical and marketing innovations of Kodak. One of Cine-Art's main lines was in these quasi-erotic but innocent "stag" films, which always involved naked girls, but stopped well short of showing sexual contact. Genitals and pubic hair were also seemingly taboo, with girls being careful to keep their legs closed and also sanitizing the pubic region by shaving or masking. Other titles released by the company around this period included **A Future Venus, Sirens Of The Sea, The Wood Nymph, Betty's Bath, The Idol: A Phantasy, Desert Nymphs**, and **Jazz Babies**, with modernist girls, or flappers, playing strip-poker. Flappers also featured in "naughty" reels – with no nudity – such as **Why Girls Walk Home** (Hollywood 16mm Co, c.1929), in which four girl swimmers are forced to walk back in their underwear after their clothes are stolen by a cheeky young negro child. Another well-known home "nudie" film of this period was **Bearcat Runs Wild**, in which a man dressed in a bear costume chases off an artist before accosting the man's two nude models. These films of naked girls were matched by photographic "art" magazine publications of the time such as *Art Classics*, *Art Studies*, *Art Studio Life*, *French Art Classics* or *Classic Art*, while even from mainstream Hollywood came the nude "pin-up" portraits of starlets taken by MGM house photographer Clarence Sinclair Bull. Kodak continued to innovate, introducing

ARTISTIC MGM PUBLICITY PHOTOGRAPHS OF STARLET MARIE HOPKINS BY CLARENCE SINCLAIR BULL, 1928 (*RIGHT AND OVERLEAF VERSO*).

Kodacolor film in 1928; but the advance which would really launch the home projection market into overdrive would come in 1932, with the first 8mm motion picture film, cameras, and projectors. Meanwhile, nude and semi-nude ladies could still be seen in the short reels produced for Mutoscope peep-show machines; Mutoscope was acquired in 1923 by entrpreneur William Rabkin, who renamed it International Mutoscope and, until around 1933, continued producing risqué subjects – which he marketed as "spicy".[1] Spicy titles from the mid to late 1920s include **Red Hot Mamma, Battling Babes, Hollywood Scandals, Arrested! Defying The Censors, Cleo The Harem Queen, Bare Facts, The Lure Of The Serpent, Black Bottom Beauties, Bare In Bear Skin, Sweet Sixteen, Forbidden Fruit, Bedroom Secrets, Unveiled, What Girls Do When Alone, The Naked Truth, The X-Ray Gown, Bedroom Follies, The Queen Of Sin, That Schoolgirl Complexion, A Modern Venus, Ladies' Night In A Turkish Bath, Oriental Fantasy, Silk Stocking Brigade, The Virgin Of Bagdad, A Midnight Maid,** and **French Dressing,** to name just a few out of hundreds.

1. Although Rabkin initially announced that no full nudity would appear in his productions, this policy – if ever adhered to – was clearly abandoned by the 1930s with reels such as **Eve's Leaves** (1930), which showed a bare-breasted female bather. Rabkin also licensed regular films from other companies, and reformatted them for Mutoscope playback.

HORO ZANMAI
("Wander-Lust"; Hiroshi Inagaki, 1928: Japan)
Starring *jidai-geki* action star Chiezo Kataoka, and produced by his own Chiezo Pro film company, **Horo Zanmai** was the second film by director Hiroshi, and one of the key works of the "itinerant gambler" sub-genre. Chiezo plays Mondo, a *samurai* who avenges the murder of his wife by killing the son of his chief retainer. Subsequently made an outcast, Mondo becomes a wanderer, accompanied by his young son, in a series of fugitive and often ferocious episodes. **Horo Zanmai** was scripted by Mansaku Itami, a regular collaborator with Hiroshi, who also directed several films such as the 2-part **Zoku Banka Jigoku** ("Elegy Of Hell", 1928), another violent *chambara* produced by and starring Chiezo. Chiezo, Itami and Hiroshi next joined forces to make **Ehon Musha-Shugyo** ("Warrior-Mission Picture-Book", 1928). Mondo, the central figure of **Horo Zanmai**, bears similar attributes to one of the Japanese cinema's most popular wandering gamblers, Kunisada Chuji, a legendary gambler-outlaw with roots in actual history. Dozens of films have been made about Chuji; these include Makino Shozo's **Kunisada Chuji** (1924, starring Shojiro Sawada), Daisuke Ito's revolutionary trilogy **Chuji Tabi Nikki**, and **Kunisada Chuji** (1933), again from the team of Hiroshi Inagaki and Chiezo Kataoka. Another popular figure was that of Kurama Tengu, the literary creation of popular novelist Jiro Osaragi who featured him a series of period adventures from 1924 onwards; Osaragi's other well-known works included *Ako Roshi* ("Loyal Retainers Of Ako", 1927). Teppei Yamaguchi's **Kurama Tengu** (1928), the first production from Arashi Kanjuro Pro – the company formed by *chambara* star Arashi in 1928 – is a fresh interpretation of the character he first played in the 1927 Makino production **Kurama Tengu: Imon Kakubeijishi** ("Kurama Tengu: Street Performers"). The first of two short but action-packed films directed by Yamaguchi, **Kurama Tengu** culminates with a dazzling swordfight sequence, in which the hood-masked hero wields a deadly, flesh-cleaving *katana* is each flashing hand. The sequel, **Kurama Tengu: Kyofu Jidai** ("Kurama Tengu: Reign Of Terror", also 1928) repeats the formula and also includes a horror sequence set in an old house haunted by a long-haired female ghost and malevolent black cats, before breathlessly reaching its frentic climax of blazing choreographed swordplay. Arashi's next films included the Keikoku Kinema *yokai* production **Tokaido Koshin-Kyoku Tanuki Taiji** ("Tokaido Road: Tanuki Extermination March", 1929), as well as a series of films from Toa Kyoto featuring the "samurai detective" Muttsuri Umon, which commenced with **Umon Ichiban Tegara Nanban Yurei** ("Umon's First Exploit: Exotic Ghost", 1929).

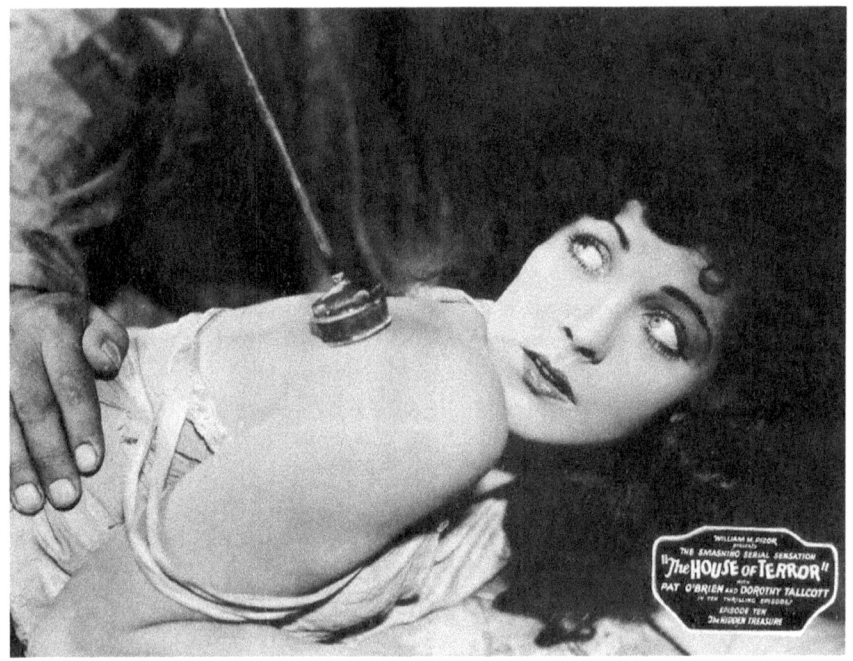

THE HOUSE OF TERROR – LOBBY CARDS (*LEFT & ABOVE*).
THE GHOST CITY (1923) – "CLUTCHING HAND" IMAGE FROM UNIVERSAL'S 15-CHAPTER WESTERN SERIAL (*OPPOSITE PAGE TOP*); PRODUCTION PHOTOGRAPH.
THE MYSTERY RIDER – PRODUCTION PHOTOGRAPH (*OPPOSITE PAGE BOTTOM*).
PHANTOM CITY – PRODUCTION PHOTOGRAPH (*OVERLEAF*).

The HOUSE OF TERROR
(Roland D. Reed, 1928: USA)

Produced by William M. Pizor, **The House Of Terror** was a striking, 10-chapter horror-western fusion serial. Although the films are apparently lost, a host of images survive which indicate a trenchant mix of action, violence, sadism (a girl's naked flesh being branded by a hot iron), and horror, as shown on a striking lobby card in which two men are seen being terrorized by hooded, superimposed ghosts resembling spectres of the KKK. The serial's chapters were: **Missing Men; Tongues Of Flame; Swirling Waters; Out Of The Night; Perilous Trails; Secret Passage; Division; Revenge; Pawns Of Evil;** and **The Hidden Treasure**. Another "weird western" from 1928 was Albert S. Rogell's **Phantom City**, starring cult cowboy star Ken Maynard and concerning a ghost town with a gold mine and a sinister spectral rider. **Phantom City** was virtually remade as **Ghost Valley** (1932), and much of its footage reused in **Haunted Gold**, a cut-up with new scenes also shot in 1932. Less compelling were the earlier **Spook Ranch** (1925), **Hoodoo Ranch** (1926) and **Haunted Range** (1926), all with fake ghosts (a plot device which can be found in westerns as least as far back as William Worthington's **The Ghost Of The Rancho**, from 1918). In many ways these films were standard "fake haunted house" stories simply transposed to a western setting, more often than not in a deserted mine. An example of this in serial format was **The Ghost City**, a 15-chapter Universal production from 1923.[1] **Silver Valley** (1927), a Tom Mix western, stood out by its unusual plot which involved Mix's character turning an automobile into a small aircraft, while Mix's **King Cowboy** (1928) managed to incorporate Arab villainy. Other even weirder westerns included Vitagraph's **The Mystery Of Lost Ranch** (1925), in which "red" Indians are subjugated by a "death ray" which vaporises living creatures; Universal's two 10-chapter serials **The Mystery Rider** (1928),[2] featuring a deformed villain named The Claw, and **The Vanishing Rider** (1927, released 1928),[3] with Boris Karloff as villain; and two serials from Mascot – the 10-chapter **The Phantom Of The West** (1931),[4] featuring a hooded gang named the League of the Lawless, and the 12-chapter **The Lightning Warrior** (also 1931),[5] with a cloaked maniac known as the Wolf Man and the final screen appearance of canine star "Rin-Tin-Tin", the German Shepherd whose films of the silent era had been phenomenally successful. These weird westerns, although they included horror-type imagery and themes of mystery and menace, were ultimately nearly always explained in rational terms.

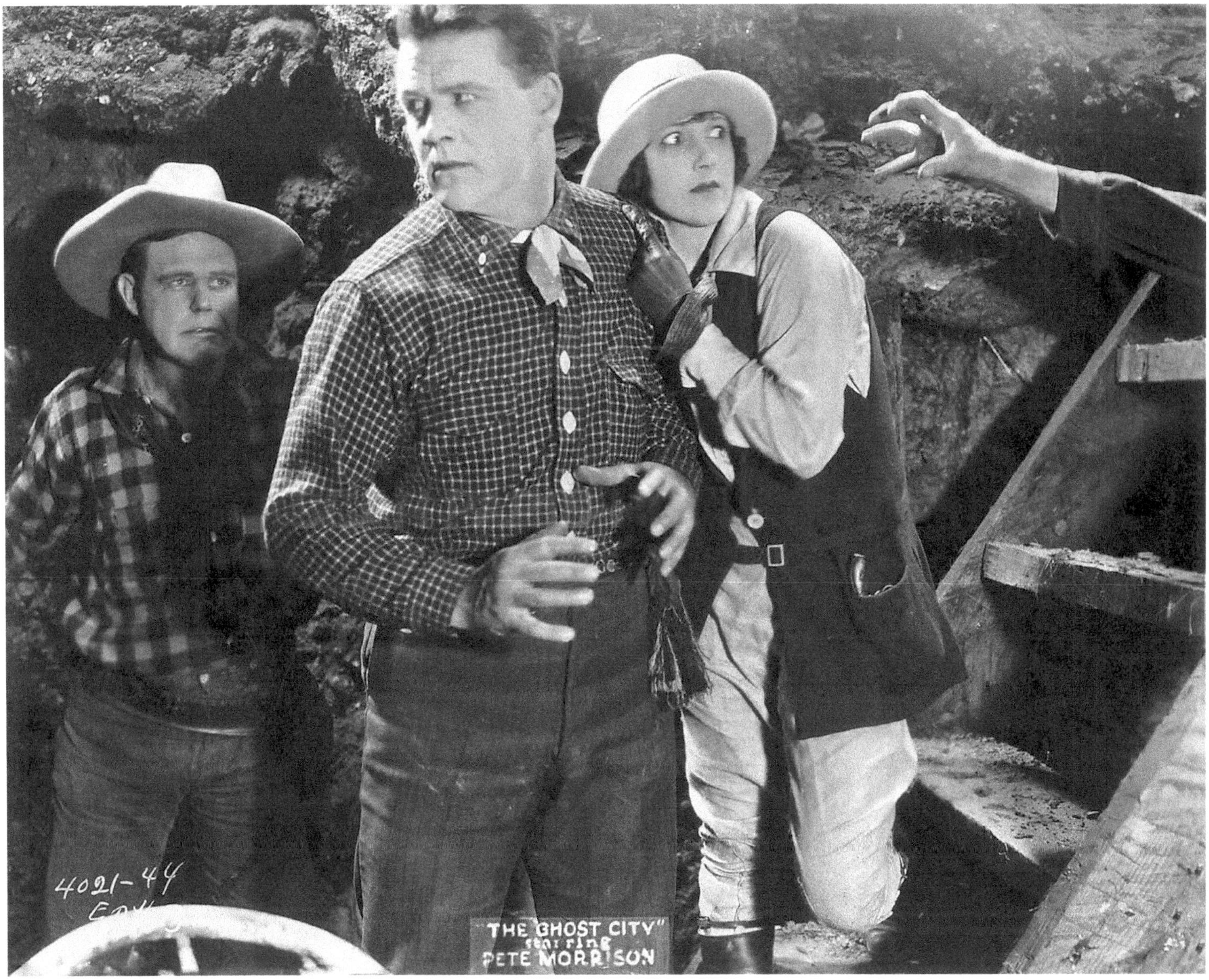
4021-44
"THE GHOST CITY"
starring
PETE MORRISON

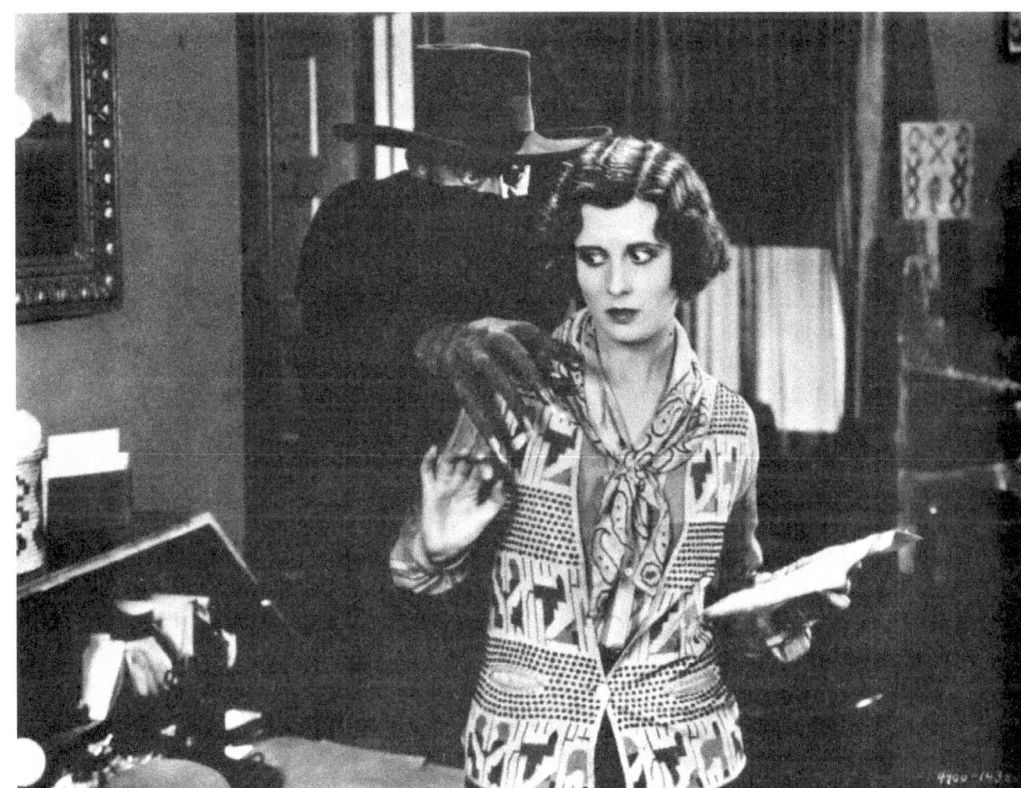

1. The fifteen chapters of The Ghost City were: The Thundering Herd; The Bulldogger; The Maelstrom; The Water Trap; Foiling The Rustlers; Death's Specter; Stolen Gold; The Midnight Intruder; Talons Of The Night; The Frame-Up; Ambushed; The Betrayal; Man To Man; Flames Of Vengeance; and Face To Face.

2. The ten chapters of The Mystery Rider were: The Clutching Claw; Trapped; The Stampede; Hands Up; Buried Alive; The Fatal Shot; Hurled Through Space; Unmasked; Doomed; and The End Of The Trail.

3. The ten chapters of The Vanishing Rider were: The Road Agent; Trapped; A Fight For Life; Brother Against Brother; The Wings Of Fury; The False Message; The Waters Of Death; The Bargain Of Fear; The Last Stand; and Vengeance. Ray Taylor was the director.

4. The ten chapters of The Phantom Of The West were: The Ghost Rides; Stairway Of Doom; Horror In The Dark; Battle Of The Strong; League Of The Lawless; Canyon Of Calamity; Price Of Silence; House Of Hate; Fatal Secret; and Rogue's Roundup.

5. The twelve chapters of The Lightning Warrior were: Drums Of Doom; The Wolf Man; Empty Saddles; Flaming Arrows; The Invisible Enemy; The Fatal Name; The Ordeal Of Fire; The Man Who Knew; Traitor's Hour; Secret Of The Cave; Red Shadows; and Painted Faces. Rin-Tin-Tin's silent films included While London Sleeps (1926), set in London's opium-riddled Limehouse district and featuring George Kotsonaros as a bestial thug known as The Monk, who perpetrates acts of heinous violence.

KING COWBOY – PRODUCTION PHOTOGRAPH (*THIS PAGE, ABOVE*). IN THIS STRANGE WESTERN, COWBOY TEX ROGERS (MIX) AND HIS GANG SOMEHOW GET TO NORTH AFRICA, WHERE THEIR BOSS IS BEING HELD CAPTIVE AFTER BEING KIDNAPPED FOR RANSOM BY ARABS. AFTER KILLING THE ARAB LEADER, ROGERS IS ELECTED TO TAKE HIS PLACE.

THE MYSTERY OF LOST RANCH – FILM POSTER (*OPPOSITE ABOVE LEFT*).

THE LIGHTNING WARRIOR – FILM POSTER (*OPPOSITE ABOVE RIGHT*).

GHOST VALLEY – FILM POSTER (*OPPOSITE BOTTOM LEFT*).
SILVER VALLEY – FILM POSTER (*OPPOSITE BOTTOM RIGHT*).

PHANTOM OF THE WEST – PRODUCTION PHOTOGRAPH (*OVERLEAF VERSO TOP*).
HAUNTED GOLD – PRODUCTION PHOTOGRAPH (*OVERLEAF VERSO BOTTOM*).
THE VANISHING RIDER – PRODUCTION PHOTOGRAPH (*OVERLEAF RECTO TOP*).
WHILE LONDON SLEEPS – MENACED BY THE MONK; PRODUCTION PHOTOGRAPH (*OVERLEAF RECTO BOTTOM*).

HUO SHAO HONG LIAN SI – PRODUCTION PHOTOGRAPH.

HUO SHAO HONG LIAN SI
("Burning Of Red Lotus Temple"; Shichuan Zhang, 1928-31: China)
Adapted from a newspaper serial entitled *Jianghu Qi Xia Zhuan* ("Strange Tales Of The Wild Swordsman"), **Huo Shao Hong Lian Sì** is among the first *wuxia* (martial arts/fantasy) movies produced in China; it is also the longest, originally running at more than 24 hours in 18 episodes, released over 3-year period, and its huge success led to the popularization of cinema – especially martial arts cinema – across Chinese society; it even inspired other film-makers to make movies with similar titles, such as **Huo Shao Qi Xing Lou** ("Burning Of Seven Stars Mansion") and **Huo Shao Bai Hua Tai** ("Burning Of One Hundred Flower Terrace"), both 1929. The film – which features swordplay, "magic" special effects, scantily-clad females, and other attractions – also cemented the popularity of its female star, Hu Die (aka Butterfly Wu). More and more *wuxia* films were produced, including **Jiu Long Shan** (Nine Dragon Mountain", 1930) and the 13-part **Huangjiang Nu Xia** ("Wild River Swordswoman", 1930) with its (typically) female protagonist (played by Xu Qinfang), until the genre was suppressed by the Guomingdang government who feared it would foment decadence and anarchy due to its conjuring of a chaotic world of magic, strange beasts, violence and "depravity" – under the rules of the NFCC (National Film Censorship Committee), formed in 1931, female nudity, not uncommon in films of the 1920s, was absolutely prohibited. Production then moved to Hong Kong, where the late 1930s saw a wave of new martial arts cinema.[1]

1. *Wuxia* films of the 1920s are credited with introducing the "wire-work" special effects which allowed actors to seemingly defy gravity during fight scenes; it should be remembered, however, that this kind of stuntwork was already prevalant in European and American slapstick films of the 1910s, in which human bodies can often be seen hurtling through space on the end of piano wires.

IM SCHATTEN DER MASCHINE
("In The Shadow Of The Machine"; Albrecht Viktor Blum, Germany: 1928)

Blum was one of the main film-makers of the Volksfilmverband, or VFV, a socialist film society based in Germany and having strong affiliations to Soviet cinema. The VFV provided funding for a series of short films made by Weltfilm, a film-cartel run by Communist producer Willi Münzenberg and writer Léo Lania, whose other associates included Heinrich Mann, Béla Balázs – author of the key film-theoretical text *Der Sichtbare Mensch* ("The Visible Man", 1924) – Käthe Kollwitz, and Erwin Piscator, whose revolutionary theatrical productions in 1920s Berlin utilised projected film as an organic part of the dramatic action. The first films from the company included **Was Wir Wollen – Was Wir Nicht Wollen** ("What We Want And What We Don't Want", Béla Balázs and Albrecht Viktor Blum, 1928) and **Zeitbericht – Zeitgeschichte** ("Time Report: History", Ernst Angel and Albrecht Viktor Blum, 1928), short counter-informative political montage-films made by splicing together newsreel clips and other footage. Supervised by Léo Lania, Blum's **Im Schatten der Maschine** is another montage-film, constructed mainly from parts of two 1928 films from the Soviet Union, Aleksandr Dovzhenko's **Zvenigora** and the last part of Dziga Vertov's **Odinnadtsatyi** ("The Eleventh") – based around the construction of the Dnepr hydro-electric station – although Blum indicated that footage was culled from as many as fifty other films. The result is a 20-minute assault of frightening industrial images, toiling human figures dwarfed by vast mechanisms and structures of concrete, steel and rock, fulminating smoke-stacks, engines and pistons, drills, cables, conveyor belts, cranes, and fiery crucibles brimming with molten ore; one sequence displays an array of crushed, mutilated and fingerless human hands in alarming close-up. Overwhelming in its impact, Blum's volcanic vision of mass production seems like nothing less than a blast-furnace panorama of Hell.[1] Another noted VFV/Weltfilm production was Phil Jutzi's pro-KDP Berlin riot-film **Blutmai 1929** ("Bloody May 1929", 1929); Jutzi, formerly with proletariat film-collective Prometheus,[2] also made **Ums Tägliche Brot** ("Our Daily Bread", 1929), documenting the misery of workers in the Lower Silesian mining district of Waldenburg, and regarded as an important proletarian film tract, and **Die Todeszeche** ("The Death Mine", 1930), both produced by Weltfilm. Jutzi also created the first sound version of Eisenstein's **Bronenosets Potyomkin**, in 1930. Other Weltfilm productions of this revolutionary period include Slaten Dudow's **Zeitprobleme. Wie Der Arbeiter Wohnt** ("Problems Of Our Times: How The Worker Lives", 1930), which utilised Soviet-style montage in contrasting the rich and poor. The first Russo-Germanic film company was Mezhrabpom-Rus, founded in 1924 by Willi Münzenberg and Russian producer Moisei Aleinikov. The VFV was just one of numerous radical film societies in 1920s and 1930s Europe; another example was Les Amis De Spartacus, established in France for the purpose of privately screening Soviet films prohibited by French censorship. 1928 also saw the founding in Madrid of the first Spanish cine-society, Cineclub Español, by Ernesto Giménez Caballero, editor of *La Gazeta Literaria*. A close associate of Luis Buñuel and Salvador Dalí, Caballero was dedicated to screening the most provocative and artistically daring films of the day. Dalí, and his wife Gala, can be seen in Caballero's short film **Noticiario De Cine Club** ("Cine-Club Bulletin", 1930), a 10-minute record of a group of the club's members.

ODINNADTSATYI – FILM POSTER BY GEORGII & VLADIMIR STENBERG.

1. A different kind of industrial horror was projected the following year by director Mikhail Dubson's **Giftgas** ("Poison Gas"), in which a disgruntled scientist sabotages a gas factory, releasing deadly chemicals which kill everyone in Berlin; the film ends with mournful spectres haunting this new city of the dead.

2. Where he directed **Mutter Krausens Fahrt Ins Glück** ("Mother Krausen's Flight To Happiness", 1929), now regarded as a seminal entry in the Neue Sachlichkeit ("New Objectivity") genre; the film is a study of poverty and class-struggle which ends in a murder-suicide. Jutzi's directorial apprenticeship was at Internationalen Film-Industrie in Heidelberg, a purveyor of low-budget pulp westerns and detective thrillers such as **Der Fremde Mit Der Teufelsmaske** ("Stranger In A Devil-Mask", 1920) or **Der Maskierte Schrecken** ("The Masked Horror", 1921).

THE LAST PERFORMANCE – PRODUCTION PHOTOGRAPH (*ABOVE*); *ERIK LE MYSTÉRIEUX* – PHOTOPLAY BY R. CHALMOND (*RIGHT*).

The LAST PERFORMANCE
(Pál Fejös, 1928-29: USA)

Fejös, also known as a bacteriologist, began directing films in Hungaria around 1920; one of his first films was **Pikk Dáma** ("Queen Of Spades", 1921), a new version of the famous Russian horror story. Moving to America in the mid-1920s, he attracted much attention with **The Last Moment** (1927), an evocation of suicide by drowning, using rapid-cutting and avant-garde techniques to show the victim's life in flashback. Fejös went on to direct several Hollywood films, notably Universal's **The Last Performance** (1928, released in 1929) with Conrad Veidt as a homicidal hypnotist, Erik, who inhabits an apartment decorated with grotesque masks. Driven mad by jealousy when his beautiful assistant (played by Mary Philbin) falls for another, he finally implicates his love rival in a death which occurs during a stage-trick involving swords. Originally shot as a gothic silent titled **Erik The Great**, **The Last Performance** was eventually also released with sound – a technological advance which saw Veidt decline to renew his contract with Universal, preferring to return to Germany. Fejös himself reportedly shot the sound sequences in not only English but also French and German – in Germany the film was released as **Doktor Gift** ("Dr. Poison"), and in France as **Erik Le Mystérieux**, supported by a photoplay published by Tallandier. Fejös would later direct a new feature-length version of **Fantômas** (1932), filmed in France; he eventually turned to ethno-documentary film-making for Scandinavian companies.

THE LAST WARNING – PRODUCTION PHOTOGRAPH (*ABOVE*).
HOUSE OF FEAR – PRODUCTION PHOTOGRAPH (*BELOW*).

The LAST WARNING
(Paul Leni, 1928: USA)

Leni returned to the murder-mystery *milieu* of his earlier hit **The Cat And The Canary** with the 1928 film **The Last Warning**, based on the play *House Of Fear* and this time set in an abandoned theatre supposedly haunted by the ghost of an actor murdered there – electrocuted and then dissolved in quicklime – a few years previously. When a producer attempts to re-open the theatre, he and his cast are menaced by a hideously-masked phantom; this central part of the film also includes some brief sequences of spider-horror. The producer ignores the phantom's last warning and goes ahead with his new project, leading to more mayhem on the opening night and a final revelation of the killer's identity. Leni also inserts some experimental montage sequences into the film, but overall fails to significantly better **The Cat And The Canary**. **The Last Warning** was to prove Leni's final film – he died from blood poisoning in 1929, aged just 44. **House Of Fear**, a new jokey screen version of the play, was made in 1939 by another German director in Hollywood, Joe May.

THE MAN WHO LAUGHS – PRODUCTION PHOTOGRAPHS.

The MAN WHO LAUGHS
(Paul Leni, 1928: USA)

Leni's renowned version of the Victor Hugo novel *L'Homme Qui Rit*, with Conrad Veidt as the facially disfigured Gwynplaine, and a dark backdrop of torture and the gibbet, the fairground, and corruption in high places. Veidt's startling appearance is sometimes cited as the inspiration for comic-book character The Joker, who first appeared in *Batman* #1 (1940). The film also stars Mary Philbin, with support from Olga Baclanova whose naked buttocks, or those of a body-double, are at one point shown through a spy-hole. Scenes deleted before release included a sequence set in a house of disfigured children.

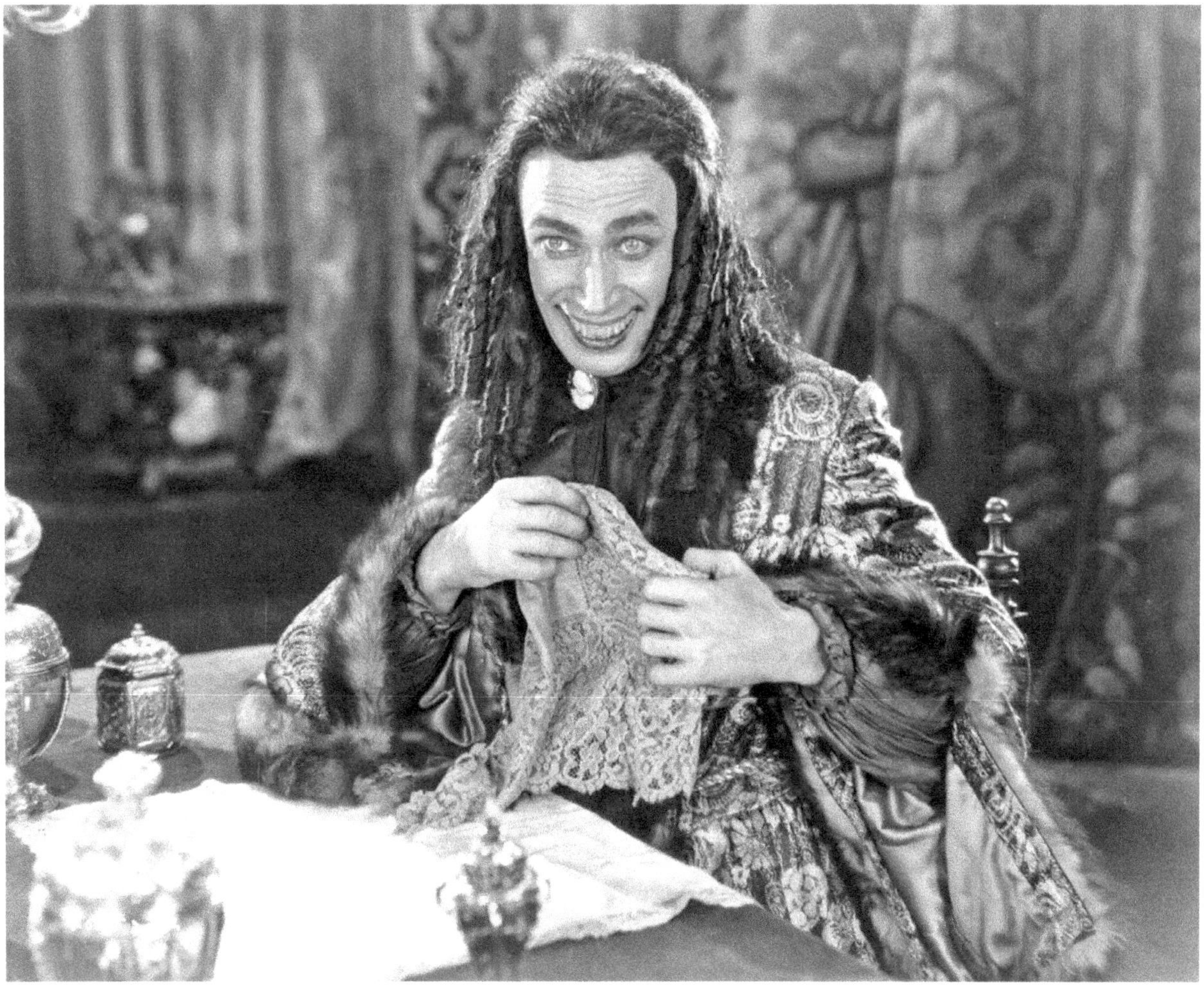

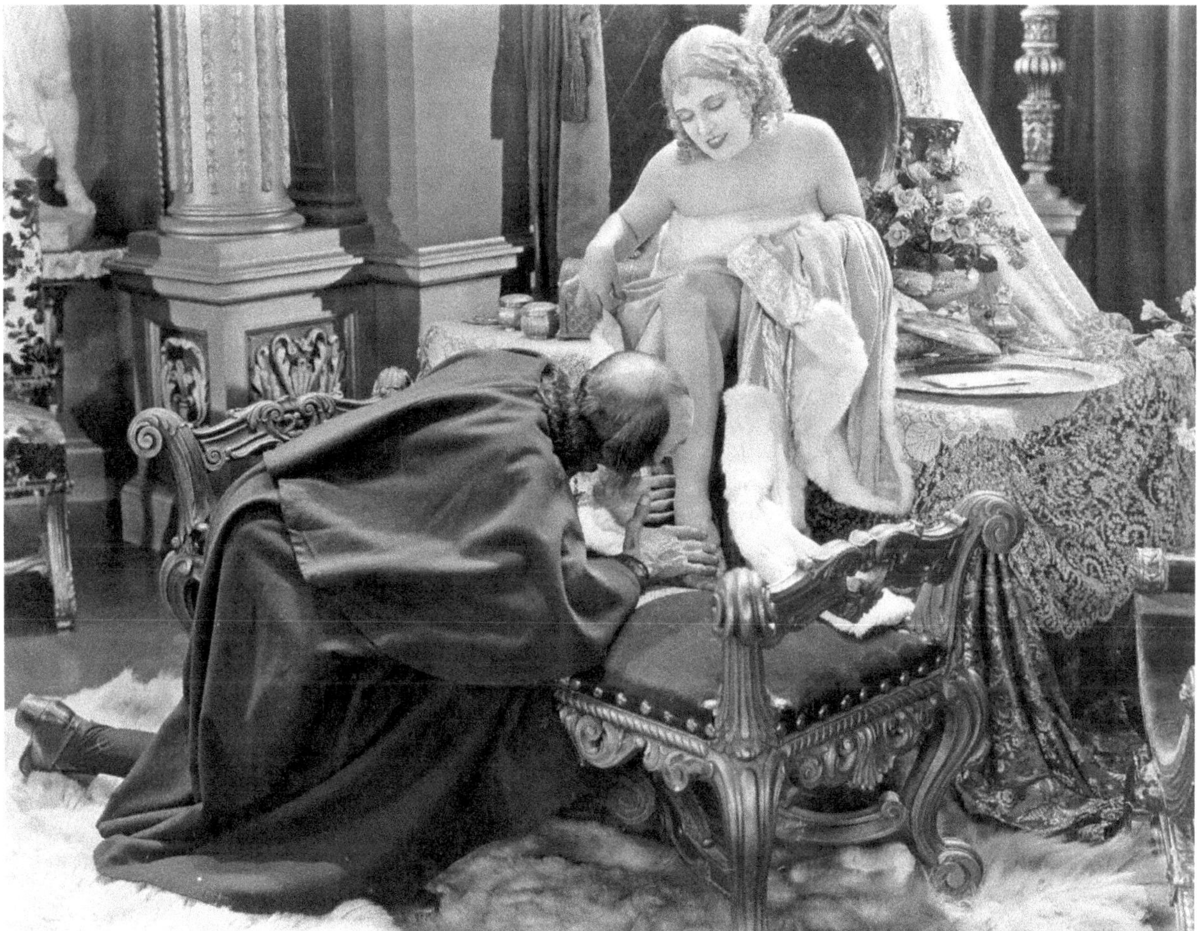

Les MYSTÈRES DU COUVENT
("Mysteries Of The Convent"; Anonymous, c.1928: France)

A short, silent underground blasphemo-porno film featuring nuns and monks engaged in various explicit sex acts, including lesbianism and sodomy; in the tradition of **Le Paysan Et La Nonne** ("The Peasant And The Nun") and **Le Moine** ("The Monk"), also from the 1920s. Another unusual French stag film from this time was **Le Professeur**, in which a horny school-teacher seduces six of his female pupils. A similar setting was used for **Fessées À L'École** ("Spanked At School"), in which a succession of schoolgirls raise their skirts and display their naked buttocks for the cane – one of them, inexplicably, wearing a rabbit-mask. Around this period it was also possible to buy erotic (though not explicit) films in France by mail order; small Parisian companies such as Ginette and Studio de la Lune would openly advertise such "sensational" stag reels as **Vierges Et Demi-Vierges** ("Virgins And Near-Virgins", c.1930), **Brutalités Feminines** ("Feminine Brutalities", c.1930), **La Belle Et La Bête** ("Beauty And The Beast", c.1932) or **Curiosa** (c.1932) in various publications. The fetishistic nature of some of these *super-galant* ("ultra-erotic") offerings of the 1930s has often invoked speculation linking their clandestine production to certain French lingerie companies of the day, particularly Yva Richard and Diana Slip, who both sold a range of fetish apparel and accoutrements alongside books on sado-masochism and erogenous photographs of their underwear ranges posed by semi-nude models – some in bondage or "anti-clerical" crucifixion poses. Also made around 1928, and similar in theme to **Les Mystères Du Couvent**, was the 8-minute German stag reel **Schwarze Messe** ("Black Mass", known in France as **Messe Noire**). The film depicts a coven of nude nuns being consecrated to Satan. This involves orgies, SM rites (including blood-letting) and lesbian scenes conducted by a masked high priest. Another 20s German stag film was **Gretchen Und Faust**, involving two couples. The earlist surviving German hardcore film is thought to be **Am Abend** ("In The Evening", c.1910), complete with fellatio and sodomy scenes; another film from that period, **Klostergeheimnisse** ("Monastery Secrets", c.1912) may be Germany's first porno-nun movie.

YVA RICHARD – MODEL PHOTOGRAPH.

NIHON-ICHI MOMOTARO
("Momotaro, Japan's Number One"; Sanae Yamamoto, 1928: Japan)

In this 11-minute animated phantasy, the revered boy-hero Momotaro leaves his parents and voyages to an island called Onigashima, where he destroys the marauding *oni* (demons or ogres) that dwell there. Momotaro as a *manga eiga* character came into his own with the advent of Japan's "15-year war" in 1930, when his propaganda value as a national hero became apparent. Seitaro Kitayama's more primitive **Momotaro** (1918) stands as the first animated incarnation of this enduring legend. Another *manga eiga* deriving from Japanese legend was Yasuji Murata's **Kobutori** ("Snatched Lump", 1929); with more refined animation techniques, Murata relays the tale of *tengu* (bird-like goblins) who claw lumps from old men's faces. Murata's most accomplished film, a short masterpiece of cut-out animation (*kirigami*), was **Tsuki No Miya No Ojosama** ("Queen Of The Moon Palace", 1934). Other phantastic *manga eiga* from this period include **Tako No Hone** ("Octopus Bones", 1927, directed by Murata), which tells how the octopus lost its skeleton, Manzo Miyashita's **Urashima Taro** (1931), an updated and more technically proficient version of the deep-sea legend, and **Chinkoro Heihei Tamatebako** ("Chinkoro Heihei's Treasure Chest", directed by Noburo Ofuji, 1936), a variation in which the mischievous Chinkoro meets the fish king.

OPIUM
(Vitaliy Zhemchuzhniy, 1928: Soviet Union)

An anti-religious montage film, inspired by Karl Marx's idiom "religion is the opium of the masses", and produced by Sovkino. Constructed from archival footage, the film contrasts poppy fields and opium factories with the churches of various religions, and further ridicules them by likening priests and worshippers to sham fortune tellers and the suckers who blindly hand over their money in return for meaningless assurances. A police raid, with men arrested and imprisoned, is also included. The scenario for **Opium** was devised by Osip Brik, leader of the radical arts collective

Levy Front Iskusstv and formerly co-editor, with Vladimir Mayakovsky, of its journal *LEF*, renowned for its Constructivist photomontage covers by Aleksandr Rodchenko and the publication of numerous radical film manifestos including Eisenstein's *Montazha Attraktsionov* ("The Montage Of Attractions"). From 1927 to 1929 *LEF* became *Novy LEF*, with Brik being replaced by Sergei Tretyakov. Brik's wife Lilya's film experiment **Steklyannyy Glaz** ("Glass Eye", 1928), also made with Vitaliy Zhemchuzhniy, was pitched as a parodic assemblage of documentary and fictive footage, a satire of American cinematic tropes.

The PACE THAT KILLS
(William A. O'Connor & Norton S. Parker, 1928: USA)

This Willis Kent production is an exploitative "anti-drugs" film, showing the evils of addiction and its attendant perils. A country boy goes to the big city, gets hooked on cocaine, and then along with his new-found girlfriend progresses to opiates; in the end she turns to prostitution and drowns herself after becoming pregnant in drug-fuelled sex bouts, and the boy, a hopeless addict, also plunges to his death in the river. The film also implicates the Chinese, with their insidious opium dens, as being culpable for the white man's addictions. Spurred on by the success of this production, Willis Kent entered into a series of exploitative low-budget movies on the perils of sex and substance abuse, such as **Hollywood Playthings** (1930), **The Primrose Path** (1931), and **Ten Nights In A Bar Room** (1931). He remade **The Pace That Kills** for sound in 1935, retaining O'Connor as director; this version also played under the title **Cocaine Fiends**, and was reportedly never given a seal of approval due to its themes of cocaine addiction and drug-dealing, prostitution, unmarried pregnancy, and opium dens, and its parading of human vice, misery and squalour.

THE PRIMROSE PATH – THE ROAD TO ALCOHOLISM AND PROSTITUTION; PRODUCTION PHOTOGRAPH.

PESN O METALLE
("Song Of Metal"; Mikhail Shapiro, Aleksandr Zarkhi, Iosif Kheyfits, & Vladimir Granatman, 1928: Soviet Union)

A 7-minute experimental montage, assembled from newsreel, and captioned by lines from the eponymouas poem by Aleksandr Zharov; designed as an exhortation to strengthen Russian economic and military power, the film follows the rhythm of the words. A somewhat different 1928 film on metallurgy came from director Yevgeniy Ivanov-Barkov, whose social drama **Geroi Domny** ("Heroes Of The Blast Furnace", from Sovkino) extolled those who rebuilt Soviet industry after the depletions and sabotage of the Civil War. This vein of industrial cinema continued with such films as Abram Room's **Manometr-1** ("Manometer-1", 1930), based on from actual events at a Moscow factory; this archetypal *agitpropfilm* combines newsreel footage and staged scenes to show how sub-standard workmanship at the Manometer Plant leads to a boiler-room explosion; an investigation reveals that the worker responsible is a drunk, who reforms and vows to expiate his crimes through hard work. Stills from this missing film – also known as **Proryv Na Zavode** ("Breakdown At The Factory") – show classic images of shirtless, begrimed, hammer-wielding workers, mythic figures from the monumental iconography of Soviet industrial culture. Room followed up with **Manometr-2**, also known as **Likvidatsiya Proryva Na Zavode «Manometr»** ("Elimination Of The Breakdown At The Manometer Factory"), in 1931. Another notable industrial agit-drama was Ivan Pyryev's **Konveyyer Smert** ("Conveyor-Belt Of Death", 1932), about workers in a Nazi arms factory and the rebellion of one female worker against her immoral, avaricious bosses. This brutal propaganda film was promoted by a brilliant poster drafted by the artist Smolyakovskiy, foregrounding a blazing machine-gun. An example of a purely documentary agit-film was Viktor Turin's **Stalnoy Put** ("The Steel Path", 1929); also known as **Turksib**, this record of trans-Siberian railway construction was a visual tribute to mechanization and industrial progress filled with stirring and iconic images.

GEROI DOMNY – UNSIGNED FILM POSTER (*BELOW LEFT*); **TURKSIB** – FILM POSTER BY GEORGII AND VLADIMIR STENBERG (*BELOW RIGHT*); **KONVEIER SMERTI** – FILM POSTER BY SMOLYAKOVSKY (*OPPOSITE PAGE*).

PODVIG VO LDAKH – THE ICE-BREAKER *KRASSIN*; PRODUCTION PHOTOGRAPH (*ABOVE*).
EROICHE GESTA DELL'ARTIDE – THE AIRSHIP *ITALIA*; NEWSREEL IMAGE (*BACKGROND*).

PODVIG VO LDAKH
("Glory On The Ice"; Georgi Vasilyev & Sergei Vasilyev, 1928: Soviet Union)

In May 1928, Italian aeronaut Umberto Nobile embarked upon his second – and final – flight across the Arctic in his airship *Italia*, a semi-rigid dirigible launched the previous month. The *Italia* crashed into the polar ice on May 25, killing one crew member and injuring several others; the survivors were stranded for several weeks, with some later accused of resorting to cannibalism. Three Soviet ice-breakers, including the *Krassin* and the *Malygin*,[1] were dispatched to help in the search and rescue operation; on each ship were Sovkino cameramen (V. Bluvshtayn, I. Vallentey, and E. Bogarov), who shot masses of raw film footage of the entire operation. This material was later handed to two editors, Georgi Vasilyev and Sergei Vasilyev, who used it to construct a montage-film with dramatic narrative, entitled **Podvig Vo Ldakh**. This docu-drama was much acclaimed, enabling the self-styled "Vasilyev Brothers" (they were not actually related) to progress as feature-film directors. Nobile's disastrous voyage was also recorded in Istituto LUCE newsreels, and LUCE cameraman Otello Martelli later edited his footage into a 30-minute documentary entitled **Eroiche Gesta Dell'Artide** ("Heroic Arctic Exploits", 1928). **Eisbrecher Krassin** ("Ice-Breaker Krassin", also 1928) was a short German documentary on the subject produced in Hamburg, and seized in 1933, along with several other films, from Film-Kartell Weltfilm, the Berlin-based producer, distributor and promoter of Communist cinema. **Il Mistero Dell'Artide** ("Mystery Of the Arctic", 1930) was a film record of a 1929 expedition to find the *Italia*, led by Gianni Albertini and financed by Mussolini.

1. The Soviet ice-breaker *Malygin* sank in 1940, drowning all 98 crew.

POLICE REPORTER – PRODUCTION PHOTOGRAPH.

POLICE REPORTER
(Jack Nelson, 1928: USA)
A 10-chapter crime/mystery serial from Weiss Brothers. The plot revolves around the Phantom, a hooded criminal whose calling-card is a skull-and-crossbones on a disk; reviews noted that the Phantom gained the upper hand more often than not (at least until the final chapter), a more downbeat scenario than the norm. The serial's ten chapters were: **The Phantom; The Code Of The Underworld; The Secret Tube; The Flaming Idol; The Phantom's Trap; The Girl Who Dared; The Wharf Rat; The Mystery Room; In The Phantom's Den;** and **The Law Wins**. Police Reporter was distributed overseas by the European Motion Picture Company, and was released in Denmark in 1931, in two parts – **Underverdenens Mystiske Hersker** ("Mysterious Ruler Of The Underworld") and **Retfaerdighedens Triumf** ("The Triumph Of Justice"). Another Weiss serial for 1928, **You Can't Win** – from a script by Arthur B. Reeve – was announced but seemingly never completed.

POLIZEIBERICHT ÜBERFALL – PRODUCTION PHOTOGRAPH.

POLIZEIBERICHT ÜBERFALL
("Police Report: Violent Robbery"; Ernö Metzner, 1928: Germany)
One of a few films directed by set designer Metzner, a short (21-minute) expressionistic tale of a man who finds a counterfeit coin that brings him nothing but bad luck, ending with a beating by a robber. In depicting the underbelly of Berlin Metzner uses several avant-garde techniques, including mirror distortions and shadowplay, recalling his complex designs for Pabst's **Geheimnisse Einer Seele**. This film was banned by the German censor on grounds of bleakness and brutality – the premise that the downtrodden, poverty-stricken people of Berlin would kill just to obtain a single fake coin. Metzner also directed a series of three short political films for the emergent Social Democrat Party during this period – **Dein Schicksal** ("Your Fate", 1927-28), **Im Anfang War Das Wort...** ("In The Beginning Was The Word...", 1928), and **Freie Fahrt** ("Free Travel", 1928).

SHANHKAYSKIY DOKUMENT
("The Shanghai Document"; Yakov Bliokh, 1928: Soviet Union)

A 6-reel propagandist ("counter-informative") documentary that opens by contrasting the lives of impoverished Chinese labourers in Shanghai with the comparative luxury enjoyed by Western residents of the city. Bliokh's film was made in the shadow of the violent suppression in 1927 of Communist Party factions in Shanghai by the ultra-nationalist Guomintang party troops under Chiang Kai-shek, with footage from the purges including an actual execution sequence in which Guomintang soldiers shoot dead two bound prisoners. Acclaimed for its political use of "parallel montage" – for example, a treadmill worked by Chinese coolies dissolves into a carousel of laughing Western children which dissolves into Chinese children toiling inside a poisonous factory – **Shanhkayskiy Dokument** was later regarded as a milestone in Soviet documentary film-making. After the massacres in Shanghai, many Communist forces relocated to Qiong Island, but were hunted down and subjected to mass executions – footage of these purges can be found in the documentary **Qiong Ya Jiao Gong** ("Record Of Qiong Exterminations", 1933). The civil war between the government forces and the Communist rebels would last until 1949, with mass atrocities committed on both sides.

SEVERED HEADS OF COMMUNIST REBELS DISPLAYED AS A WARNING, SHANGHAI 1927– DOCUMENTARY PHOTOGRAPH.

P.W. MELROSE
BIG CIRCUS SIDE SHOW

THE SIDESHOW – MIDGET "LITTLE BILLY" RHODES; PRODUCTION PHOTOGRAPH (*OPPOSITE PAGE*).

SIDE SHOW – GIANT RALPH "TEX" MADSEN AND MIDGET BILLY PLATT; PRODUCTION PHOTOGRAPH (*BELOW*).

The SIDESHOW
(Erle C. Kenton, 1928: USA)

A freak-film starring midget "Little Billy" Rhodes as a carnival operator who suffers from unrequited love for a "normal" woman, and a series of deliberate "accidents" staged by a ruthless competitor.[1] Stuntgirl Janet Ford plays a knife-thrower's assistant. Other human anomalies glimpsed in the movie include a man with no arms (Paul Desmuke, who also acted as "stunt double" for Lon Chaney in Tod Browning's **The Unknown**), a fat lady, a "human skeleton", and Schlitze, the world-famous microcephalic ("pinhead"). Schlitze was of Mexican birth, and also had a pinhead sister. He found fame in Barnum's circus, where he was billed as the last of the Aztecs.[1] Schlitze was generally exhibited as a female and wore dresses, apparently to facilitate diaper-changing. He remained a roadshow exhibit until 1971. Freaks were also glimpsed in other carnival films of this period, such as Duke Worne's **Wheel Of Destiny** (1927), George Fitzmaurice's **The Barker** (1928), and Roy Del Ruth's **Side Show** (1931) – all three featuring Russian "human oddity" Bynunsky Hyman – but none could match the uncanny terror which would be unleashed in Tod Browning's skin-crawling **Freaks** – again showcasing Schlitze – which began filming in 1931. The 1920s were perhaps the peak years for the American freakshow, a phenomenon at whose epicentre was the sprawling pleasure complex of Coney Island, especially the Dreamland Circus Sideshow which in 1928 time boasted freak attractions such as Lionel the hypertrichotic lion man, dwarfs and midgets including the 24-inch Baron Paucci, 34-inch Princess Pee-Wee, Bonita the "midget fat lady" (height undetermined), and the 34-inch Duchess Leona, fat ladies Jolly Trixty, Jolly Irene, Baby Carrie and Baby Alpine, the albinos Rob Roy and Princess Lilian, Toney the alligator-skin boy, Schrief Afendl the human salamander, half-girls Mademoiselle Gabrielle and Violetta, Ursa the bear girl, half-man Eli Bowen, the pinheads Zip, Pip

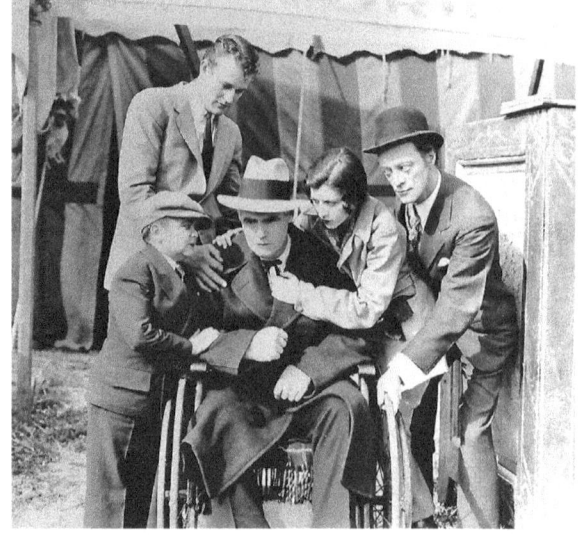

THE BARKER – BYNUNSKY HYMAN AS FIRE-EATER;
PRODUCTION PHOTOGRAPH (*LEFT*).
SHADOW OF THE EAGLE – WITH MIDGET BILLY RHODES;
PRODUCTION PHOTOGRAPH (*ABOVE*).
MAXIMO AND BARTOLA, THE ORIGINAL "AZTEC" PINHEADS;
PUBLICITY PHOTOGRAPH (*BELOW*).

and Flip, tattooed ladies Mademoiselle Burilian and Rosita, Moe and Joe the boxing dwarfs, Souse the elephant girl, Jean Libera and his parasitic twin, Alsoria the turtle girl, and Mortado, the human fountain, who claimed to have been crucified by savages and spurted blood from his wounds. Other sideshows included The Strand, which at that time boasted pinheads Kaki and Kako, Arkoff the human fountain, snake lady Belle Bonita, and armless wonder Martha Morris. During 1928 a select troupe of these acts and exhibits was assembled under the banner "A Night At Coney Island", a show which toured right across America – those in the show included Ajax, the sword-swallower; Harry Bulson, the Spider Boy (who had escaped from a lunatic asylum); living skeleton Pete Robinson and his wife, fat lady Baby Bunny; Mrs. Tiny, a midget billed as the world's smallest mother; half-man half-woman Albert-Alberta; bearded lady Olga Roderick; giant Paul Herold; Nina, the snake charmer; and Koo-Koo, the bird-girl. It was this cultural climate which soon enabled Browning to create **Freaks**, his masterwork of human horrors.

1. Midget Rhodes later featured in the 12-chapter Mascot serial **Shadow Of The Eagle** (1932), in which a carnival is stalked by a homicidal airman. The serial's chapters were: **The Carnival Mystery; Pinholes; The Eagle Strikes; The Man Of A Million Voices; The Telephone Cipher; Code Of The Carnival; Eagle Or Vulture?; On The Spot; When Thieves Fall Out; The Man Who Knew; The Eagle's Wings;** and **The Shadow Unmasked.**
2. The Barnum tradition of exhibiting microcephalics as Aztecs dates back to around 1848, when two pinheads – male and female siblings named Maximo and Bartola – were presented as "Aztec children", supposedly discovered lurking in the ruins of a lost jungle city temple.

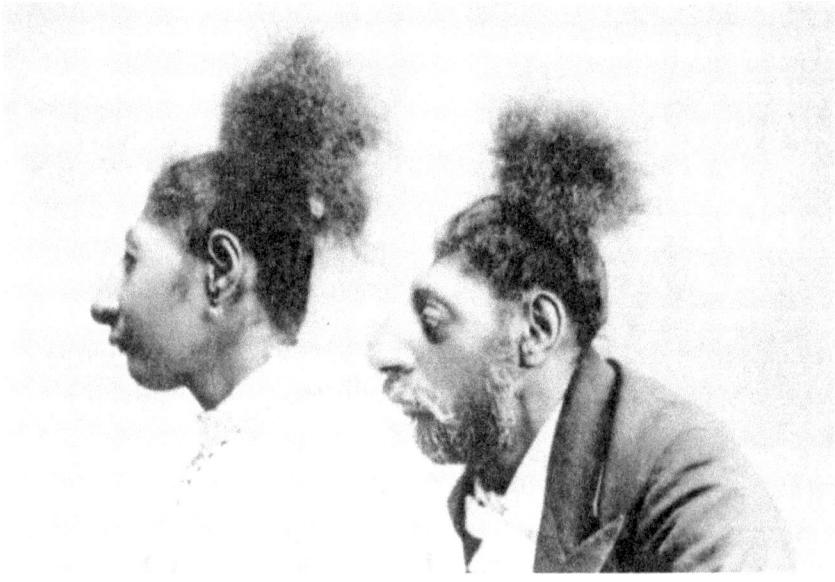

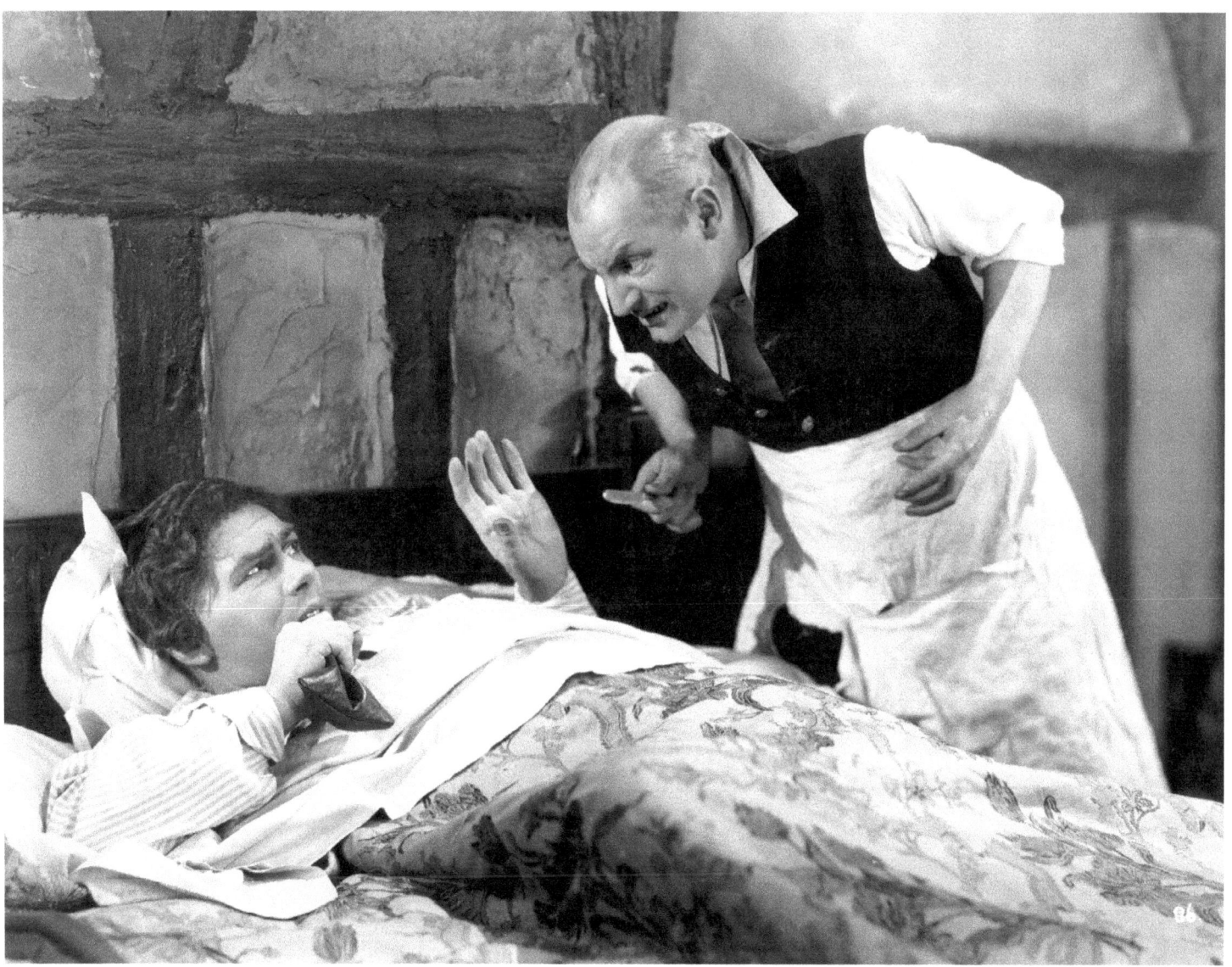

SWEENEY TODD – PRODUCTION PHOTOGRAPH. CHARACTER ACTOR MOORE MARRIOTT, WHO PLAYED TODD, ALSO APPEARED IN ANOTHER HORRIFIC LITERARY ADAPTATION, THE MONKEY'S PAW (1923).

SWEENEY TODD
(Walter West, 1928: UK)

The first dramatic adaptation of the literary legend of Sweeney Todd, otherwise known as the demon barber of Fleet Street; Todd was that most feared figure, the serial killer, a man who butchered his victims using the tools of his trade (in this case, a cut-throat razor). The legend of Todd also ventures into the taboo zone of cannibalism – his victims were made into meat pies, and sold to unsuspecting customers on the streets of London. Perhaps to mitigate the horrors of this tale, West's film is framed as a nightmare – an atrocity which could never happen in real life. The character of Sweeney Todd first appeared in the British pulp serial (or "penny blood") *The String Of Pearls* (1846–1847), believed to have been authored by James Malcolm Rymer, who also wrote the infamous *Varney The Vampire* (although another pulp author, Thomas Preskett Prest, may actually be responsible for one, or both, or parts of these classic horror tales). **Sweeney Todd** is actually based on the 1847 play *The String Of Pearls, or The Fiend Of Fleet Street* by George Dibdin-Pitt, which in turn drew directly from Rymer's weekly pulp missives.

TARZAN THE MIGHTY – PRODUCTION PHOTOGRAPHS.

TARZAN THE MIGHTY
(Jack Nelson & Ray Taylor , 1928: USA)

The first of two 15-chapter Tarzan serials from Universal,[1] both starring Frank Merrill (replacing Joe Bonomo, who fractured a leg prior to shooting) as Tarzan and Natalie Kingston as Jane – the second serial was **Tarzan The Tiger** (1929),[2] notable for nude swimming scenes by Kingston aa well as topless nudity in slave-market scenes. Both serials featured sequences with actors in gorilla suits, with an extremely vicious-looking specimen named Taug in **Tarzan The Mighty** being played by Charles Gemora. Gemora returned in **Tarzan The Tiger** to play another dangerous ape, named Taglat. Physically bested by Tarzan, Taglat takes revenge by ambushing and abducting Jane, presumably in order to subject her to trans-species rape. **Tarzan The Mighty** is said to have been based upon the short story collection *Jungle Tales Of Tarzan*, published in 1919, and pits Tarzan against a villain named Black John. The serial's fifteen chapters of were: **The Terror Of Tarzan; The Love Cry; The Call Of The Jungle; The Lion's Leap; Flames Of Hate; The Fiery Pit; The Leopard's Lair; The Jungle Traitor; Lost In The Jungle; Jaws Of Death; A Thief In The Night; The Enemy Of Tarzan; Perilous Paths; Facing Death;** and **The Reckoning**. Based on Edgar Rice Burroughs' 1916 novel *Tarzan And The Jewels Of Opar*, **Tarzan The Tiger**

featured a lost civilization with a malevolent High Priestess, played by an exotic Eurasian dancer named Kithnou. It was released both as silent and with partial sound, the latter with jungle sound effects and the very first "jungle scream" of Tarzan. A third serial starring Frank Merrill – **Tarzan The Terrible**, based on Burroughs' 1921 novel of a hidden valley with dinosaurs and demi-human tribes – was projected but cancelled, possibly due to Universal's concerns over the transition to sound which would be required of the actor. Merrill had previously starred in **Perils Of The Jungle** (1927, directed by Harry L. Fraser),[3] a 10-chapter serial from Louis Weiss which included a feral ape-man creature and cannibal tiger-men amongst its low-budget attractions. Weiss' productions were known as bottom-of-the-barrel circuit fodder, and years later Weiss and Fraser even cut up their own negative of **Perils Of the Jungle** to use as stock footage in a new, hallucinatory montage entitled **White Gorilla**. Former Tarzan Elmo Lincoln also returned to the cinematic jungle scene in 1927, starring in a cash-in serial, Webster Cullison's 10-chapter **The King Of The Jungle**;[4] it is reported that actor Gordon Standing was attacked and killed by a lion during filming, resulting in Lincoln's decision to quit the movie business (he returned a decade later).

TARZAN THE MIGHTY – PRODUCTION PHOTOGRAPH (*OPPOSITE PAGE*).
TARZAN THE TIGER – JANE IN THE SLAVE MARKET; PRODUCTION PHOTOGRAPH (*ABOVE*).

1. The Universal serials were immediately preceded by **Tarzan And The Golden Lion** (FBO, 1927), a feature based on Burroughs' 1923 novel of that name and starring James Pierce as Tarzan. The film, which was not commercially successful, notably featured Boris Karloff as Owaza, a jungle savage with a human skull emblazoned upon his head-dress, as well as a Chinese giant named Lin-Yu-Ching who was claimed to be eight feet tall.

2. The fifteen chapters of **Tarzan The Tiger** were: Call Of The Jungle; The Road To Opar; The Altar Of The Flaming God; The Vengeance Of La; Condemned To Death; Tantor The Terror; The Deadly Peril; Loop Of Death; Flight Of Werper; Prisoner Of The Apes; The Jaws Of Death; The Jewels Of Opar; A Human Sacrifice; Tarzan's Rage; and Tarzan's Triumph. It was directed by Henry MacRae.

3. The ten chapters of **Perils of The Jungle** were: Jungle Trails; The Jungle King; The Elephant's Revenge; At The Lion's Mercy; The Sting Of Death; The Trail Of Blood; The Feast Of Vengeance; The Leopards' Attack; The Tiger Men (also known as The Gorilla's Bride); and One-Eyed Monsters (also known as The Tiger's Den).

4. The ten chapters of **The King Of The Jungle** were: A Great Tragedy; The Elephant Avenger; Battling For Her Life; Into The Lion's Jaws; The Striped Terror; Gripped By The Death Vice; The Slinking Demons; The Giant Ape Strikes; No Escape; and The Death Trap. Movie heavy George Kotsonaros reprised his usual role as a violent brute-man.

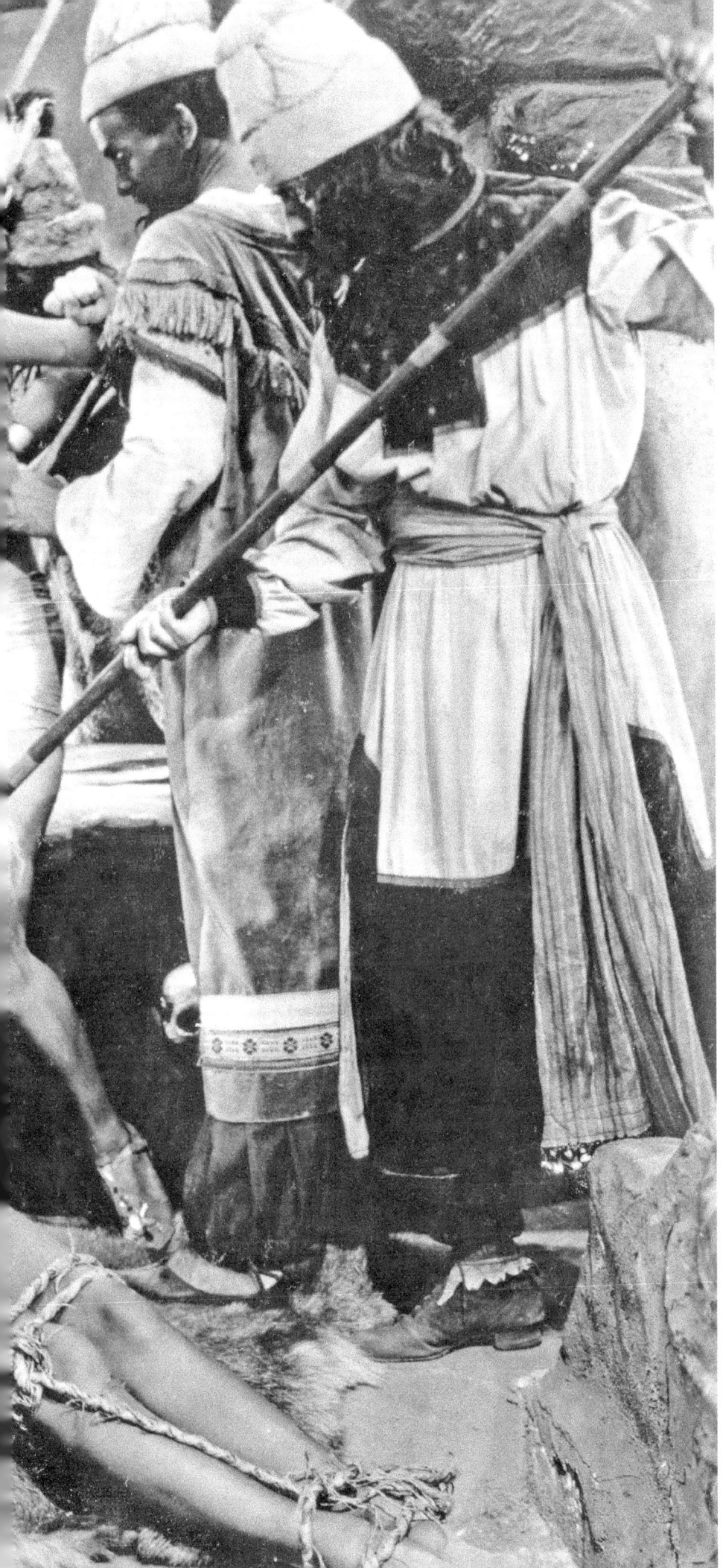

TARZAN THE TIGER – PRODUCTION PHOTOGRAPH (*LEFT*).
PERILS OF THE JUNGLE – PRODUCTION PHOTOGRAPHS (*OVERLEAF VERSO*).

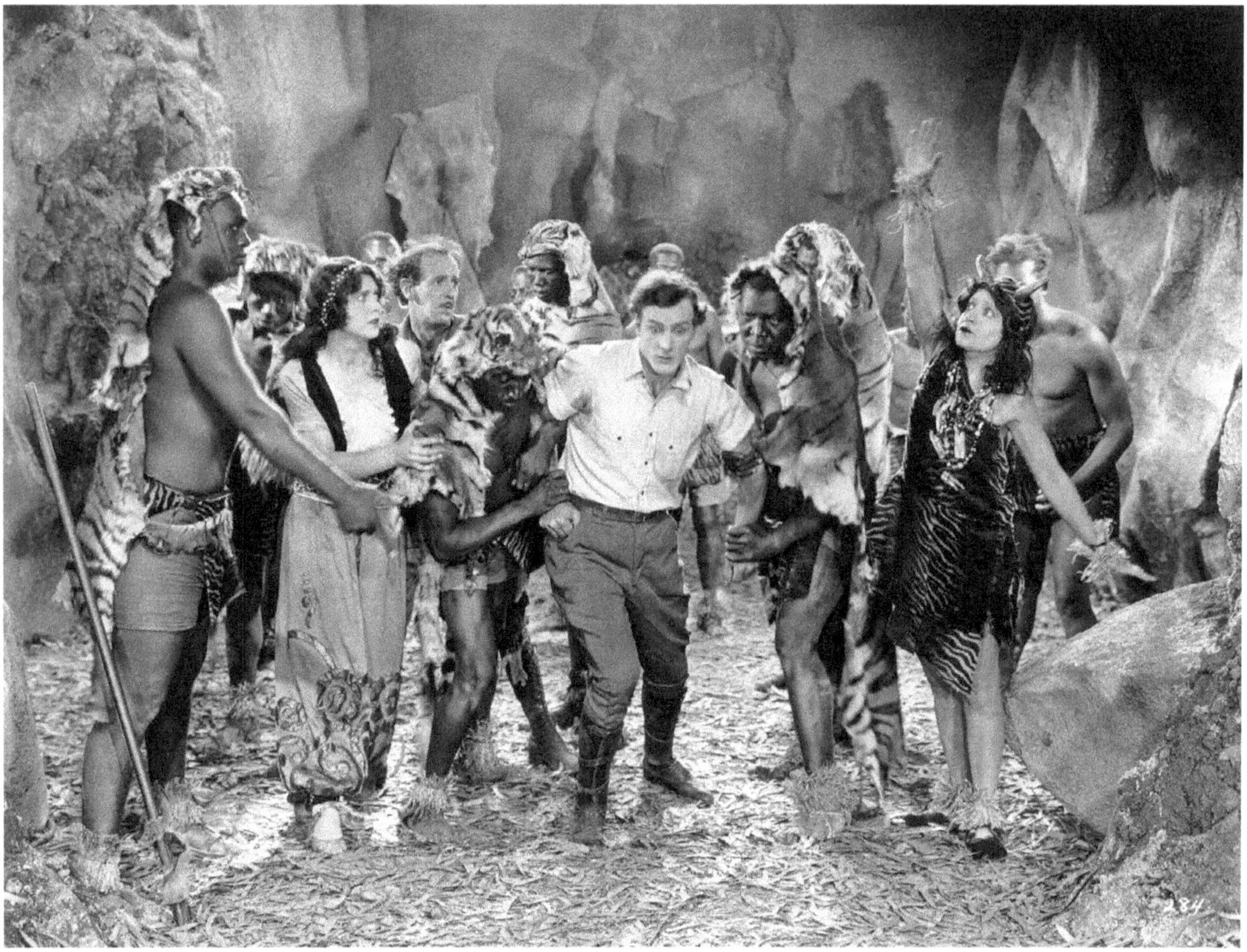

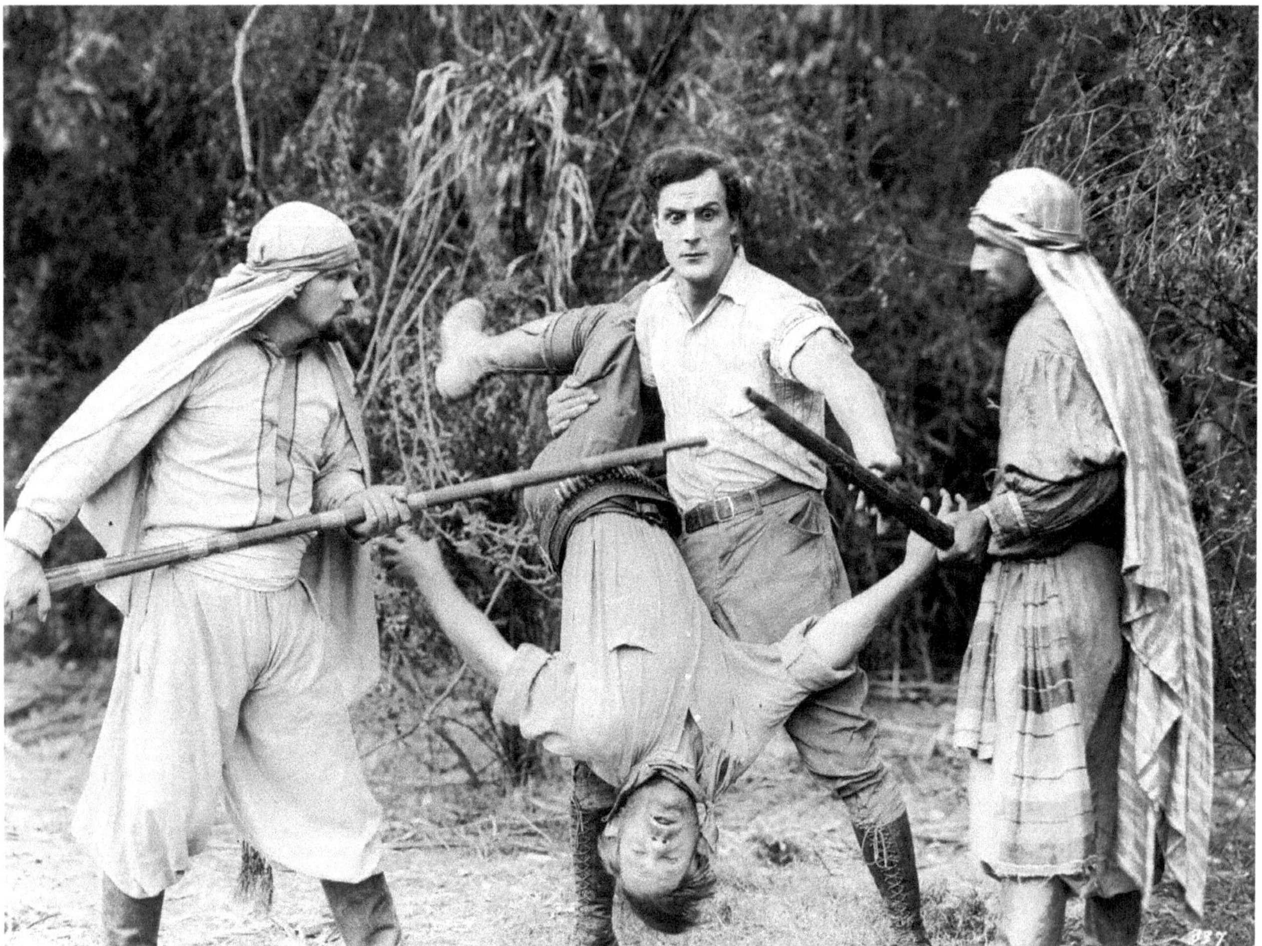

THE TELLTALE HEART – PRODUCTION PHOTOGRAPH (*BELOW*).

DRAWING FOR "THE TELL-TALE HEART" BY HARRY CLARKE (*BACKGROUND*).

"THE TELL-TALE HEART" WAS ONE OF MANY STORIES BY POE WHICH WERE PUBLISHED UNDER THE TITLE *TALES OF MYSTERY AND IMAGINATION* FOR THE FIRST TIME IN 1908, AN ANTHOLOGY WHICH HELPED ESTABLISH THE AUTHOR AS MASTER OF THE HORROR GENRE. NEW ILLUSTRATED EDITIONS WOULD FOLLOW – IN 1919 WITH MACABRE DRAWINGS BY ARTIST HARRY CLARKE, AND IN 1935 WITH DEPICTIONS BY ARTHUR RACKHAM. IT IS NOT RECORDED WHETHER OR NOT CLARKE'S DRAWINGS WERE AN INFLUENCE ON SHAMROY AND KLEIN'S FILMIC VISION OF THE STORY.

The TELLTALE HEART
(Leon Shamroy & Charles Klein, 1928: USA)
The first true adaptation of one of Poe's classic tales (it had previously been misused – diluted with religious visions – by D.W. Griffith in his 1914 effort **The Avenging Conscience**), running at around twenty-four minutes. Very bizarre angular sets modelled after **Caligari,** plus distorting double exposures and frames overwritten with text, help visualize the terror and paranoia of a murderer haunted by the mortal remains of his victim. The first sound version of Poe's "The Tell-Tale Heart" was made in England by Brian Desmond Hurst, in 1934.

THE TERROR – PRODUCTION PHOTOGRAPHS (*ABOVE & OPPOSITE*).

The TERROR
(Roy Del Ruth, 1928: USA)

Based on a 1927 stage-play by Edgar Wallace, and set in an old English countryside inn, this Warner Brothers production was one of the very first "talking" pictures, with a roughly-synched soundtrack played on Vitaphone recorded discs.[1] A typical "old dark house" mystery, **The Terror** features a hooded maniac who haunts the inn

and perpetrates various acts of murderous nocturnal outrage. The film's phantom killer and "haunted house" setting may qualify it as the first "horror" movie made with accompanying sound. After **The Terror** was released, Wallace produced a novelization of the play, which was published in 1929. The film was immediately preceded by another Wallace adaptation, **The Terrible People**, a 10-chapter Pathé Exchange serial whose first chapter was released in August 1928.² Taken from Wallace's 1926 novel of that title (originally serialized in *Detective Story Magazine* in 1925 as *The Gallows Hand*), **The Terrible People** also boasts images of a hooded killer menacing a female victim, and concerns a gang of "living dead" criminals. It was directed by Spencer Gordon Bennet, who began as a stuntman and later joined Astra Films. In 1928 Wallace also scripted Arch Heath's 10-chapter **Mark Of The Frog**, again for Pathé; not greatly reputed, the serial depicted a secret New York crime syndicate headed by the Frog, a hooded cripple. It was seemingly based on Wallace's original novel, *The Fellowship Of The Frog*, published in serial format in the *Chicago News* in 1923. Edgar Wallace was a prolific writer of crime and mystery fiction, who self-published his first crime thriller *The Four Just Men* in 1905. After several years in the British film industry, he moved to Hollywood in 1931. Notable silent films based on Wallace's work include **The Green Terror** (British Gaumont, 1919), from the novel *Green Rust*, a science-fictional tale of bio-terrorism and a mad scientist threatening to destroying the world's crops; and **The Green Archer** (1925), Spencer Gordon Bennet's first Wallace-inspired serial, from a 1923 novel. Regarded by some as one of the best silent serials, **The Green Archer** concerned an old castle, supposedly haunted by the hooded archer, where a villain keeps his wife locked away in a dungeon. It was filmed by Pathé Exchange in 10 chapters, and remade in fifteen chapters by Columbia in 1940.³ **The Terror** was remade as a feature in 1938, by Associated British Picture Corporation. The First National production **Return Of The Terror** (1934) was not a sequel to **The Terror**, but a mystery-thriller set in a sanitarium, with elements of drug addiction and insanity, and a strange X-ray machine; although supposedly based on the same Wallace play as **The Terror**, its plot appears substantially different. A masked menace could also be seen in **On Trial**, another experimental 1928 sound thriller from Warners.

1. The Vitaphone film sound system was inaugurated in 1926 by Warner Brothers, who first used it in conjunction with their production **Don Juan**, premiered in August that year. The system involved playing pre-recorded sound discs of a musical soundtrack in synchronization with film projection. Vitaphone was also established as a subsidiary film production unit, initially specialising in short musical numbers.

2. The ten chapters of The Terrible People were: The Penalty; Disaster; The Claws Of Death; Hidden Enemies; The Disastrous Rescue; The House Of Peril; In The Enemy's Hands; The Dread Professor; The Death Trap; and The Capture.

3. The ten chapters of Mark Of The Frog were: The Gas Attack; Decoyed; The Jail Delivery; Triple Vengeance; The Enemy Within; Cross Fire; Framed; A Life At Stake; A Race With Death; and Paying The Penalty. The Frog (1937) was a UK production based on the same Wallace novel, but its 1939 sequel The Return Of The Frog was based on Wallace's The India Rubber Men, a novel first published in 1929.

4. The ten chapters of Pathé's The Green Archer were: The Ghost Of Bellamy Castle; The Midnight Warning; In The Enemy's Stronghold; On The Storm King Road; An Affair At The River; The Mystery Ship; Bellamy Baits A Trap; The Cottage In The Woods; The Battle Starts; and The Smoke Clears Away. The fifteen chapters of Columbia's The Green Archer were: Prison Bars Beckon; The Face At The Window; The Devil's Dictograph; Vanishing Jewels; The Fatal Spark; The Necklace Of Treachery; The Secret Passage; Garr Castle Is Robbed; Mirror Of Treachery; The Dagger That Failed; The Flaming Arrow; The Devil Dogs; The Deceiving Microphone; End Of Hope; and The Green Archer Exposed.

THE TERRIBLE PEOPLE – PRINTED PRODUCTION PHOTOGRAPH (*TOP RIGHT*); MARK OF THE FROG – PRODUCTION PHOTOGRAPH (*CENTRE RIGHT*); RETURN OF THE TERROR – PRODUCTION PHOTOGRAPH (*BOTTOM RIGHT*).
ON TRIAL – PRODUCTION PHOTOGRAPH (*OPPOSITE TOP*);
THE TERROR (1938) – PRODUCTION PHOTOGRAPH (*OPPOSITE BOTTOM*).

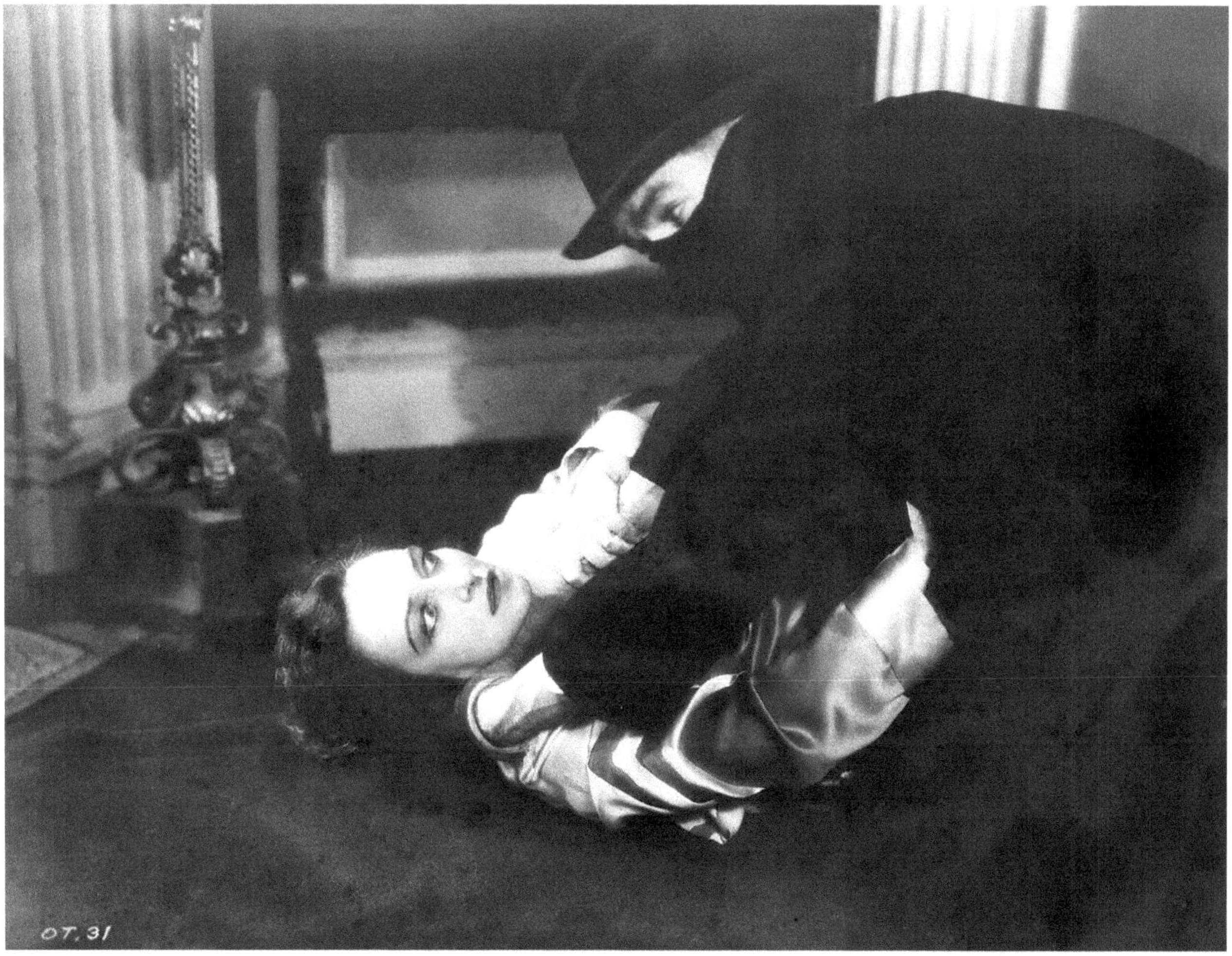
OT. 31

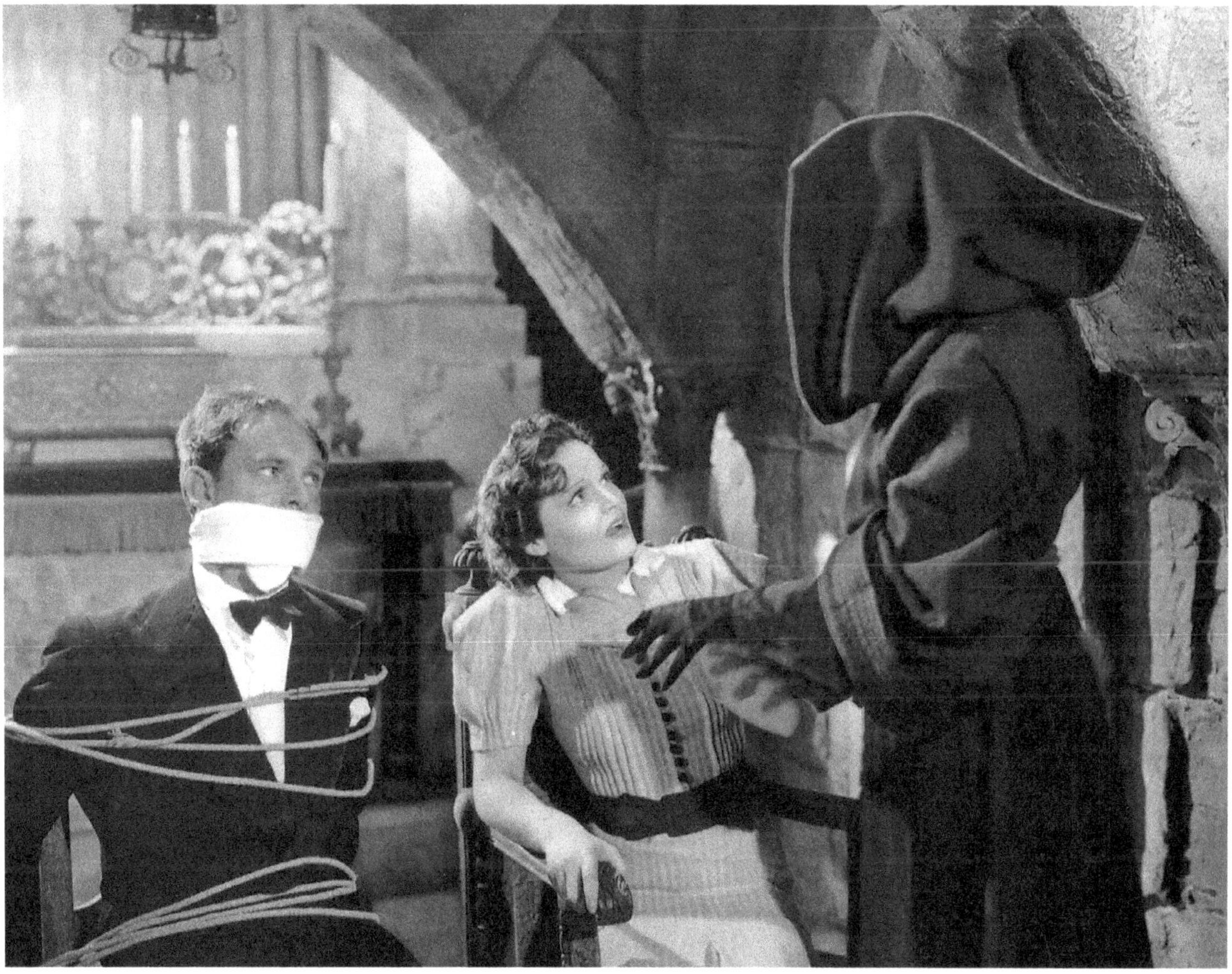

THERE IT IS – PRODUCTION PHOTOGRAPH.

THERE IT IS
(Charles R. Bowers & Harold L. Muller, 1928: USA)
At the apex of the slapstick fantasies created by Bowers and Muller, **There It Is** is an absurdist masterpiece in the tradition of Segundo de Chómon, one of Bowers' most readily identifiable predecessors. Using the "haunted mansion" theme much favoured by Chómon, Bowers adds a dash of lunatixploitation – the film is set in a nuthouse – to his customary mixture of stop-motion animation,[1] knockabout, and nightmarish non-logic. Bowers plays an officer of Scotland Yard – depicted as a playpen filled with men in kilts – who, assisted by his (animated) insect assistant, must solve the mystery of a house which seemingly has a mind of its own. Some of the effects featured include a cart which dissolves into a brick wall, a fully-grown hen springing from a cracked egg, a picture of the ocean which gushes torrents of water, and a deranged, bald "phantom" who perambulates through the proceedings on wheels. The phantom was played by Buster Brodie, a human anomaly who also appeared as an "egghead" in Bowers' **Goofy Birds** (1928), and can be seen as a pig-man in **Island Of Lost Souls** (1932), and a jack-in-the-box in the Laurel and Hardy feature **Babes In Toyland** (1934). **There It Is** and **Goofy Birds** were two of six Bowers shorts released by Educational; the others were **Hop Off, Whoozit, Say Ah-h!**, and **You'll**

Be Sorry (all 1928). Bowers went on to make his first sound film, **It's A Bird** (1930), a bizarre animation featuring a junk-metal-eating bird that was acclaimed by the likes of André Breton, who deeemed it to have originated from "the very heart of the black star". Produced by J.H. Hoffberg, **It's A Bird** was scripted by Lowell Thomas as an ethnographic spoof. Thereafter Bowers turned to working as a cartoonist, only returning to puppet animation again in the mid-1930s with a project entitled **Believe It Or Don't** (1935), containing imagery such as a xylophone-playing lobster.[2] In 1939 he collaborated on **Pete Roleum And His Cousins**, a 25-minute colour film designed to promote the oil industry and screen at the New York World's Fair. Filled with surrealistic imagery and the antics of anthropomorphic oil droplets, the film was supervised by future feature-film director Joseph Losey. Bowers' last films were **A Sleepless Night** (1940) and **Wild Oysters** (1941), a pair of 10-minute adventures with grotesque animated animal figures.

1. Some Bowers-style animation can also be seen in another 1928 short, Larry Semon's final film **A Simple Sap** (co-directed by Hampton Del Ruth). This valedictory mayhem of slapstick destruction, flying food, shotgun blasts and blackface jokes contains sequences of an animated woodpecker – which projectile-vomits over Semon's head – and an animated half-hatched alligator egg. A similar sequence of animated chicken eggs can also be found in Jack White's earlier Mermaid comedy **Fast And Furious** (1924), while Semon's 1925 short **The Dome Doctor** featured an animated onion.

2. **Believe It Or Don't**, produced by Novelty Pictures, is seemingly related to a project between Bowers and Lowell Thomas, announced in 1934 and entitled **Tall Story Comedies**, and may be the only completed or surviving film from this collaboration.

GOOFY BIRDS – LOBBY CARD.

A TRAGEDY OF SPEED!!
(Pathé, 1928: UK/USA)

On April 25, 1928, American racing driver Frank Lockhart attempted to set a new land speed record at Daytona Beach, Florida. Driving a supercharged Stutz Black Hawk automobile, Lockhart exceeded 200 miles per hour before one of his tires blew out, sending the vehicle airborne. As it rolled over and over across the sand, disintegrating, Lockhart was thrown out and died instantly as he landed. The whole event was captured on film by Pathé cameras, and edited into the short **Pathé Gazette** newsreel **A Tragedy Of Speed!!**. The film opens with an aerial tracking shot of Lockhart's car as it races along the beach, then cuts to medium range as the accident occurs; Lockhart's body can be seen hurtling from the spinning car and violently impacting as it lands. The mangled wreckage is then shown in close-up, but Lockhart's corpse is not. One of the first documentary film captures of high-velocity death and the effects of speed upon the human body. One year later, mechanic Lee Bible was killed in a similar Daytona accident which was filmed and covered in the **Gaumont Graphic** newsreel **One Was Taken** (1929); the twisted wreckage of Bible's car, the Triplex, is shown, but Bible's actual death is not, despite almost certainly being recorded. A Pathé newsreel cameraman, Charles Traub, was also killed when he was struck by the hurtling car which effectively sliced him into two pieces. Another deadly high-speed car-crash filmed by Gaumont occurred during a 1949 race at Del Mar in California, when driver Rex Mays was hurled from his vehicle and broke his neck upon landing, dying instantly. Gaumont's subsequent newsreel replays the crash in slow-motion, showing Mays' fatal ejection and collision with the track. Singled out as news because of his celebrity status, Mays was just one of hundreds of racing drivers who died during the sport's primitive years of motorized carnage and bloody destruction, much of which was doubtless recorded by local film cameras.

A TRAGEDY OF SPEED!! – FRAME ENLARGEMENT (*ABOVE*).
THE DEATH-WRECKAGE OF LEE BIBLE'S TRIPLEX;
DOCUMENTARY PHOTOGRAPH (*BELOW*).

WEST OF ZANZIBAR – PRODUCTION PHOTOGRAPH (*ABOVE & FOLLOWING PAGES*).

WEST OF ZANZIBAR
(Tod Browning, 1928: USA)

The penultimate silent film collaboration between Browning and Chaney, a twisted tale of revenge set in East Africa. Chaney plays Phroso, a stage magician, who is paralyzed from the waist down in a fight with his wife's lover, Crane. The wife dies a year later, leaving behind a female child who Phroso assumes to be Crane's. When he next see Phroso, some eighteen years later, he has turned into the cruel, baldheaded Dead Legs, holed up in Africa where he spell-binds the natives with crude magic tricks. Dead Legs has a plan for revenge on Crane, who is also on the dark continent hunting ivory; he has condemned Crane's daughter (played by a former Ziegfeld Follies girl, Mary Nolan) to life as an alcohol-addicted prostitute. Chaney's portrayal of Dead Legs, crippled in both body and soul, is one of his outstanding performances, exacerbating the film's aura of exotic evil to a climactic shatteringpoint. He would only appear in three more movies, dying of cancer in 1930. **West Of Zanzibar** is also of interest for the contributions of photographer/artist William Mortensen, the pictorialist who created notoriously provocative composite images of horror, sex and the grotesque through various manipulative techniques, including scratching, superimpositions, and chemical treatment of his negatives. Browning commissioned Mortensen to create a set of tribal masks for the film; the results were some of the most bizarre and nightmarish props of any Hollywood production. **West**

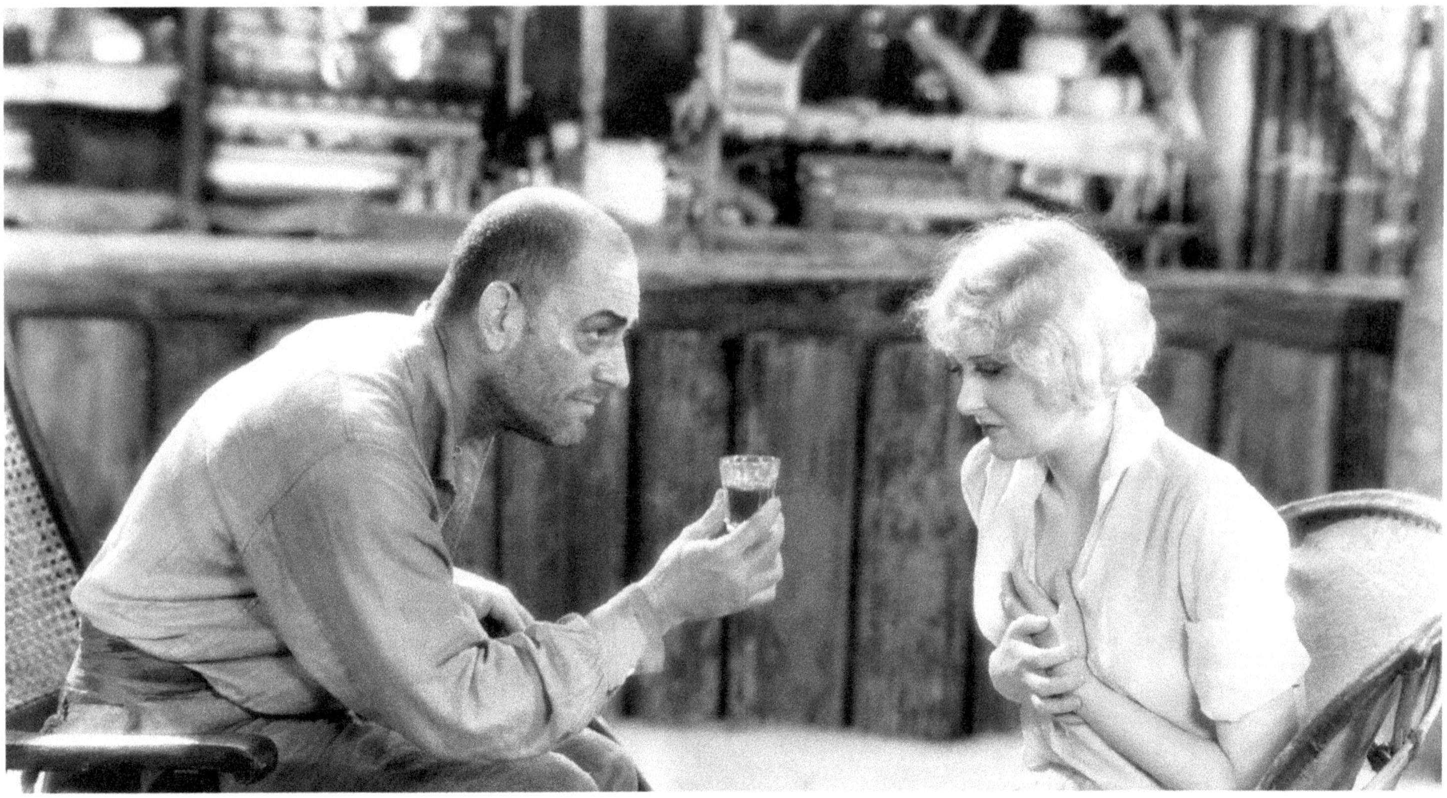

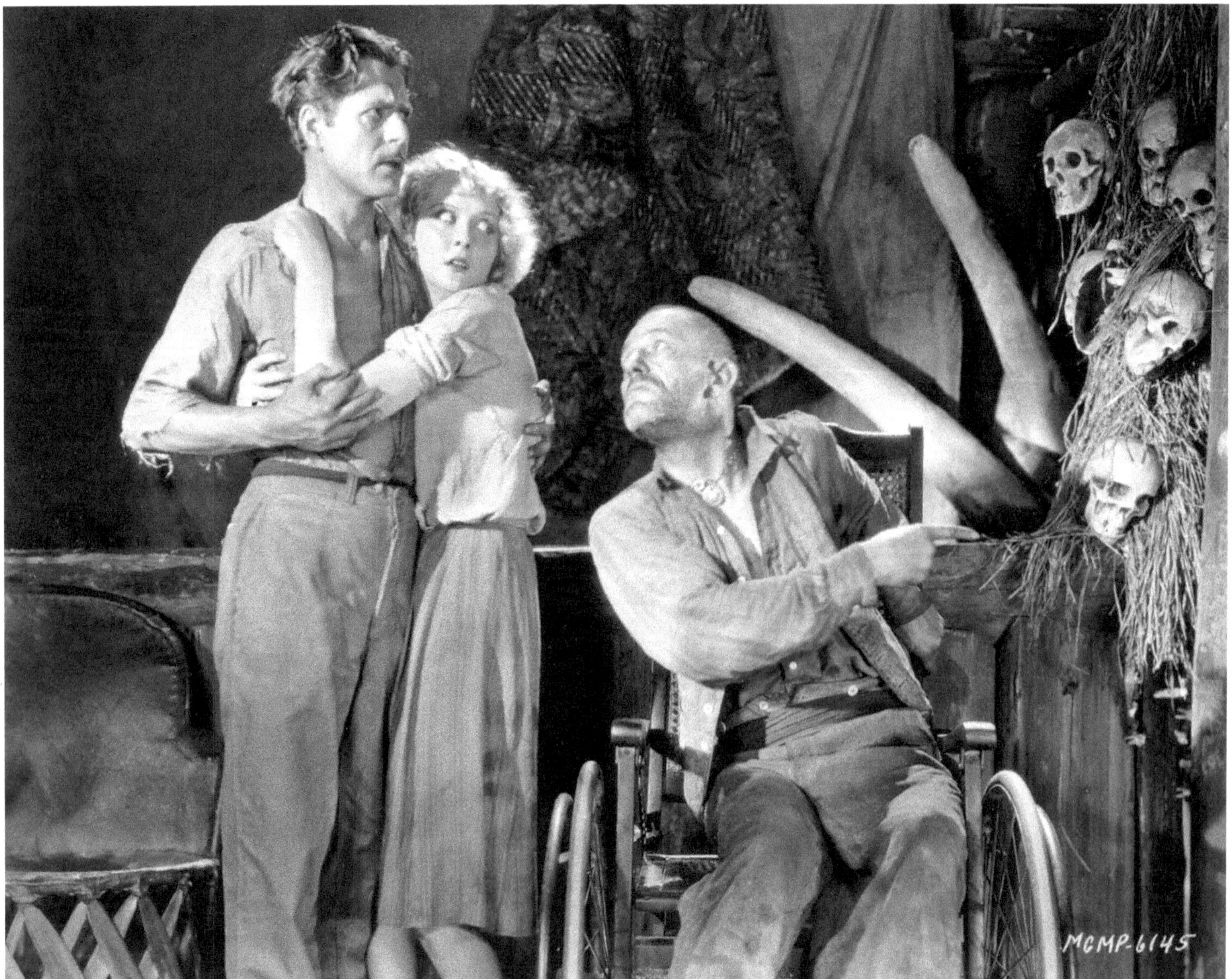
MGMP-6145

WEST OF ZANZIBAR – PRODUCTION PHOTOGRAPH (*OPPOSITE PAGE*).
WHERE EAST IS EAST – PRODUCTION PHOTOGRAPHS (*BELOW & OVERLEAF VERSO*).
MAMBA – PRODUCTION PHOTOGRAPH (*OVERLEAF RECTO TOP*); WHITE CARGO – PRODUCTION PHOTOGRAPH (*OVERLEAF RECTO BOTTOM*).

Of Zanzibar was based on *Kongo*, a sensational Broadway play staged in 1926, starring Walter Huston as Flint (the basis for Dead Legs in Browning's version). *Kongo* was vilified in the mainstream press for its blend of horrors and taboos, which included drug addiction, miscegeny, abortion, and venereal disease – elements toned down for **West Of Zanzibar**,[1] but gloatingly restored for another film version, the notoriously sleazy **Kongo**, shot and released in 1932 just before the Hays Code clampdown. Browning and Chaney next created their final film collaboration, **Where East Is East** (1929), set in Indo-China. Chaney played Tiger Haynes, a heavily scarred animal-trapper, and Mexican starlet Lupe Velez featured as his daughter; when the girl's estranged mother tries to seduce her fiancée, Tiger lets loose his trained, homicidal gorilla, leading to a climax of carnage. Some sources credit Richard Neill, a bit-part player, as the actor in the gorilla-suit, which resembles those designed by Charles Gemora. Another film set in East Africa and featuring a memorable villain was **Mamba** (1929), a Tiffany Pictures production touted as the first dramatic feature to be shot in 2-strip Technicolor. Jean Hersholt played the monstrous German plantation owner known as Mamba, who buys a young wife and cruelly mistreats her until he is killed by tribal savages. Aligned with these jungle-sex films was a part-sound British production, **White Cargo** (1929), also based on a popular play, and set on a rubber plantation where a savage native girl poisons her white husband.

1. Several scenes were still cut by the studio before the film's release, among them a "freak-show" sequence in which Chaney appears as a half-human, half-bird creature. Browning would re-use the effect for the coda of his later horror film **Freaks**.

2. By 1929, Chaney's position as a protean icon of weird cinema was cemented to the extent that MGM's self-congratulatory **The Hollywood Revue Of 1929** included a special tribute to him, a sketch entitled "Lon Chaney Will Get You If You Don't Watch Out" in which young chorines were menaced by figures wearing an array of hideous and horrific masks (again sculpted by William Mortensen).

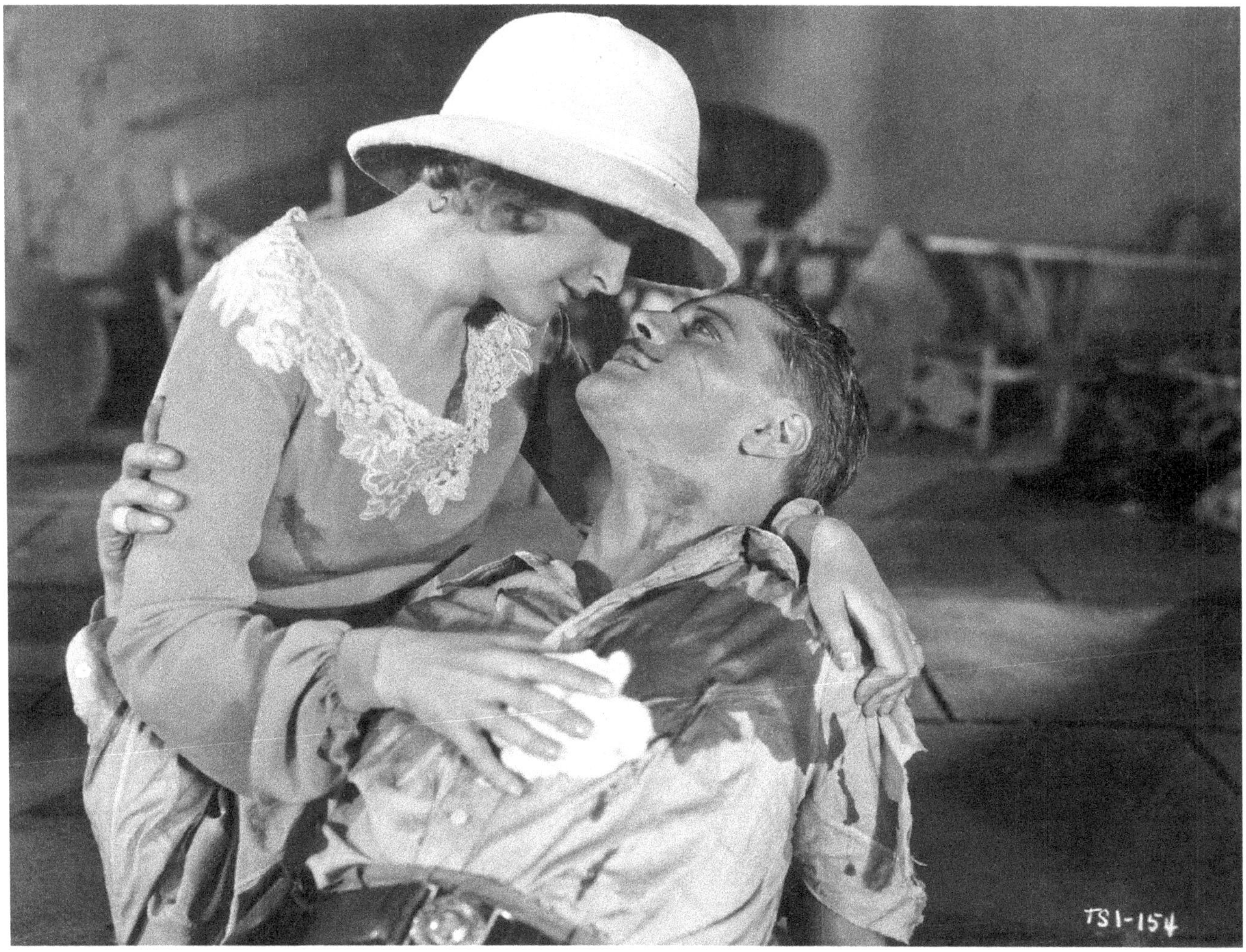
TS1-154

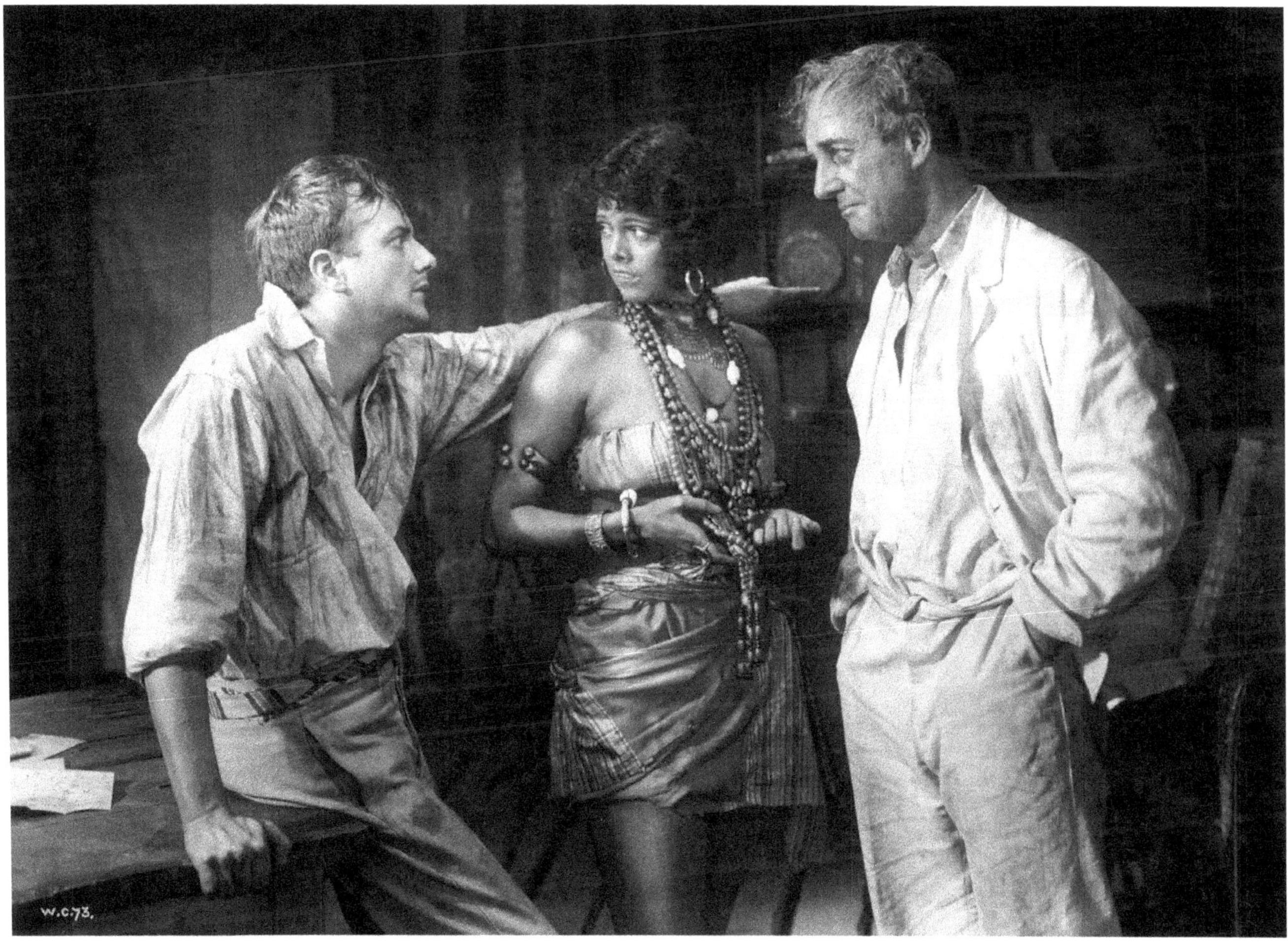
W.C.73.

WHITE SHADOWS IN THE SOUTH SEAS – PRODUCTION PHOTOGRAPH (*ABOVE*).

FROM HEADQUARTERS – PRODUCTION PHOTOGRAPH (BELOW).

WHITE SHADOWS IN THE SOUTH SEAS
(W.S. Van Dyke, 1928: USA)

One of very few films praised by the Surrealist group (for its "savage love") in their 1930 manifesto for Luis Buñuel's **L'Âge D'Or**; others included a few Mack Sennett slapstick comedies, Picabia and Clair's **Entr'acte**, and Eisenstein's **Bronenosets Potyomkin**. White Shadows In The South Seas no doubt appealed to the ethnographic leanings of Breton, Leiris and other Surrealists,[1] depicting as it does a European derelict (played by Monte Blue) adopted by a Tahitian tribe, who dies trying to protect them from exploitation by white traders. The result is a mixture of exotic documentary and doomed romance, enhanced by stunning panchromatic cinematography, and with glimpses of native nudity. Robert J. Flaherty was co-director during the initial stages of filming, but quit citing lack of artistic control. Monte Blue's other "exotic" films of this period included **From Headquarters** (1929), an unremarkable adventure set in South America notable only for some bizarre scenes with a midget magician.

1. Leiris actually left the Surrealist Group in 1929 and wrote a number of ethnographical texts for Georges Bataille's revue *Documents*, including *L'Île Magique*, a review of William Seabrook's voodoo handbook *The Magic Island*, a book which would soon inspire one of cinema's seminal horror narratives, **White Zombie**. He also contributed to the anti-Breton pamphlet *Un Cadavre* ("A Corpse"), published at the start of 1930. During 1931-33 Leiris took part in an ethnographic expedition across Africa, Marcel Griaule's Dakar-Djibouti mission which was part-sponsored by the Vicomte de Noailles; his journal of this trip was

published in 1934 as *L'Afrique Fantôme* ("Phantom Africa"). Over 1600 metres of film were shot by cameraman Eric Lutten during the expedition, including footage of Dogon masks and dances, sorcery, and funerary and circumcision rituals.

THE WIND – PRODUCTION PHOTOGRAPHS (*ABOVE & OVERLEAF VERSO*).

The WIND
(Victor Sjöström, 1928: USA)

Director Sjöström's final silent film production, a striking but flawed – due to a bland studio-imposed ending – adaptation of the 1925 novel by Dorothy Scarborough, set in an arid frontier zone where the incessant wind and heat drive people insane. Lillian Gish plays the unfortunate young woman forced by poverty to seek refuge at an isolated desert ranch, where a psycho-drama unfurls leading to rape and killing. The woman shoots her attacker dead and buries his corpse; the next morning, the wind has as if by magic erased all traces of the crime, and she recovers her mind. This is diametrically opposite to the novel's climax, in which the wind in fact reveals the dead rapist's body and the woman, by now insane, staggers away to die in the wilderness. Sjöström still conjures some powerful images of horror and incipient madness, making **The Wind** his final film of any note; unable to adjust to film-making with sound, he returned to Sweden in 1931 to concentrate on acting and theatre.

WU NU FUCHOU
("Five Female Avengers"; Gao Xiping, 1928: China)
In the huge explosion of *wuxia* films between 1928 and 1931, **Wu Nu Fuchou** was perhaps the first to establish a now-familiar genre storyline, that of a gang of five female fighters bent on reaping justice or retribution. The film tells how the five women, all victims of rape by monstrous men, decide to retaliate; after months of training in the ancient martial arts of sword-fighting, hand combat and magic, they return as an unstoppable force of violent revenge. The actresses involved in this Minxin production included Dong Pianpian, Lin Chuchu, and Lin Dandan. A similar rape-revenge theme, although involving a lone female, featured in Yimin Wen's **Hong Xia** ("Red Warrior", 1929), a 13-part serial in which Yun Gu, a peasant girl (played by Xueming Fan), is brutally violated by a bandit chief whose rampaging horde has just killed her family and razed her village. She is rescued by White Monkey, a feral martial arts hermit-priest, who teaches her the Daoist fighting tools she needs to return as a flying swordswoman and wreak vengeance on the rapist (whose lair is stocked with scantily-clad female servants).

La ZONE
("The Zone"; Georges Lacombe, 1928: France)
Lacombe's unusual city-film eschews the bright lights and tall buildings of other documentaries to focus on a strip of wasteland on the outskirts of Paris, inhabited by a race of urban outcasts who live in shacks or caravans, scavenging for scraps and bones. Lacombe uses a fixed camera to examine the faces and gestures of these impoverished foragers, given the self-appointed rank of *chiffonniers* ("rag-pickers") in their alternative society of the damned. Among their number is La Goulue ("The Greedy Bitch"), a former Moulin Rouge *can-can* dancer once known as the Queen of Montmartre, who posed not only for dwarf artist Toulouse Lautrec, but also for a series of nude photographs by Achille Delmaet. La Goulue ended up a destitute alcoholic after a failed business venture, and was reduced to scratching a living from the streets.

THE PARIS ZONE, 1928 – DOCUMENTARY PHOTOGRAPH.

DAS SCHIFF DER VERLORENEN MENSCHEN ("SHIP OF LOST SOULS", MAX GLASS FILM, 1929) – PRODUCTION PHOTOGRAPH.

1929

ALIBI – PRODUCTION PHOTOGRAPHS.

ALIBI
(Roland West, 1929: USA)

In **Alibi**, the first classic crime/gangster film of the sound era, director West embraced the new sonic technology by creating experimental sound collages, an aural mesh of police sirens and whistles, gun-shots, and roaring car engines, used in the same way as a visual montage, but concurrently with action scenes of violent robbery and murder. The camerawork, by former Signal Corps operator Ray June, includes mobile subjective shots and "phantom ride" sequences. The film was further enhanced on the imagistic level by a series of amazing set designs by art director William Cameron Menzies, together producing a revolutionary fusion of annihilatory architectonic spaces and crushing, claustrophobic sound. Based on the hit Broadway play *Nightstick* (1927), **Alibi** was also one of the first sound heist movies, showing a robbery carried out during a theatre intermision, so that the perpetrator can use his escort – a policeman's daughter – to verify his whereabouts. West's regular lead, Chester Morris, plays the mob-connected crook, while Mae Busch plays a masochistic moll. As customary during 1929, a silent version was also released for movie theatres not yet converted for sound.

ALL QUIET ON THE WESTERN FRONT – PRODUCTION PHOTOGRAPH.

VÄSTFRONTEN 1918 – FILM POSTER FOR THE SWEDISH RELEASE BY A.B. BIOGRAFERNAS OF WESTFRONT 1918 (*OPPOSITE*).

ALL QUIET ON THE WESTERN FRONT

(Lewis Milestone, 1929-30: USA)

The final silent WWI film of note was an American production, also released in a 1930 sound version. Based on the 1928 novel *Im Westen Nichts Neues* ("No News From The West") by German author Erich Maria Remarque, the film is most memorable for its 8-minute battle sequence, a depiction of hellish carnage which includes a shot of the severed forearms of a soldier, still gripping a barbed wire fence, after his body is blasted to pieces. A similar film from Germany, also released in 1930, was G.W. Pabst's **Westfront 1918**, which also features grim battle sequences in France and, back in the homeland, scenes in which one soldier's unfaithful wife has allowed herself to be bedded – perhaps even sodomised – by the village butcher.

BIG BUSINESS – PRODUCTION PHOTOGRAPH (*ABOVE*).
WRONG AGAIN (1928) – PRODUCTION PHOTOGRAPH (*OPPOSITE TOP*); DOUBLE WHOOPEE (1929) – PRODUCTION PHOTOGRAPH (*OPPOSITE BOTTOM*).

BIG BUSINESS
(James W. Horne, 1929: USA)

The apotheosis of silent screen slapstick. Although Laurel and Hardy's silent films seldom match their later sound 2-reelers in terms of sustained invention, **Big Business** ranks amongst the most delirious of their short films in either format. Here they play a pair of Christmas tree salesmen who, unable to make a sale in July, get drawn into a pitched battle with a customer (their eternal nemesis, James Finlayson), leading to the utter demolition of both his house and their automobile. Finally, the wanton destruction of bourgeois property and the infantile outpourings of naked aggression and violence raise **Big Business** to a level of atavistic intensity that Laurel and Hardy would only reach again in select moments of their sound output. The duo's other stand-out shorts released in 1929 included **Wrong Again**, featuring weird scenes with a piano and a horse which inevitably evoking the rotting donkeys from Dalí and Buñuel's **Un Chien Andalou** (released later the same year), and **Double Whoopee**, notable mainly for an eye-catching turn by aspiring starlet Jean Harlow who appears in extremely scanty attire (presumably as a high-class hotel hooker). Harlow also appeared in the Laurel and Hardy silent short **Bacon Grabbers** a couple of months later, not long before she was abruptly scooped up by Howard Hughes and given a lead role in the sound reshoot of his ongoing project **Hell's Angels**. As for Laurel and Hardy, their next challenge – the transition to talking pictures and the definition of a new genre, slapstick in sound – was just around the corner.

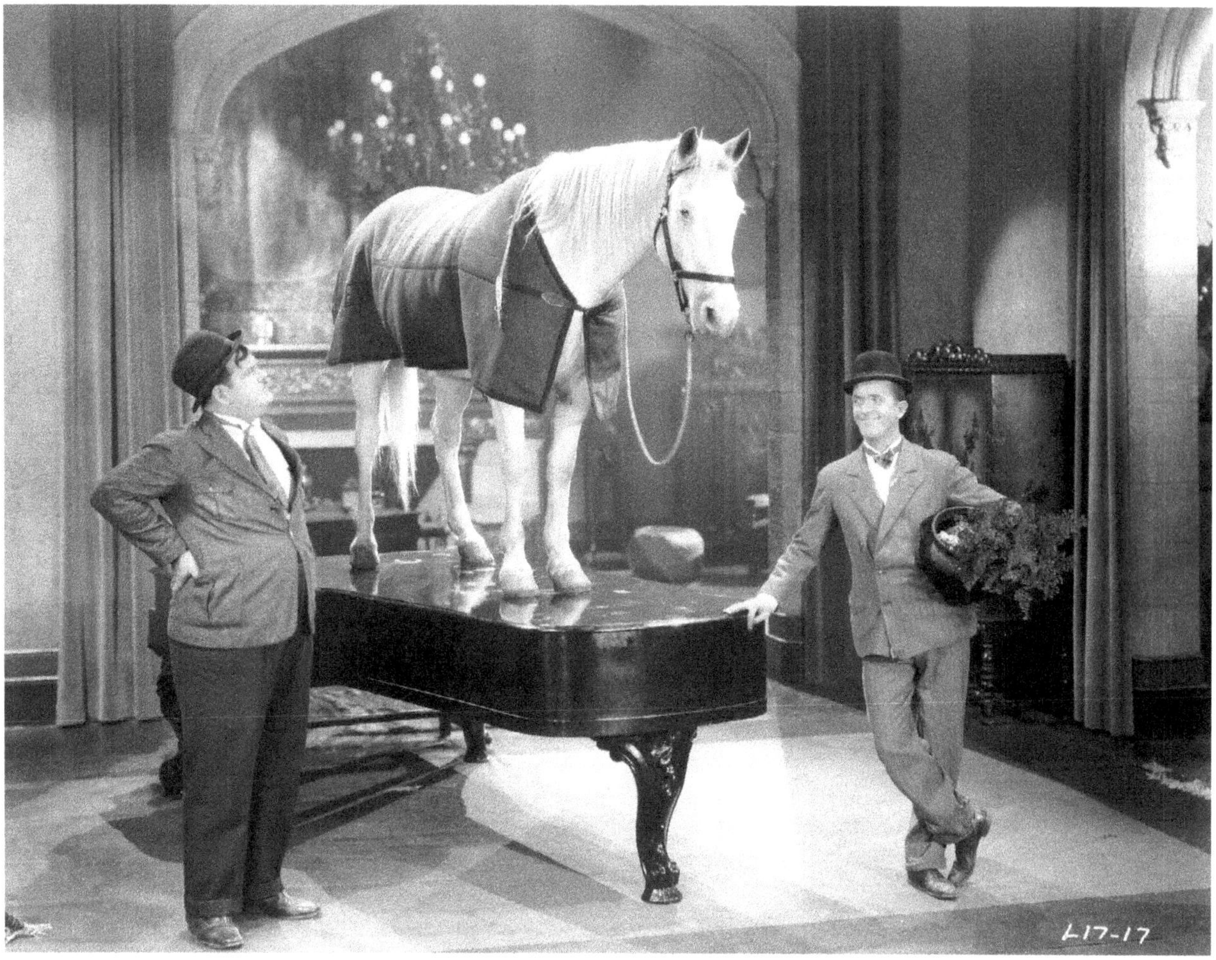
L17-17

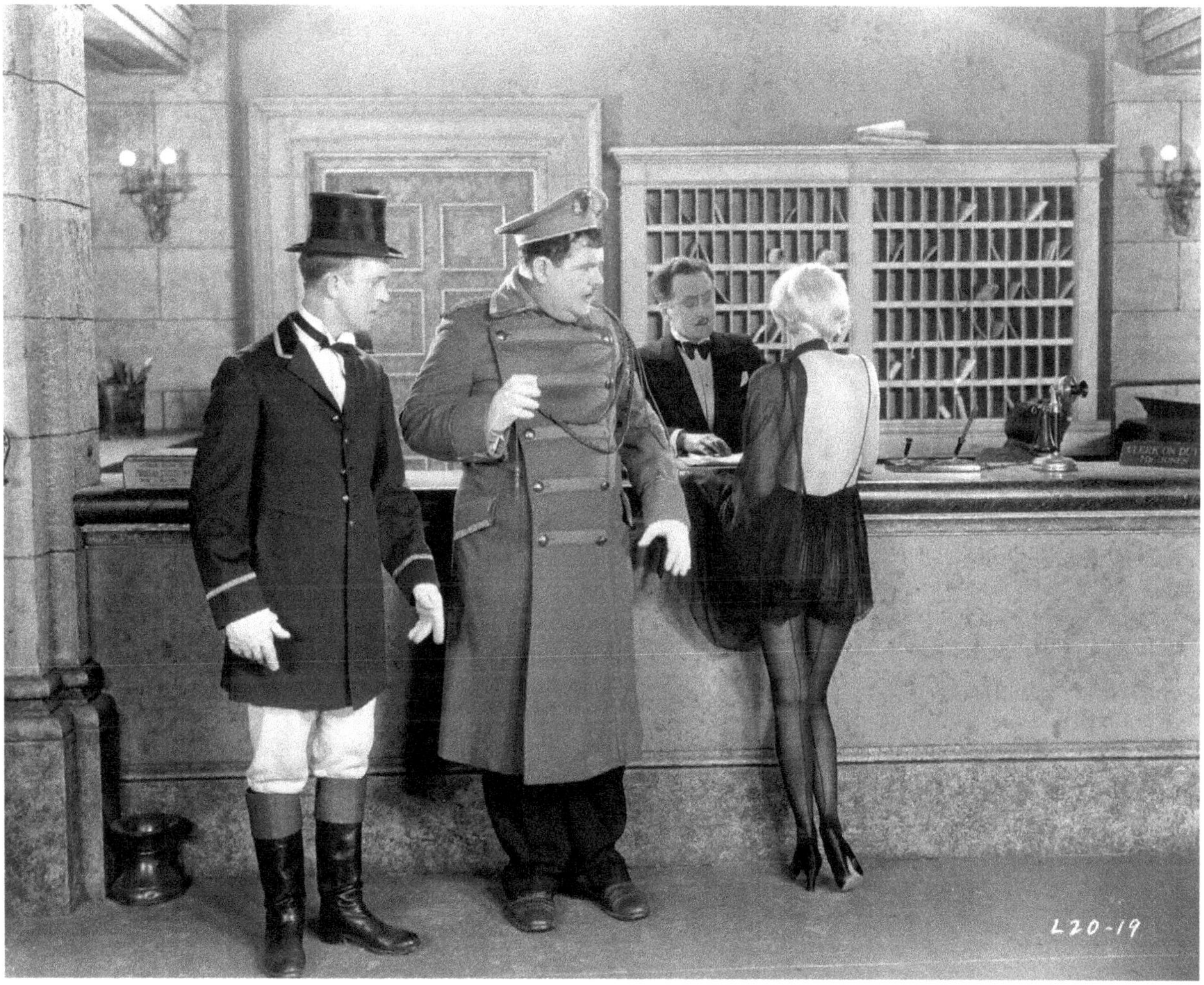
L20-19

BLACKMAIL – PRODUCTION PHOTOGRAPH (LEFT).
DÖDSSKEPPET ("DEATH SHIP") – FILM POSTER FOR THE SWEDISH RELEASE OF THE HATE SHIP (ABOVE).

BLACKMAIL
(Alfred Hitchcock, 1929: UK)

Hitchcock's first sound film was also the first integrated British sound feature made in England.[1] A dark thriller, **Blackmail** deals with a girl (played by Anny Ondra) who stabs to death a would-be rapist, is protected by her boyfriend (a police officer), and then is blackmailed by a man who finds out their secret. In the film's finale, the blackmailer falls to his death after a chase through the British Museum, a sequence achieved using the Schüfftan Process (first used by Fritz Lang in **Metropolis**), whereby live action and model-work can be combined in a single shot through mirror masking. Hitchcock's willingness to embrace new technologies is also demonstrated by the famous "sound montage" sequence in which the guilt-stricken girl is haunted by a recurring echo of the word "knife". **Black Waters**, a horrific murder-mystery filmed in sound earlier that same year by a British company, was actually produced in the USA; it was set onboard a ship at sea, as was another early British sound mystery, **The Hate Ship** (also 1929).[2] Adapted from *Fog*, a play by John Willard, and directed by Marshall Neilan, **Black Waters** depicts a homicidal lunatic's "party in Hell", held aboard the drifting ship and attended by such characters as a demented clergyman and a native "cannibal", played by Noble Johnson.

1. **Blackmail** was preceded by **Der Rote Kreis**, a 1928 German silent feature which in 1929 was produced in an English version, **The Crimson Circle**, with the Phonofilm optical sound-on-film system, and by **The Clue Of The New Pin**, a UK production made with the experimental Phototone sound-on-disc system; these two films, both crime mysteries based on stories by Edgar Wallace, were trade-screened together to British exhibitors in March 1929.

MELODIE DES HERZENS – PRODUCTION PHOTOGRAPH (*BELOW TOP*); DER ROTE KREIS – PRODUCTION PHOTOGRAPH (*BELOW BOTTOM*).

2. Another early British sound production with a nautical theme was **Atlantic** (1929), directed by Ewald André Dupont, and based on the sinking of the *Titanic*; a German-language version, **Atlantik**, was shot simultaneously and became the first all-sound film released in Germany. The first German sound feature, **Melodie Des Herzens** ("Melody Of The Heart"), was produced by UFA in May-September 1929 and is otherwise notable only for some scenes with show-midgets.

DER BLAUE ENGEL – PRODUCTION PHOTOGRAPHS
(*OPPOSITE PAGE*)

Der BLAUE ENGEL
("The Blue Angel"; Joseph Von Sternberg, 1929-30: Germany)

The film that made Marlene Dietrich into an overnight star, renowned for its sado-masochistic undercurrent and scenes of decadence. Dietrich plays a singer in a sleazy nightclub in Berlin, Emil Jannings plays the middle-aged school teacher who becomes infatuated with her and allows her to humiliate him and then abandons him; he dies a broken man. Visually, the film is filled with symbolic detail, a mounting montage of sex, cruelty and ineluctable death. **Der Blaue Engel** was the first sound film made in Germany; an English language version, **The Blue Angel**, was produced simultaneously. Sternberg and Dietrich were quickly signed up by Paramount Pictures and relocated to Hollywood, where they collaborated on an uneven series of six further films starting with **Morocco** (1930), of which **The Scarlet Empress** (1934), with its lavish sets, exotic costumes and striking compositions, is the most aesthetically outrageous. **Shanghai Express** (1932), set on a train moving across civil-war-torn China with Dietrich as a high-class prostitute, was memorable for the participation of actress Anna May Wong as her companion, who is raped and then takes murderous revenge; a scene showing the severed skull-heads of rebel fighters was subject to a removal request by the censor. After Paramount, Sternberg worked for various companies, but only recaptured the oneiric and quasi-erotic magnificence of his earlier work, briefly, in the bizarre **The Shanghai Gesture** (1941), a concoction of drugs, alcohol, gambling and sex starring Ona Munson as dragon-lady Mother Gin Sling. Dietrich's only post-Sternberg film of vague interest was Fritz Lang's **Rancho Notorious** (1952), one of several gynocentric "Freudian westerns" made in the 1950s. The English-language version of **Der Blaue Engel** is also notable as being

MOROCCO – PRODUCTION PHOTOGRAPH (*ABOVE*). DIETRICH WAS A NOTORIOUS CROSS-DRESSER, WHOSE BISEXUAL EXPLOITS WERE AN OPEN HOLLYWOOD SECRET.

SHANGHAI EXPRESS – PRODUCTION PHOTOGRAPH (*ABOVE RIGHT*).

the first film to be reviewed by the newly-formed Hays Code censorship committe, at that time headed by Jason Joy. The Hays Code – officially known as the Motion Picture Production Code – was a raft of puritanical, religion-inspired censorships designed to "clean up" the US movie industry, published in 1930 but not effectively enforced until 1934, with the appointment as chief of Joseph I. Breen, a religious fanatic;[1] this brief gap created what is known as the "pre-code" era, during which Hollywood created some of its most transgressive and challenging productions. The Code was an expansion of the 1927 MPPDA guidelines, culminating with new a list of strictly prohibited "repellent subjects", including actual executions, brutality and gruesomeness, branding, cruelty, white slavery, and surgical operations. With full enforcement of the Code, film companies were required to submit all scripts to the PCA (Production Code Administration) for approval before they could begin shooting, and the finished works were also subject to close scrutiny before release. Like all prohibitions, this created a climate where underground, unlicensed producers could cash in by manufacturing and selling product on the black market – the product in this case being on-screen sex and sin. Just like liquor bootleggers, film entrepreneurs were able to make a fine living peddling forbidden fruit to the masses who, according to the dictates of human nature, craved only what they were told they couldn't have. These new moonshiners of on-screen immorality were able to concoct low-budget, low-quality films shot purely to highlight nudity, prostitution, narcotics abuse or other sleazy material, and drive them from town to town setting up independent screenings, grabbing the cash and then quickly moving on. In this way, exploitation producers like Louis Sonney, S.S. Millard, Samuel Cummins and Dwain Esper forged a veritable dark carnival of the moving image, an ever-rolling roadshow of voyeuristic attractions circuiting the country's seamy underbelly. Their roadshow programs usually consisted of the "main feature" supplemented by other short, often found, items; these would range from striptease films to newsreel footage of executions, war atrocities or the bullet-riddled corpses of gangsters, and medical films detailing human anomalies, drug abuse, live births, graphic surgeries or the treatment of venereal disease. Lectures on addiction, sexology and other subjects of prurient interest were given by (often fake) doctors as part of the show, backed up by the sale of lurid books or pamphlets.

1. Catholic Breen was also a notorious Jew-hater, whose recorded description of Jews as "the scum of the Earth" exactly matched that used by his German contemporary, Adolf Hitler.

BLUTMAI 1929
("Bloody May 1929"; Phil Jutzi, 1929: Germany)

Originally entitled **1. Mai – Weltfeiertag Der Arbeiterklasse** ("May 1st – International Holiday Of The Working Class"), Jutzi's production for Volksfilmverband/Weltfilm is a classic of counter-informative cinema, the first political documentary riot film. Doubtless influenced by the riot scenes recreated by Eisenstein in earlier Soviet cinema, Jutzi set out to make a politicized record of violent events which unfurled in Berlin's Bülow Square on 1st May 1929, where demonstrations by the KPD (Kommunistische Partei Deutschlands) were brutally broken up by SPD (Sozialdemokratische Partei Deutschlands) police forces. In resulting clashes between police and the KPD's paramilitary wing the RFB (Roten Frontkämpferbund – "Red Front Fighters' League"), at least thirty-three protestors were killed over three days, eliciting a strike call from the KPD on May 2 which ended with the revolutionary admonition *Das Gemetzel unter der Berliner Arbeiterschaft – das ist das Vorspiel für die imperialistische Massenschlächterei!* ("The butchery of Berlin workers is the prelude to Imperialist mass-slaughter!"). Using shots from multiple camera set-ups plus photographic inserts, Jutzi creates a vivid and potent document designed to highlight the crushing oppression of workers by those in power. Footage from **Blutmai 1929** reoccurred in Soviet newsreels such as **Perwoje Maja W Berline** ("Berlin, May 1", 1929), and was also employed perjoratively in such works as Johannes Häussler's **Blutendes Deutschland** ("Bleeding Germany", 1933), a Nazi propaganda film designed to show the Weimar Republic in terminal collapse.

The BRIDGE
(Charles Vidor, 1929: USA)

Hungarian-born film-maker Karoly Vidor was an editor at Berlin's UFA before he moved to America and started his directorial career with this short fantasy film based on the 1891 Ambrose Bierce story "An Occurrence At Owl Creek Bridge", in which the protagonist – a man hanged for espionage – imagines whole episodes of experience during the split-second of his death. Using experimental techniques such as double exposure, Vidor made one of the more stark and thought-provoking silent debuts (also known as **The Spy**). His next significant film work would be as an uncredited co-director on the classic yellow peril horror film **Mask Of Fu Manchu**, released in 1932.

Die BÜCHSE DER PANDORA
("Pandora's Box"; G.W. Pabst, 1929: Germany)

The film for which actress Louise Brooks is always remembered; it was director Pabst who in 1928 lured her away from Hollywood, where she was a fast-rising star, to the decadent Berlin of the Weimar Republic. Brooks, a former Ziegfeld Follies showgirl, plays Lulu, a sexually wanton young woman who captivates and ruins all men (and lesbian women) who cross her path; she finally meets her inevitable destruction at the hands of Jack the Ripper, in London – death as terminal ecstasy. Lulu was created by the playwright Wedekind, in his two works *Erdgeist* ("Earth Spirit") and *Die Büchse Der Pandora*; he envisioned her as the purest essence of the female sexual impulse, an avatar of physical consciousness and the child-like victim of an unassuagable nymphomania, and Brooks manages to convey the character perfectly. This led many to speculate whether she was simply playing an amplified version of herself, and her eventual memoirs, *Lulu In Hollywood*, certainly indicated a life of promiscuity: she ended up working as a paid escort in New York.[1] *Die Büchse Der Pandora* was first adapted to film by Arzén von Cserépy in 1921; notable amongst numerous later versions of Wedekind was Walerian Borowczyk's **Lulu** (1980), with Udo Kier as Jack the Ripper.

---

1. Brooks' Hollywood career was effectively ended when, during her sojourn in Europe, she was asked to return and record a vocal soundtrack for a sound reworking of the last film she made before leaving America in 1928, **The Canary Murder Case**; Brooks refused, and was reportedly blacklisted by Paramount. She made just a handful of further film appearances before quitting in 1938.

DIE BÜCHSE DER PANDORA – PRODUCTION PHOTOGRAPHS (*OPPOSITE & OVERLEAF VERSO*).
THE CANARY MURDER CASE – LOUISE BROOKS AS DOOMED SHOWGIRL; PRODUCTION PHOTOGRAPHS (*OVERLEAF RECTO*).

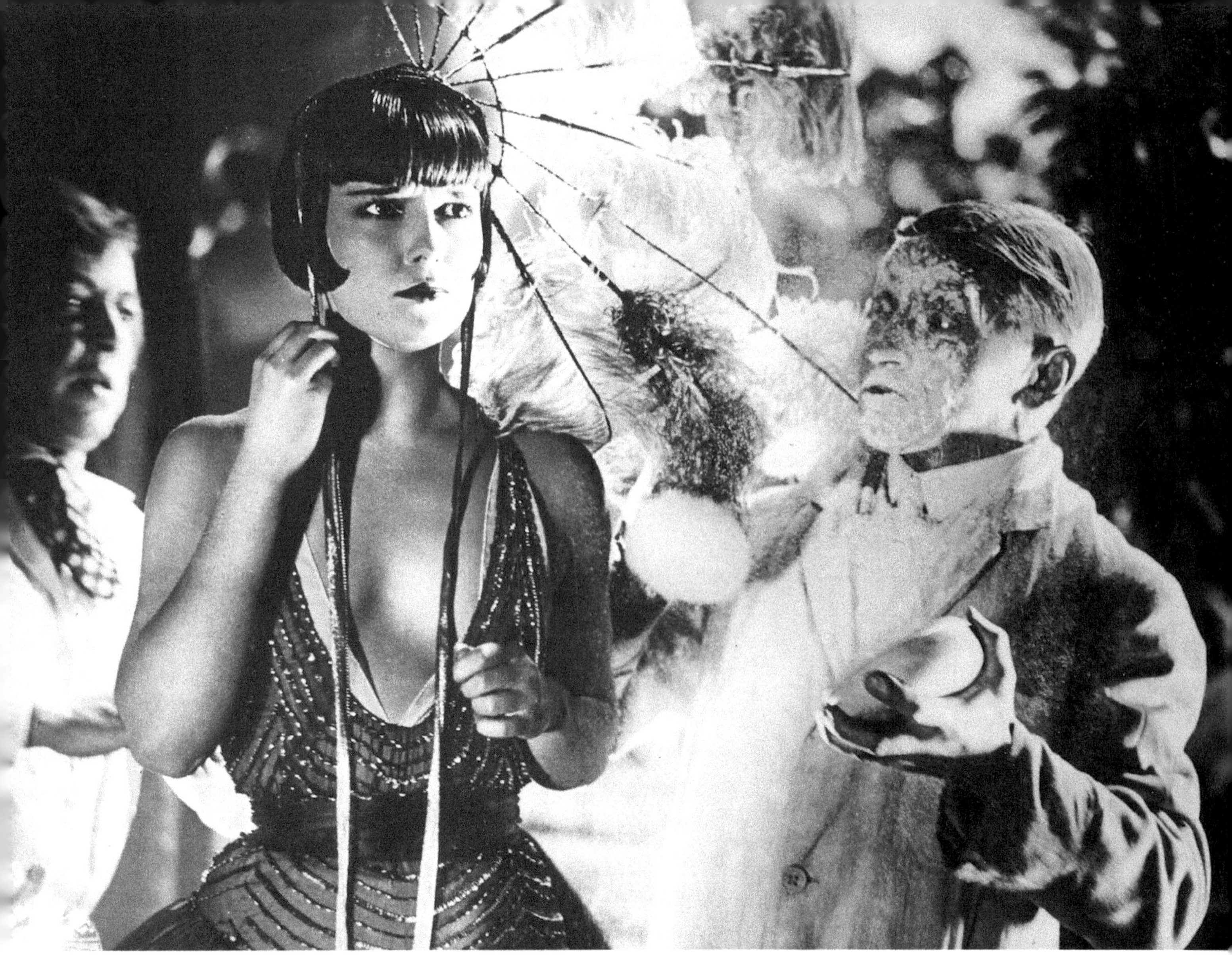

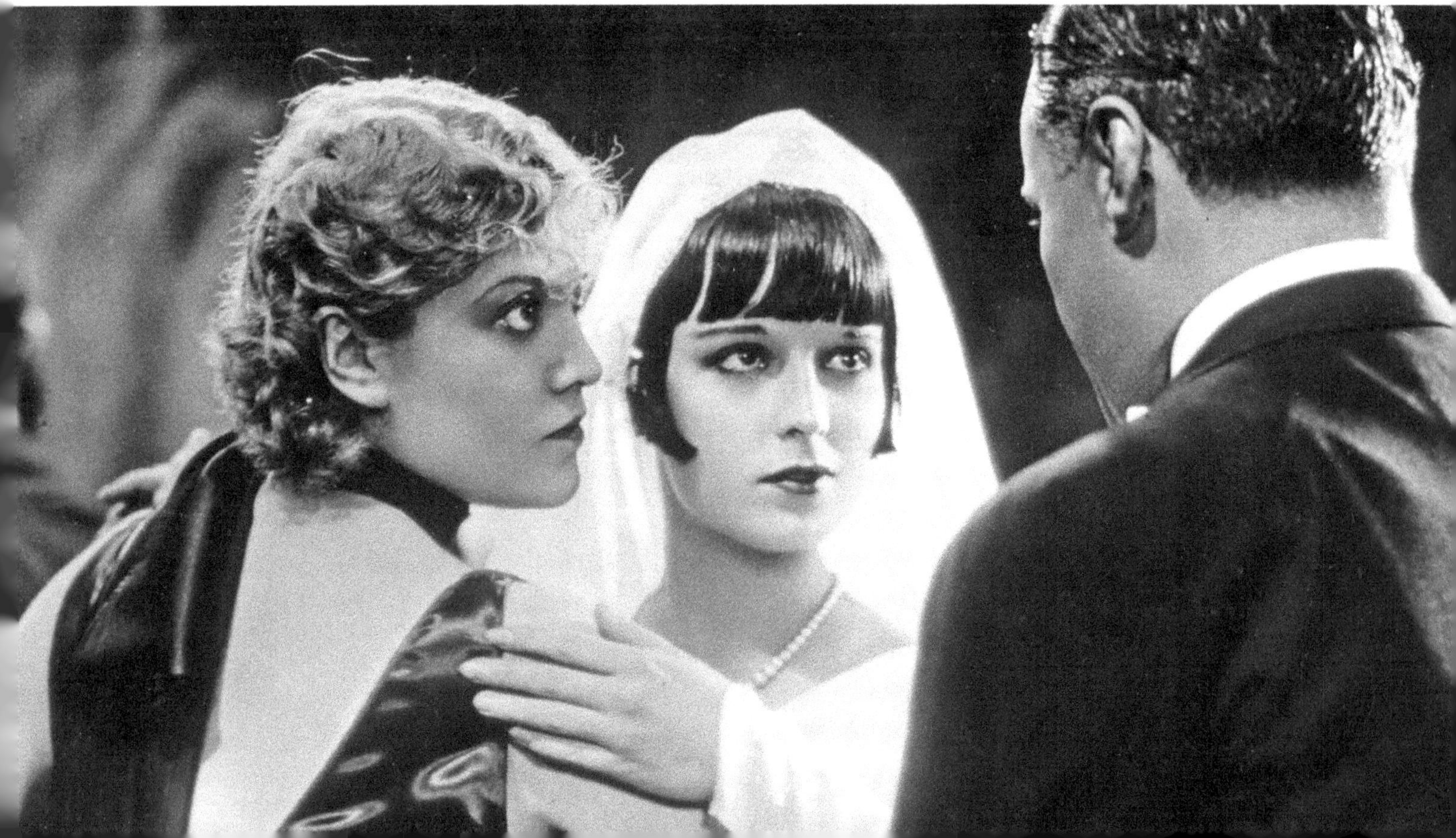

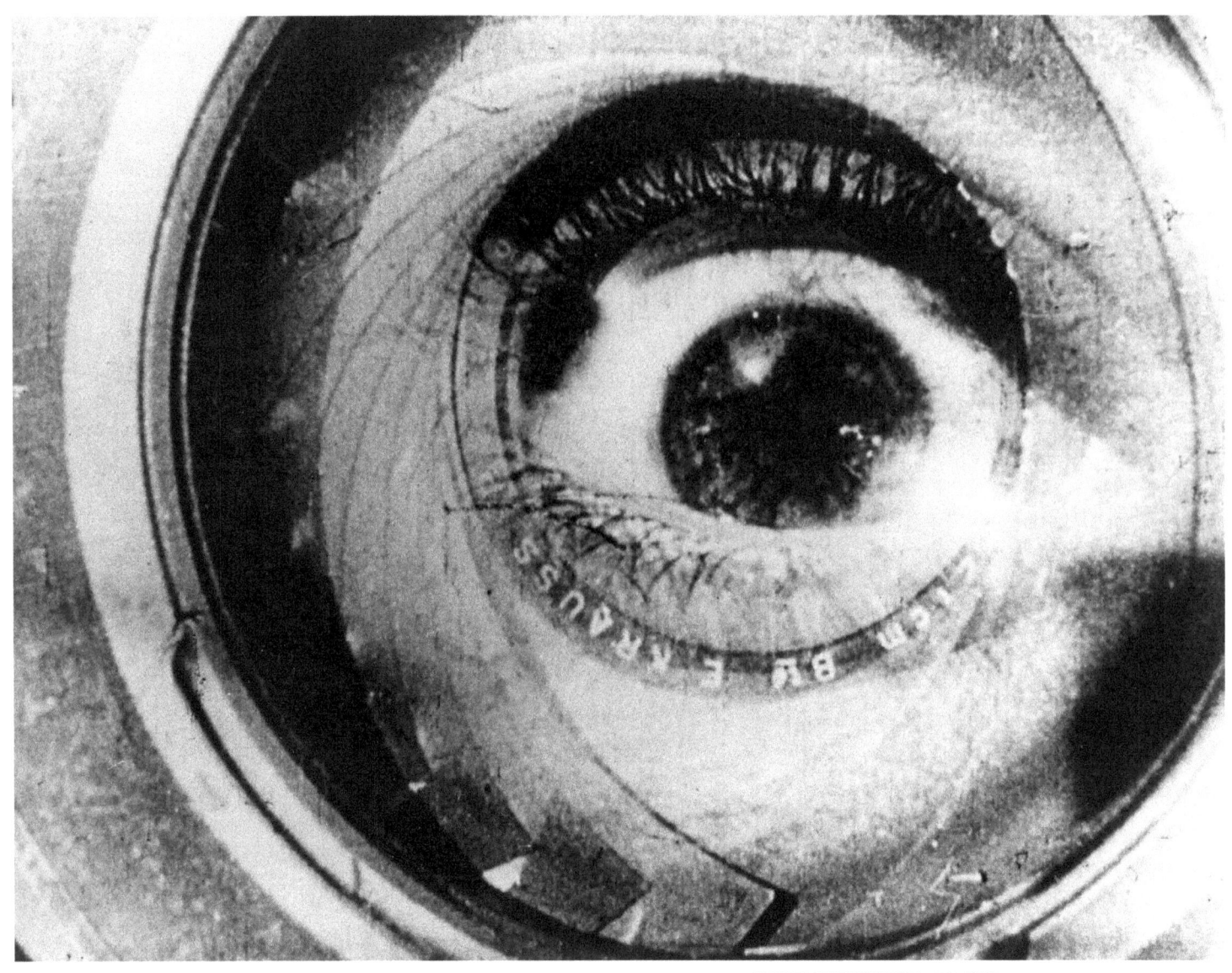

CHELOVEK S KINOAPPARATOM – PRODUCTION PHOTOGRAPHS (*THIS PAGE, OPPOSITE & OVERLEAF VERSO*), AND FILM POSTER BY GEORGII AND VLADIMIR STENBERG (*OVERLEAF RECTO*).

CHELOVEK S KINOAPPARATOM
("The Man With The Movie Camera"; Dziga Vertov, 1929: Soviet Union)

Vertov's last silent feature, a Soviet "city-film" in which all is subjugated to the camera's lens, a fragmented and spiralling mechanical eye of unparalleled retinal rapidity and rapacity. Decried by Eisenstein as an act of "film hooliganism", this sweep of technical virtuosity was edited from almost two thousand separate shots, a process which is shown within the film itself, as is the act of filming, and of viewing the film, presenting an accelerating reality of total cinematic immersion. Other notable example of "city-films" from that year include Robert Florey's experimental **Skyscraper Symphony**, examining the architectural surfaces of New York's skyline; **São Paulo, Sinfonia Da Metrópole** ("Sao Paulo, Symphony Of The Metropolis") made by Rodolpho Lex Lustig and Adalberto Kemeny, a first feature-length glimpse of the Brazilian master-city; **Prater**, an avant-garde evocation of the Viennese fairground made by Friedrich Kuplent, co-founder of the Kinoamateure Österreichs (Austrian Amateur Film Club); and **Fukko Teito Shinfoni** ("Symphony Of The Imperial Capital Reconstruction"), a film documentary on replacing Tokyo's earthquake-destroyed building with new edifices of concrete and steel, commissioned by the Tokyo municipal council. Another, little-known, Japanese city-film from 1929 was the experimental **Gogo Kara Asa Made** ("From Afternoon Until Morning"), shot by amateur film-maker Masuji Tejima.

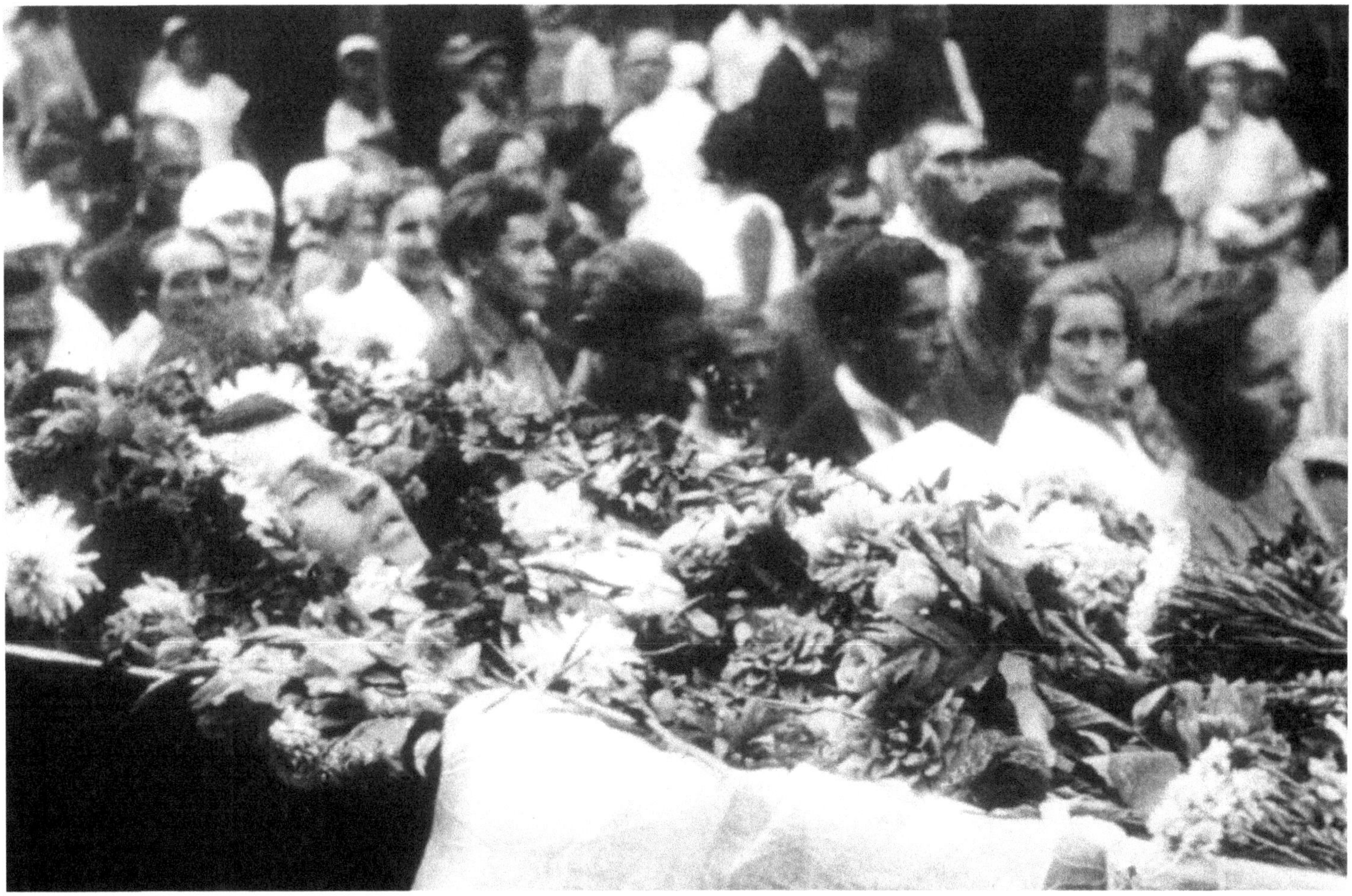

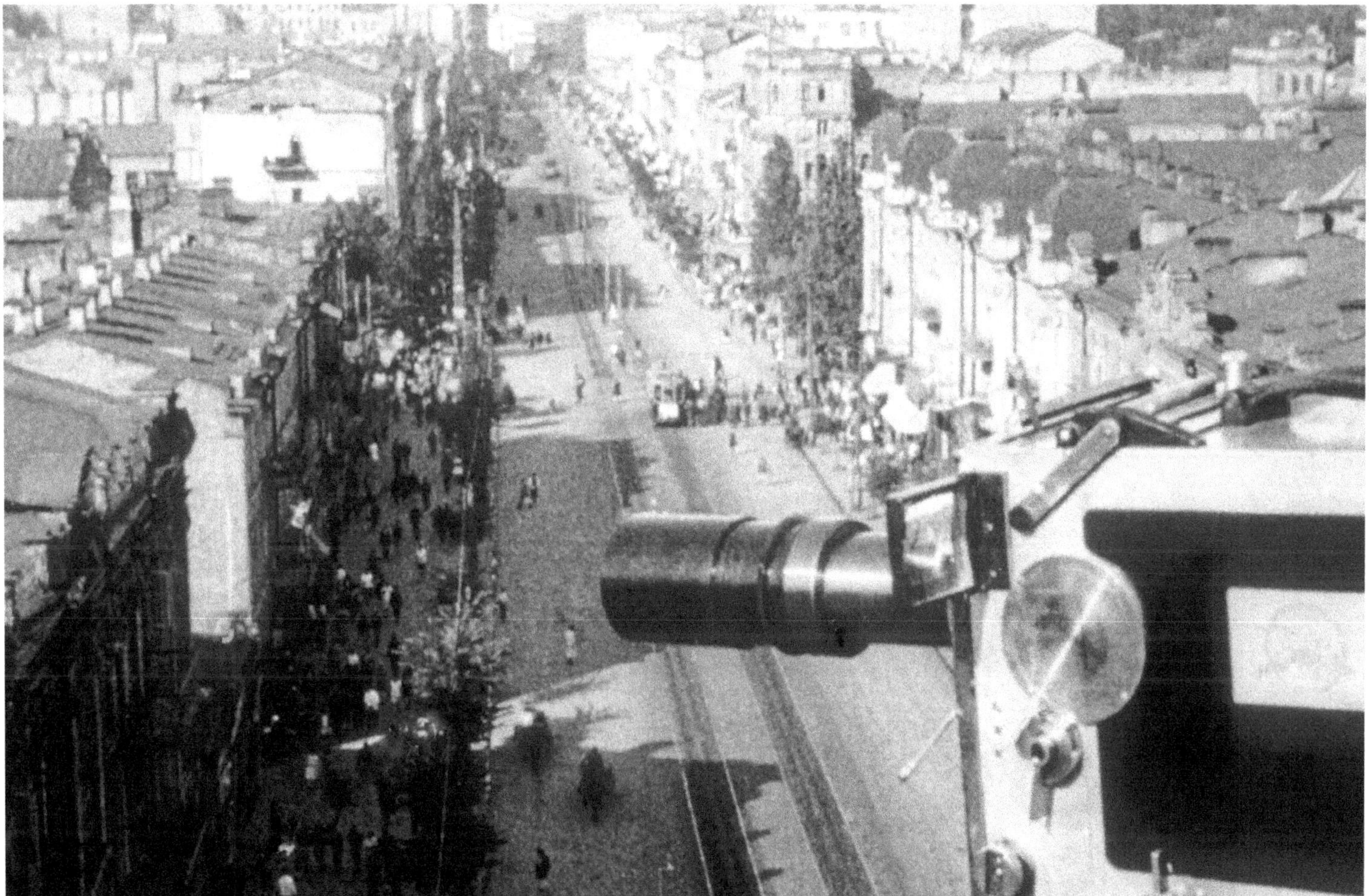

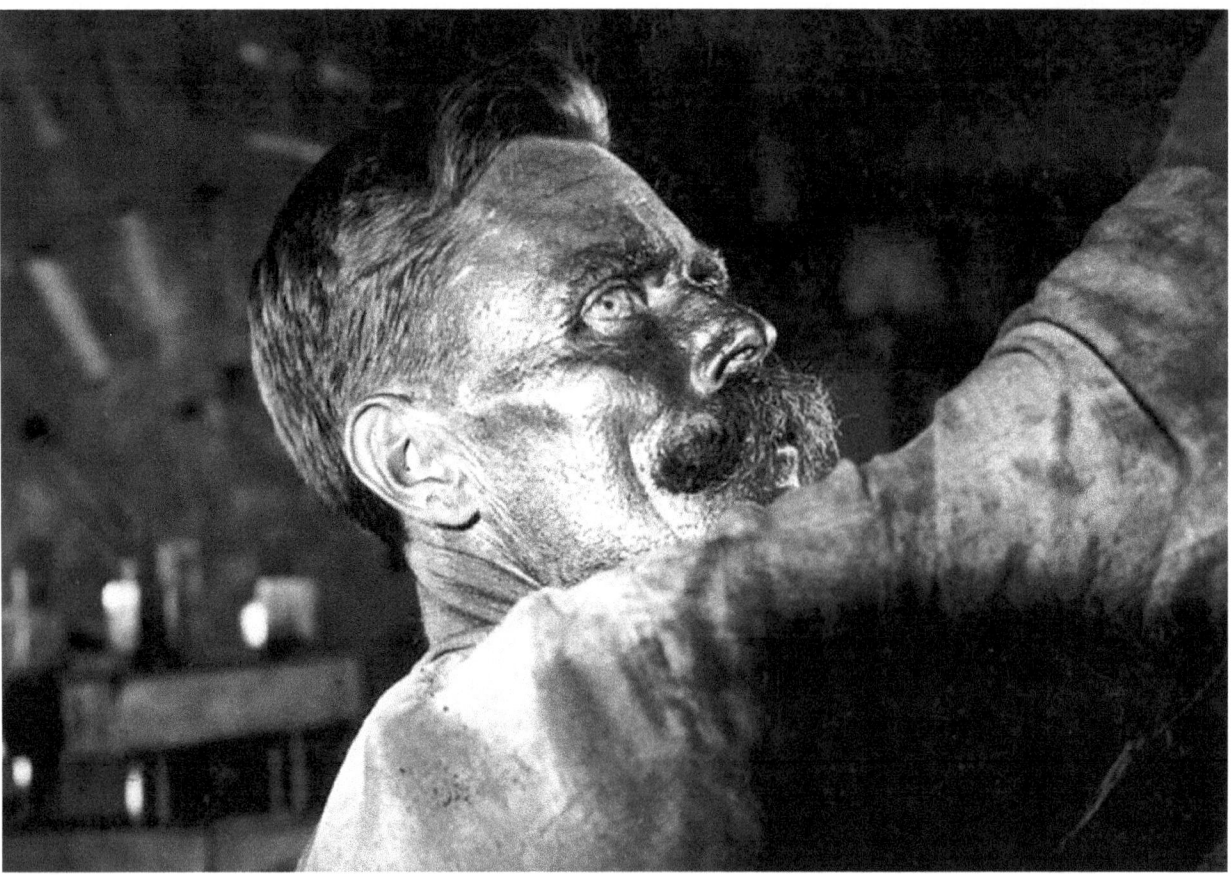

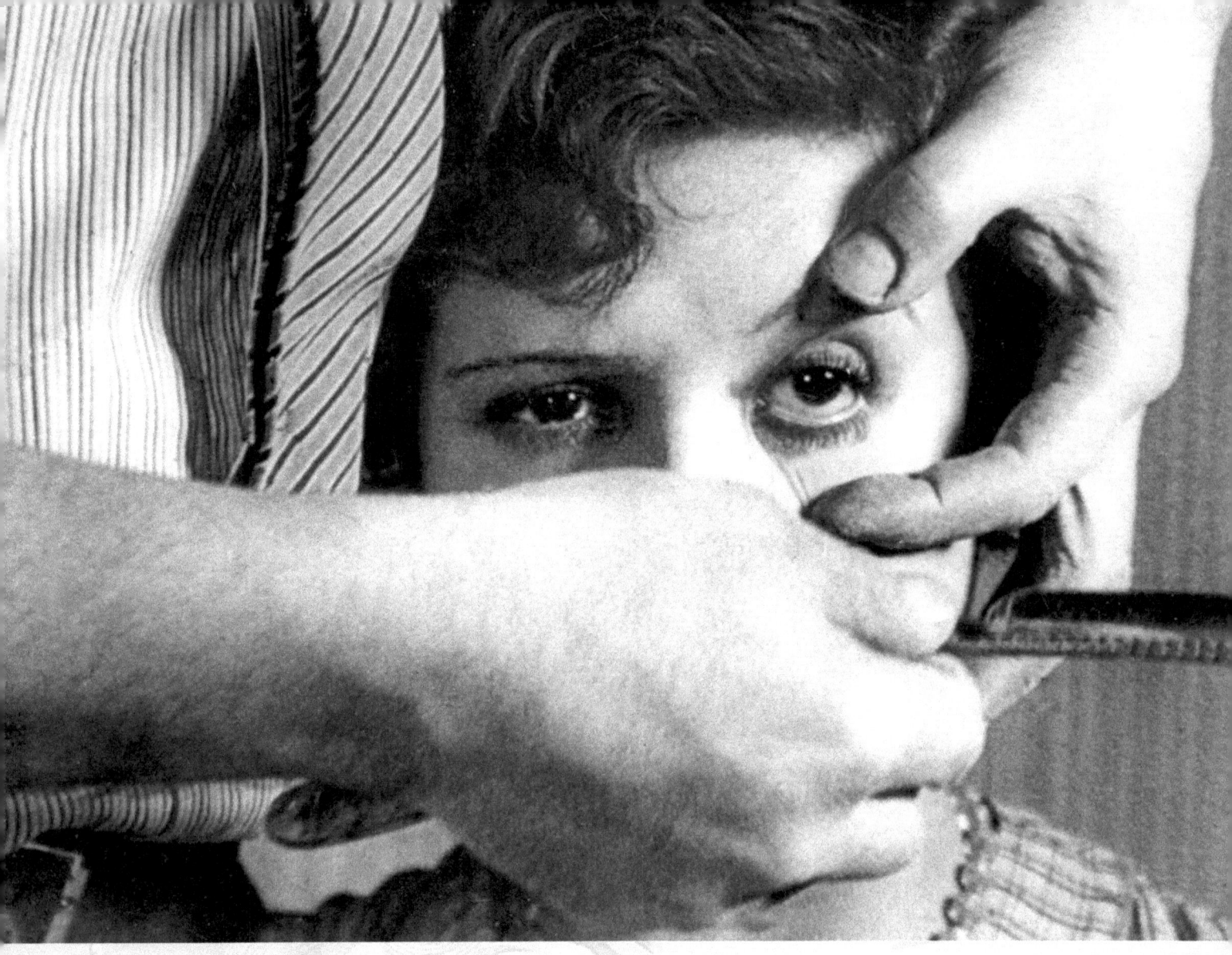

Un CHIEN ANDALOU
("An Andalusian Dog"; Luis Buñuel & Salvador Dalí, 1929: France)

By the end of 1928, Luis Buñuel had already graduated from Paris film school, filled with anti-religious venom, and was apprenticed to both film-maker Jean Epstein and the Surrealist Group. Salvador Dalí was on the verge of painting such early scatological masterpieces as *Le Jeu Lugubre* ("The Lugubrious Game") and *Le Grand Masturbateur* ("The Great Masturbator"), and was at the peak of his seething psychosexual mania. When these two renegades collided and transmuted the seed of their polyplasmic union into celluloid, the result was iconoclastic and cataclysmic. Dead, rotting donkeys mutilated and stuffed into pianos, priests on ropes, hands both ant-covered and severed, and graphic eyeball-cutting are just a few snatches of the uncanny visual beauty on display in the 17-minute **Un Chien Andalou**, an oneiric, libidinal affront to the senses. The first part of the film, entitled "One Upon A Time", sees a man (Buñuel) hold open a woman's eye, take a straight razor, and – as a cloud bisects the full moon – slice open her eyeball, shown in graphic close-up. Building on the unprecedented savagery of this opening, **Un Chien Andalou** presents a concatenation of bizarre events which comprise one of the most unsettling representations of psychosexual revolt ever constructed on film, a revolt symbolised by mutilation and ocular excavations, by mutinous and transmutant body parts, by delirium, murder, rape, and blasphemy. **Un Chien Andalou** – later described by Buñuel as a "desperate impassioned call for murder" – made its sensational debut at Studio des Ursulines in Paris, in 1929. It stands as the first true underground movie, and among the few greatest films of all time. Four years after its release, the film's main actor, Pierre Batcheff, committed suicide by taking a drug overdose; the film's leading actress, Simone Mareuil, followed suit in 1954, dousing herself in gasoline and setting herself on fire.

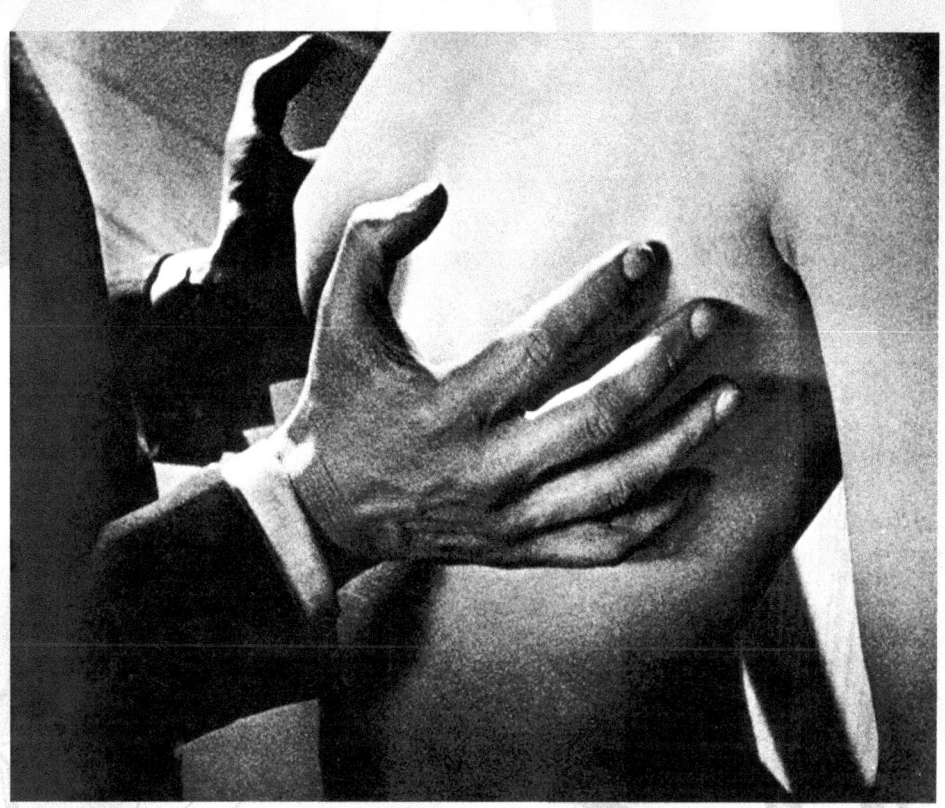

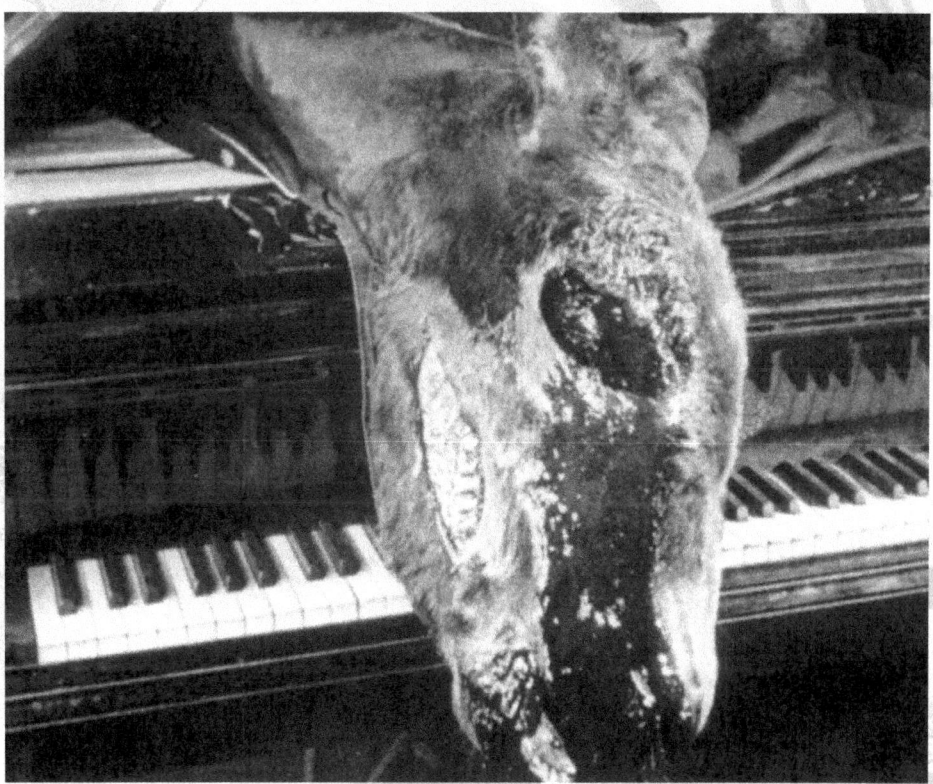

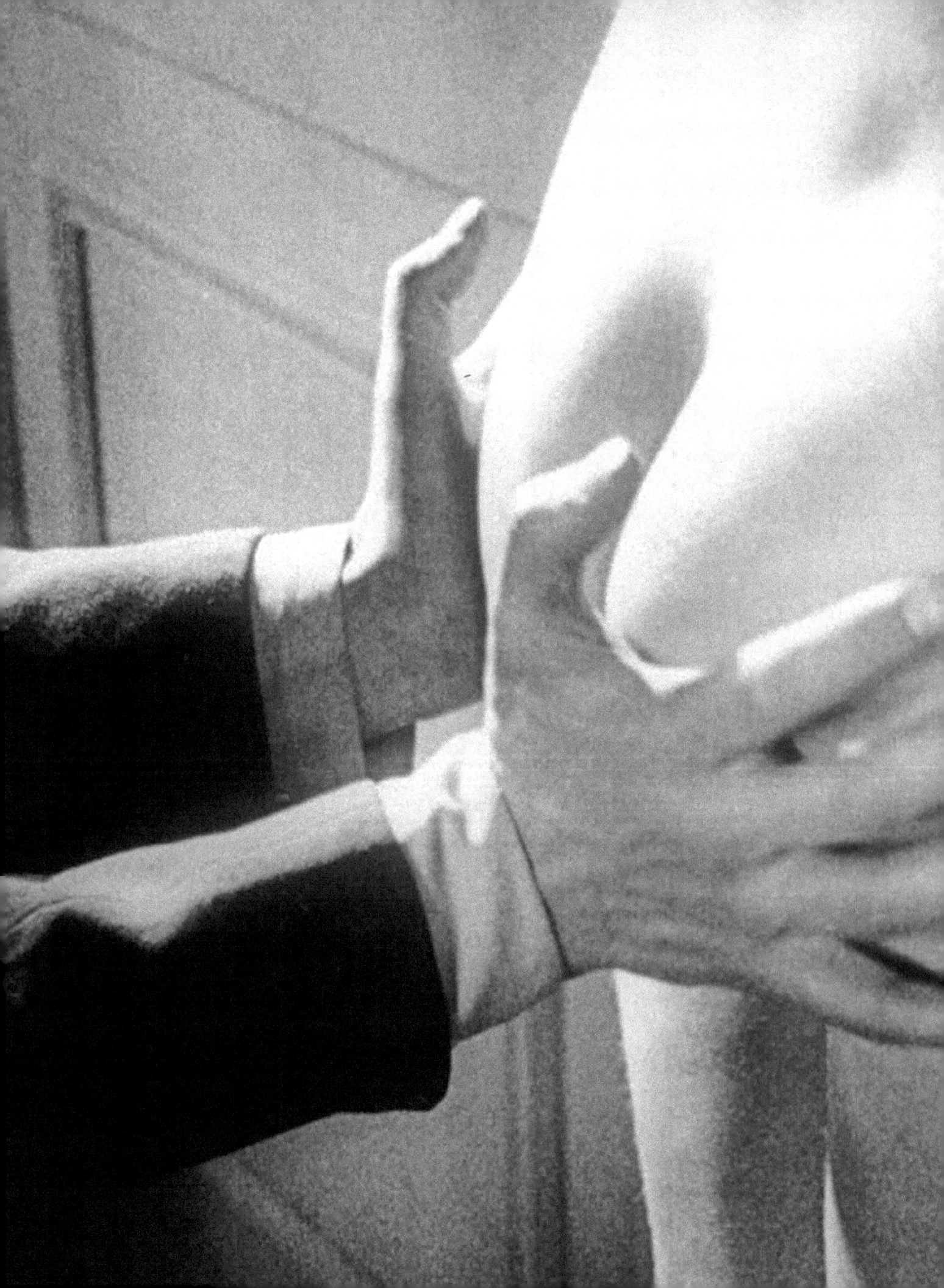

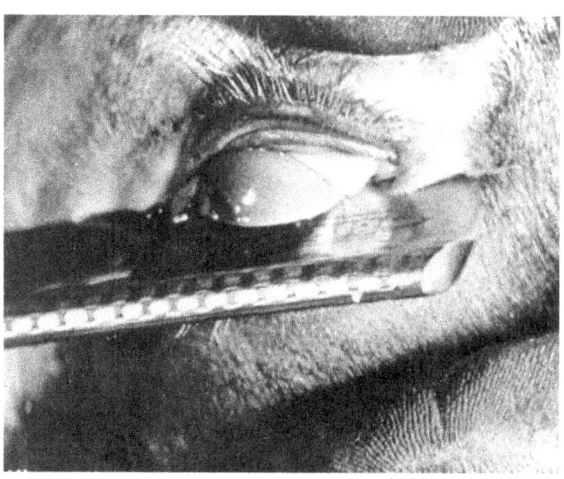

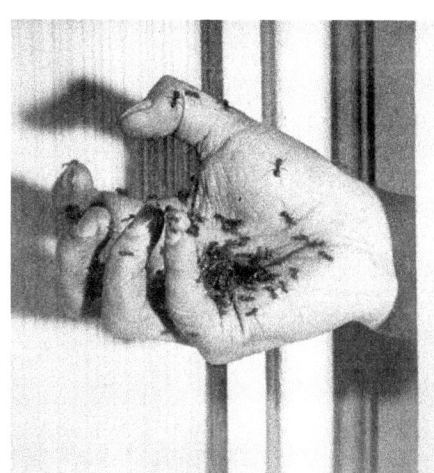
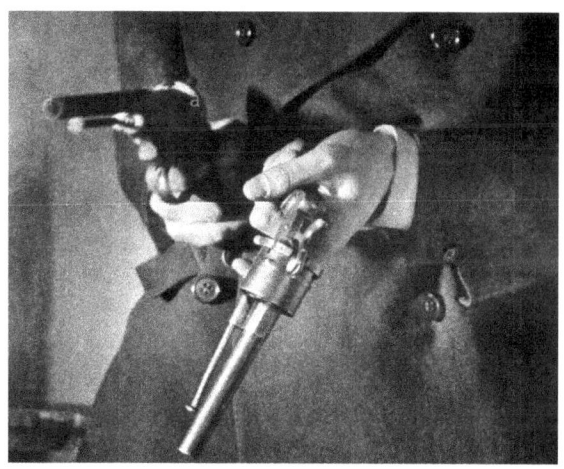

DARKENED ROOMS – PRODUCTION PHOTOGRAPH (*ABOVE*).
THE THIRTEENTH CHAIR – PRODUCTION PHOTOGRAPHS (*OPPOSITE*).

DARKENED ROOMS
(Louis Gasnier, 1929: USA)

One of several films of this period exposing clairvoyance, hypnosis and especially spiritualism as callous grifts, **Darkened Rooms** illustrates a typical set-up involving fake spirit photos and phoney seances. Other films in a similar vein include Albert Ray's **A Thief In The Dark** (1928); Tod Browning's **The Thirteenth Chair** (1929, with Bela Lugosi); **The Unholy Night** (1929, with Boris Karloff), also filmed in French by Jacques Feyder as **Le Spectre Vert** ("The Green Ghost"); Edgar Lewis' **Unmasked** (1929), a Craig Kennedy mystery; and George Melford's **The Charlatan** (1929, originally conceived as a vehicle for Conrad Veidt). A notable German contribution to this shadowy sub-genre was Adolf Trotz's **Somnambul** ("Sleep-Walking", 1927-28), which involved "criminal telepathy" in the form of both spiritism and hypnotism.

LE SPECTRE VERT – PRODUCTION PHOTOGRAPH (*FOLLOWING PAGES*).

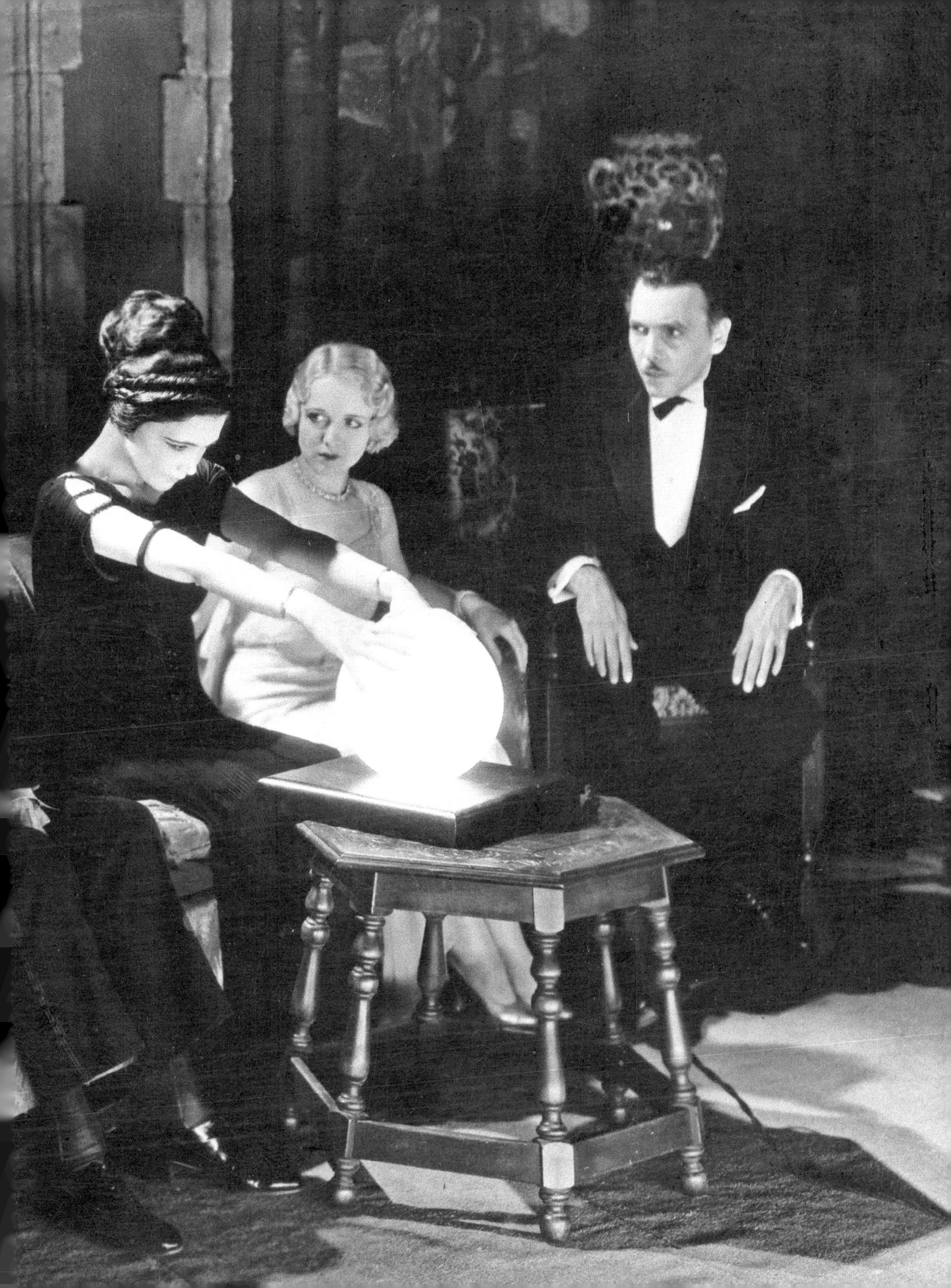

THE UNHOLY NIGHT – PRODUCTION PHOTOGRAPH (*ABOVE*).
THE CHARLATAN (*LEFT*).
A THIEF IN THE DARK – FILM POSTER (*OPPOSITE PAGE*).

ENTUZIAZM – PRODUCTION PHOTOGRAPH.

ENTUZIAZM (SIMFONIYA DONBASSA)

("Enthusiasm: The Donbas Symphony"; Dziga Vertov, 1929-1930: Soviet Union)
Films with sound, although firmly established in most major countries by the end of 1929 (with the notable exception of Japan), came more slowly to the Soviet Union. One of the sound cinema's leading theorists was Dziga Vertov; another was Sergei Eisenstein, who in 1928 published a technical "statement" on sound film, co-written with Vsevolod Pudovkin and Grigori Alexandrov. However, whilst Eisenstein advocated asynchrony as the optimal soundtracking method, Vertov was determined to achieve a more integrated and complex fusion of image and sound, hinted at in his own 1926 text *Ot Kino-Glaz Om Radio-Glaz* ("From Kino-Eye To Radio-Eye"). Vertov's chance to realise his sonic experiments came with a new project, commissioned by production company Ukrainfilm (formerly VUFKU), and designed to mark the progress of Stalin's 5-Year Plan – a military-style "shock labour" campaign of rapid industrialization – by documenting workers in the coal-mining region of Donbas. The resulting documentary, **Entuziazm**, combined Vertov's visual virtuosity with a soundtrack added post-shooting, and comprised of music mixed with industrial noise and background noise – engines, machines, hammers, whistles, factories, bells, train stations, crowds. In the tradition of Arseny Avraamov's "industrial symphonies" (1922-23) and such avant-garde musical works as Aleksandr Mosolov's *Zavod: Muzyka Mashin* ("The Iron Foundry: Machine Music", 1927), Vertov's montage of hand-recorded noise pointed at new directions in sound not only for Soviet cinema, but for the film documentary in general. Along with Abram Room's **Pyatiletka: Plan Velikih Rabot** ("5-Year Plan: Plan Of Great Works", 1929), **Entuziazm** was one of Russia's very first sound films; others – all themed around construction – included Yuli Raizman's **Zemlya Zhazhdet** ("The Earth Thirsts", 1930 – soundtrack added in 1931) and Nikolai Ekk's "feral children" drama **Putyovka V Zhizn** ("The Path To Life", 1931), which included scenes of rear male nudity. Several short films in sound were also produced in 1930; these ranged from popular cartoons (notably featuring the negro boy character, Tip-Top) to agit-prop and documentaries, such as **13 Dney. Delo Prompartii** ("13 Days: The Industrial Party Case"), which covered the trial of Leonid Ramzin and other "engineers" accused of plotting to overthrow the Soviet regime. Notable amongst early sound features were two films, Aleksandr Macheret's **Dela I Ludi** ("Affairs And Men", 1932) and Boris Yurtsev's **Iziashnaya Zhizn** ("A Graceful Life", 1932), which boasted futuristic electronic soundtracks composed by the noise musician Nikolai Krukov, using noise machines created by Vladimir Popov as well as theremins. Similar soundtracks were created by Gavriil Popov for Esfir Shub's **K.S.E. – Komsomol Shef Elektrifikatsii** ("Komsomol: Patron Of Electrification", 1932) and Aleksandr Macheret's **Rodina Zovyot** ("Motherland Calls", 1936), a quasi-SF film predicting war with Nazi

Germany. And Joris Ivens, working with German Marxist composer Hanns Eisler, created another complex industrial soundtrack for his Soviet blast-furnace documentary **Pesn O Geroyakh** ("Song Of Heroes", 1933). Moscow's first sound cinema, the Khudozhestvennyi, started operating in March 1930; although the vast rural areas beyond were slow to follow, silent film production in Russia had been completely phased out by 1936. As for Vertov, he took **Entuziazm** on a European tour, with screenings in major cities including London where, reportedly, he excitedly cranked up the volume so high that many audience members were forced to leave.

EROTIKON
(Gustav Machatý, 1929: Czechoslovakia)

Machatý's final silent feature, made in collaboration with the leading Czech Surrealist Vítezslav Nezval. An eroticized love story, daring for its time, **Erotikon** first used the facial close-up orgasm shots which, with added frontal nudity, would cause an international sensation in Machatý's **Extase** ("Ecstasy", 1932). The film is also noteworthy for its sublime visual style, design and camerawork, provided by art director Alexander Hackenschmied and cinematographer Václav Vích (Hackenschmied, an avant-garde artist, moved to America in 1938, abbreviating his name to Hammid, and continued to create works of cinema, also marrying the underground film-maker Maya Deren). Machatý, who legend tells ran away to Hollywood as a teenager in order to learn film technique from Erich von Stroheim, was part of the Devetsil modernist movement in Prague which, influenced by German Expressionism, Dadaism and French Surrealism, morphed into the Czech Surrealist Group in the 1930s, led by Nezval. Remarkable for their predilection towards erotica and pornography, the Czech surrealists included Karel Teige, known for his photomontages of naked women juxtaposed with random objects, and the androgynous Toyen (Marie Cernunova), who created many explicit works in the 1930s. Toyen was allied to the artist Jindrich Styrský, who published a pornographic magazine entitled *Erotika Revue*, as well as *Edice 69* ("Edition 69"), a series of books such as Nezval's *Sexuální Nocturno* ("Sexual Nocturne") and a Czech translation of Sade's *Justine*, for which Toyen executed several explicit illustrations. Other works by Toyen include *Mladá Snící Dívka* ("Young Girl Who Dreams", 1930), depicting a sleeping girl with exposed genitals, surrounded by erect penises. It was in this climate of sexual revolution that Machatý conceived his erotic film masterpiece, **Extase**, inspired by Nezval's unfilmed scenario *Chtíc* ("Lust"). Nezval's 1945 novel *Valerie A Týden Div* ("Valerie And Her Week Of Wonders") was later filmed by Jaromil Jireš in 1969, during a seminal period of post-reform Czech cinema.

EROTIKON – PRODUCTION PHOTOGRAPH (*ABOVE RIGHT*).
EROTIK – FILM POSTER FOR THE SWEDISH RELEASE OF EROTIKON (*ABOVE*).

LE FIN DU MONDE – PRODUCTION PHOTOGRAPH.

Le FIN DU MONDE
("The End Of The World"; Abel Gance, 1929-30: France)

A decimated masterpiece all but destroyed by commercial interference, Gance's first sound film was also one of the first "natural disaster" movies, inspired by an 1893 science fiction novel of the same name by Camille Flammarion. Gance conceived his film as an epic project, dealing with the full range of political, social and religious consequences of an imminent comet strike on the earth, threatening mankind with extinction. As with many French films of the 1930s, **Le Fin Du Monde** includes orgy scenes with bare-breasted female nudity, as well as scenes of violence. It ends with a stunning vision of apocalyptic destruction. Production began in 1929 and lasted for a year, after which Gance assembled an initial edit of around 180 minutes. At that point, the film's backers abruptly intervened and took control of the editing, cutting Gance's vision down to 105 minutes. Gance disavowed the result, declaiming his film as "abortive"; the final version premiered in January 1931, and was not well received by critics. The film was later bought for US distribution by exploitation producer Harold Auten, who further hacked it down to a running time of 54 minutes and retitled it **Paris After Dark** for roadshow audiences (presumably with the nude scenes intact). Perhaps the most primitive, strange and elusive "comet-disaster" film of this period was a 9.5mm Hungarian production, Lénárd Endre's **A Föld Halála** ("The Death Of The Earth", 1933), which was screened at the Third Festival of Amateur Films in Paris under the title **La Mort De La Terre**; only 18 minutes of fragments survive from the 45-minute original.

THE APE MAN – SCENE FROM CHAPTER 7 OF THE FIRE DETECTIVE; PRODUCTION PHOTOGRAPH (*ABOVE*).
THE BLACK BOOK – PRODUCTION PHOTOGRAPH (*BELOW*).

The FIRE DETECTIVE
(Spencer Gordon Bennet & Thomas Storey, 1929: USA)

The criminals in this 10-chapter Pathé mystery-crime serial are a gang of deadly arsonists, who engage the help of scientists to produce advanced devices and methods of fire-starting. The most bizarre of these creations is a genetically-engineered human-ape hybrid, who is able to scale tall buildings and spread fire across the rooftops. From a story by Frank Leon Smith, the serial's chapters were: **The Arson Trail; The Pit Of Darkness; The Hidden Hand; The Convict Strikes; On Flaming Waters; The Man Of Mystery; The Ape Man; Back From Death; Menace Of The Past;** and **The Flame Of Love.** Spencer Gordon Bennet also directed Pathé's 10-chapter **The Black Book**, released in July 1929;[1] it was not only the company's last silent serial, but their final serial, full stop – whilst the other film companies scrambled to make the transition to sound, Pathé simply decided not to bother. By the beginning of 1931, the company was gone – merged with a recently-formed sound production and distribution corporation, RKO Pictures.

1. The ten chapters of **The Black Book** were: The Secret Of The Vault; The Death Rail; A Shot In The Night; The Danger Sign; The Flaming Trap; The Black Dam; The Fatal Hour; The Mystery Mill; The Assassin Strikes; and Out Of The Shadows.

The FLAGELLENTES
(Roger Hilson, c.1929: Philippines)

Roger Hilson, serving in the Philippines from 1928 to 1930, was commissioned by the local government to make several short film documentaries of life on the islands. **The Flagellentes** is a record of the bizarre and bloody Easter rituals performed by the Catholic sect known as *flagellentes* or *penitentes*, whose devotions involve scourging themselves with whips, chains and other weapons as a means of identifying with Christ, who legend tells was subjected to brutal flagellations at the hands of the Romans. Entertaining on the level of a violent freakshow, and yet another example of how the world's masses, incapable of original thought, are doomed to follow absurd religious tenets set by unknown others, blindly, even to the point of self-destruction. Hilson's other films ranged from **Leprosy**, which shows horribly disfigured lepers emerge from the jungle colony of Culion, to **The Eruption Of Mount Mayon Volcano**.

FOX MOVIETONE FOLLIES OF 1929 – "PEARL OF OLD JAPAN"; PRODUCTION PHOTOGRAPH.

FOX MOVIETONE FOLLIES OF 1929
(David Butler, 1929: USA)

Among the very first musical revue films with accompanying sound (on disc) was **Fox Movietone Follies Of 1929**, whose simple narrative revolved around one night's theatre performance, with numbers that included a vignette of shop dummies that come to life. The film is most notable for the number "Pearl Of Old Japan", a

FOLLOW THRU – "I WANT TO BE BAD"; PRODUCTION PHOTOGRAPH (*ABOVE*).

HELEN KANE, ROLE MODEL FOR BETTY BOOP (*LEFT*).

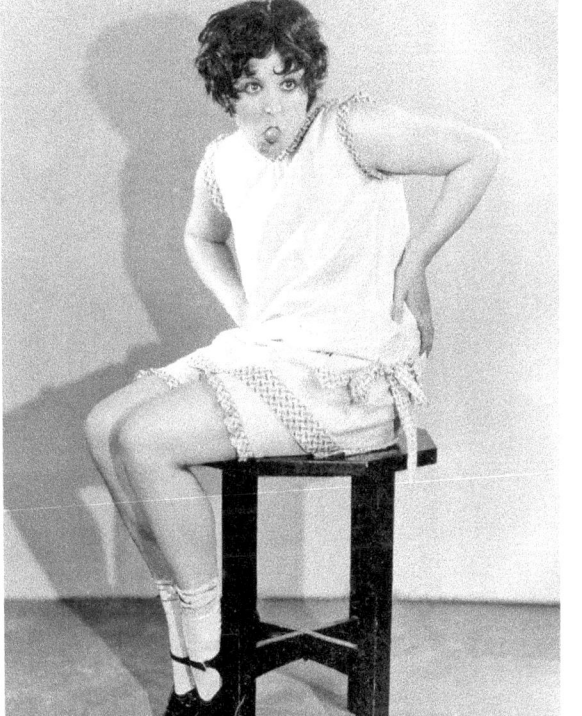

piratical/sub-aquatic tableau in the style of Georges Méliès with water-nymphs, sunken galleons, pirate-girls, and dancers dressed as devilish skeletons. This was one of two sequences in the film which were produced in Multicolor (a subtractive 2-colour process introduced in 1928, and used until 1932); the film was also one of several filmed in Fox Grandeur, an early 70mm widescreen film format. There were numerous other experiments with sound and colour – 2-strip Technicolor was used early musical film productions such as Paramount's **Follow Thru** (1930), which featured Zelma O'Neal performing her 1929 hit song "I Want To Be Bad" accompanied by hellfire and children dressed as pitchfork-wielding devils; the song was also covered in 1929 by Helen Kane, who was supposedly the inspiration for the cartoon character Betty Boop, introduced as a canine prototype in the Fleischer Studios cartoon **Dizzy Dishes** (1930).

FRAU IM MOND – PRODUCTION PHOTOGRAPH.

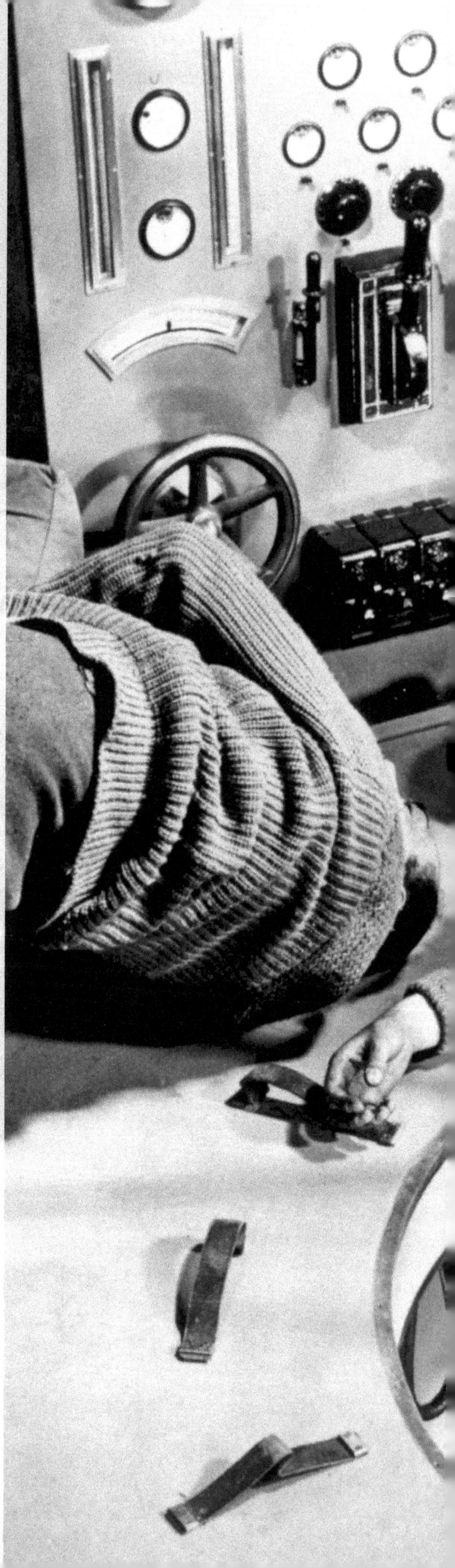

FRAU IM MOND
("Woman On The Moon"; Fritz Lang, 1929: Germany)

After **Metropolis, Frau Im Mond** was the second SF film collaboration betwen Lang and Thea von Harbou, this time investigating the possibilities of manned rocket flights to the moon. The story involves a small group of scientists and investors who build a rocket in order to prospect for gold on the lunar surface, but find their project jeopardised by a cabal of greedy businessmen. Lang went to great trouble over the technical aspects of rocket technology, working with rocket scientist Hermann Oberth – author of *Die Rakete Zu Den Planetenräumen* ("By Rocket Into Interplanetary Space", 1923) – and the launch sequences, aided by the cinematography of Oskar Fischinger, were among the most compelling yet created on film. The Nazis actually had **Frau Im Mond** suppressed in the 1930s, destroying existing negatives and even the original model rockets, believing that it revealed liquid-fuel technology secrets too close to the development of their V-2 ballistic missile. The V-2 was indeed the forerunner of all subsequent rocket and space-program technology, which indicates the unprecedented level of authenticity in Lang's film.

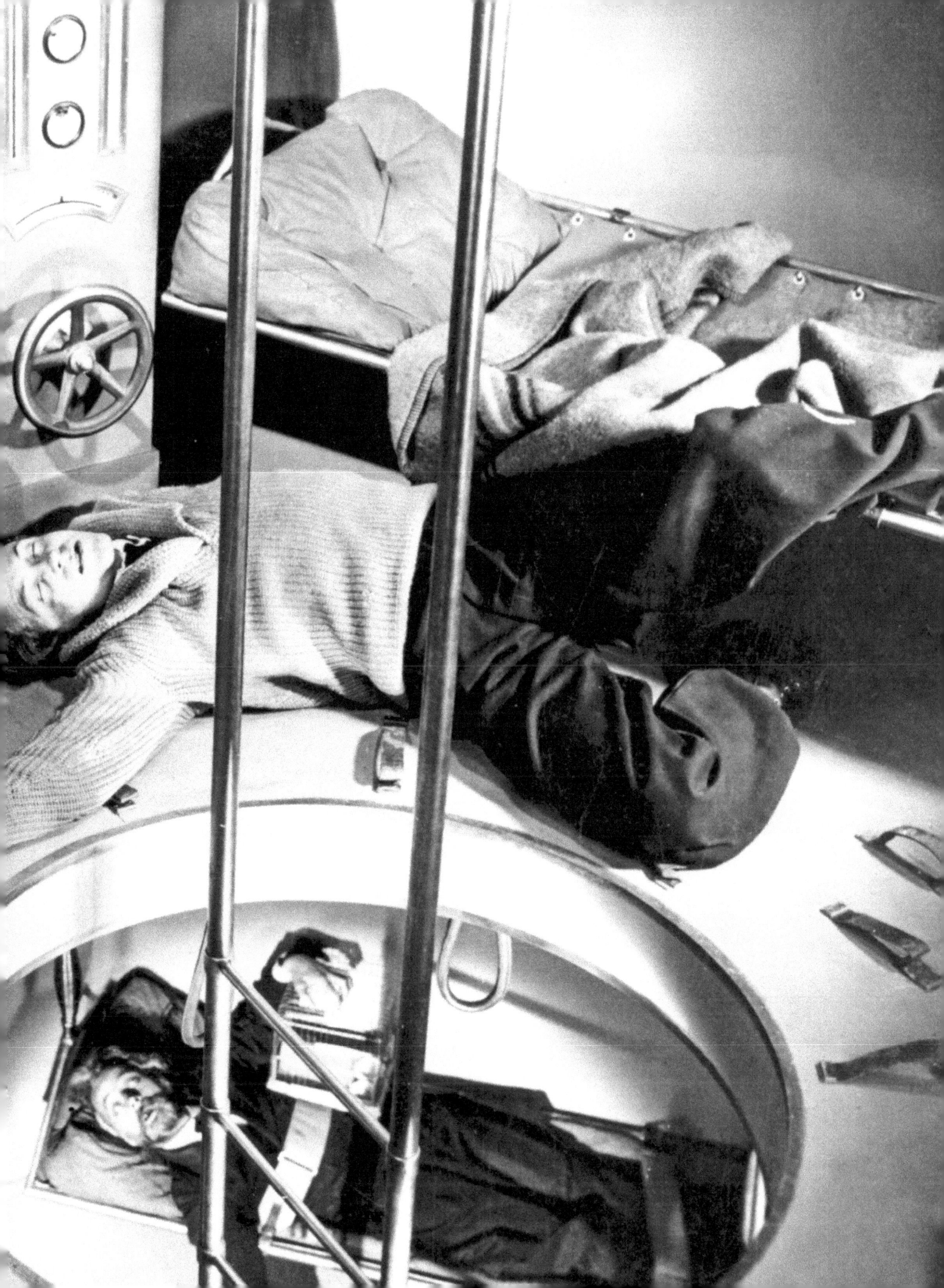

FRAUENNOT-FRAUENGLÜCK
("Women's Misery, Women's Joy"; Eduard Tissé, 1929: Switzerland)

Before the three Russian film-makers Grigori Aleksandrov, Sergei M. Eisenstein and Eduard Tissé rolled into Hollywood in 1930, they visited several European countries, including England, France, Germany and Switzerland. In Switzerland, they were commissioned by Praesens-Film to make a "social hygiene" film warning of the dangers of unlicensed abortion. Mainly shot by Tissé, who was of Swiss parentage, the result was **Frauennot-Frauenglück**, completed in 1929. The second half of **Frauennot-Frauenglück** features contrasting scenes between sanitary clinic treatment and filthy, backstreet abortions which cause sickness and death. The film includes graphic scenes of electrocution, medical gore, a tiny aborted foetus, and live birth (both vaginal and Caesarian), plus some gruesome gynaecological diagrams. It ends with a shot of a coffin. The film was released in the US in 1930, and was soon appropriated by roadshow entrepreneur Samuel Cummins, who distributed it under the title **Birth**. Cummins also released an 8-minute "adults only" extract in 1938, under the title **Childbirth With Caesarian Operation**, complete with misspelled intertitles, as well as an item entitled **Child Bride**. A Caesarian birth was also featured in the 1931 German film **Das Lied Vom Leben** ("Song Of Life"), which also included foetus footage and was reportedly acquired by exploitation producer Dwain Esper for roadshow distribution in later years. At least two other films are known to have been shot during Eisenstein's travels. The first, made during the 1929 Congress of Independent Film-Makers at La Sarraz in Switzerland, was an experimental short entitled **Die Erstürmung Von La Sarraz** ("Storming La Sarraz"); with contributions from Hans Richter and Ivan Montagu, this was apparently a farce symbolising the war between 'commercial" and "independent" cinema – it was confiscated at a customs crossing, and never retrieved. The second, co-directed with Aleksandrov, was **Romance Sentimentale**, a short experimental confection of images and music reportedly made for a private commission. Eisenstein's main gestatory cine-project of this period was a concept entitled *The Glass House*, a film set in an apartment block whose walls, both outer and inner, would be made of sheer glass; despite this, only the camera's eye would penetrate the walls – the tenants, at least initially, would not be able to view each other. This precarious social order would eventually break down with the "unfilming" of the tenants' eyes, resulting in a revelatory meltdown of scopophiliac delirium, crime, suicide, insanity and catastrophe. To Eisenstein, the glass construct would offer unprecedented visual overlaps, 3-dimensional angles, figures suspended in space, and multiple narratives in the iris of a single lens – montage without editing.

1. A theme also addressed that year in E.W. Emo's **Zwischen Vierzehn Und Siebzehn** ("Between Fourteen And Sixteen"), in which a 15-year-old is impregnated and subsequently dies during an illegal procedure.

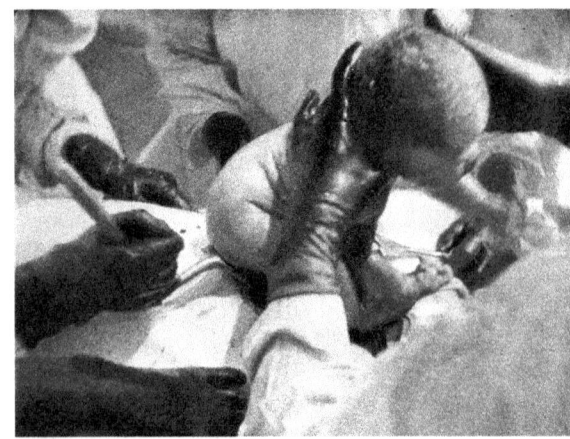
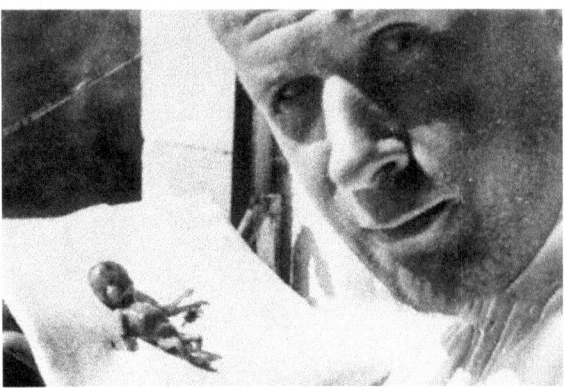

FRAUENNOT-FRAUENGLÜCK – FRAME ENLARGEMENTS.

GLORIFYING THE AMERICAN GIRL
(Millard Webb, 1929: USA)

The advent of sound inaugurated a rush to bring Broadway musical revues to the cinema screen, and no Broadway entrepreneur was bigger than Florenz Ziegfeld, who started his legendary show *Ziegfeld Follies* in 1907 and in 1915 augmented it with a racier version entitled *Danse De Folles* (later *Midnight Frolic*), with girls (some without underwear) viewed through glass from below. One of the very first musicals, MGM's **The Broadway Melody**, featured a character named the Great Zanfield. Ziegfeld himself was said have an ambivalent relationship with the film industry; Hollywood plundered his star girls for years, but he had used film in his shows as far back as 1910, when he commissioned a short trick-reel of singing star Anna Held as a comet (just as Halley's Comet veered into sight). **Glorifying The American Girl**, produced by Paramount, was Ziegfeld's first attempt at developing an original film project; most of it is tedious nonsense, enlivened only by some spectacular footage of his show-girls in action.[1] The following year Ziegfeld co-produced **Whoopee!**, a kind of sexy musical western, but that was his only official credit as a film producer.

1. The "glorification" of a racially pure, white-skinned American female archetype was Ziegfeld's pinnacle aim, one which aligned him with the Eugenics movement. Many of Ziegfeld's star girls – who were strongly discouraged from sun-bathing or any other activity which might sully their whiteness – were

GLORIFYING THE AMERICAN GIRL – JOHNNY WEISMULLER AS ADONIS IN "LOVELAND"; PRODUCTION PHOTOGRAPH (*OPPOSITE PAGE*).
GOLDWYN GIRL VIRGINIA BRUCE IN **WHOOPEE!** – PUBLICITY PHOTOGRAPH (*OVERLEAF VERSO*).

photographed for publicity by Alfred Cheney Johnston, who often extended his sessions to include eroticized and semi-nude poses which, having mainly come to light after the photographer's death, only added to the retrospective allure of the Ziegfeld mythology. Another famous Ziegfeld-related artwork was a memorial portrait by pin-up artist Alberto Vargas of Olive Thomas, the Hollywood actress and former *Midnight Frolic* girl who died in Paris in 1920 in a death variously linked with suicide, syphilis, drug abuse and murder. She was married to Jack Pickford, younge

UNIDENTIFIED ZIEGFELD GIRL (*ABOVE*); ZIEGFELD GIRL AND FILM STARLET JEAN ACKERMAN (*BELOW*); ZIEGFELD GIRL AND FILM STARLET HAZEL FORBES (*BELOW RIGHT*) – PHOTOGRAPHS BY ALFRED CHENEY JOHNSTON, c.1929.

PIN-UP PAINTING OF OLIVE THOMAS BY ALBERTO VARGAS, 1920 (*RIGHT*).

THE GREAT GABBO – PRODUCTION PHOTOGRAPHS.

The GREAT GABBO
(James Cruze, 1929: USA)

After his terminal film as director, **Queen Kelly**, collapsed into maniacal fragments, Erich von Stroheim, cursed genius of the silent cinema, was forced to reinvent himself as an actor in the "talkies". In **The Great Gabbo** he plays an insane ventriloquist, the first in a long series of roles in which he would feature as an inwardly or outwardly disfigured madman or psychotic. Some say that Stroheim directed certain sequences of the film, uncredited. Besides Stroheim's disturbing scenes with his seemingly possessed, one-eyed dummy, this bizarre film (from an outline by Ben Hecht) features a series of *outré* sub-Ziegfeld musical production numbers – including one with a girl-spider hybrid monster, human flies, and giant web. Like certain other films of the late 1920s, **The Great Gabbo** hinted at dark new directions for the cinema of dolls.

HELL'S BELLS
(Ub Iwerks, 1929: USA)

The fourth in Walt Disney's cartoon series **Silly Symphonies**, an early animated descent into Hell. Here we meet Satan himself, plus assorted demons, monsters and verminous creatures. The main featured music is Charles Gounod's *Marche Funèbre D'Une Marionnette* ("The Puppet's Funeral March", 1872-79), which later became famous as the theme tune for the long-running television show **Alfred Hitchcock Presents** (1955-62). Iwerks and Disney parted company in 1930, and Iwerks opened

HELL'S FIRE – FRAME ENLARGEMENT.

his own animation studio, backed by Disney's rival Pat Powers. **Hell's Fire** (1934), one of the Willie Whopper cartoons which he made from 1933-34, is a return visit to the Inferno featuring Satan on a throne of skulls, an array of rascals including Rasputin, Nero, Dr. Jekyll and Mr. Hyde, and Napoleon, and the twitching corpse of Prohibition (which Satan revives by pumping it full of liquor).

HUN SHI MO WANG
("The Devil Incarnate"; Ma-Xu Weibang, 1929: China)
Hailed as the first Chinese horror film, and a huge success on its release. Writer/director Ma-Xu also starred, creating for himself the most hideous make-up effects conceivable, and becoming a star in the process. He next filmed **Hei Yi Guai Ren** ("Freak In The Night", 1929), and a tribute to the "mad ape" movies of Hollywood entitled **Kong Gu Yuan Sheng** ("Screaming Ape In The Valley Of Death", 1930), with a plot involving kidnapped females, organ transplants, rejuvenation experiments and a man dressed as a gorilla. Another silent film from this period with horror elements was Zhushao Quan's **Fan Deng Gui Ying** ("Devil Shadows Of The Temple Lamp", 1930), in which a haunting by demons is revealed to be the work of monks who oppress the local peasants through fear of the supernatural. Ma-Xu returned to the horror genre in 1937, with **Yeban Gesheng** ("A Song Sounds At Midnight"), his tribute to **The Phantom Of The Opera**.

The IRRESPONSIBLES
(Mary Field, 1929: UK)
Produced by the British Social Hygiene Council, this short sex education film was one of the relatively few VD warning documentaries made in England. As its title suggests, the film sheds light on the reckless behaviour of "loose" women who sleep around and become vectors of sexual plague. Mary Field, a prolific educational filmmaker, also directed **Any Evening After Work** (1930) for the BSHC, another VD warning film showing the plight of a young man who contracts syphilis from a promiscuous woman. Other British VD warning films include **Deferred Payment** (1929), **Trial For Marriage** (1936), **A Test For Love** (1937 – a docudrama directed by Vernon Sewell), **The Road Of Health** (1938 – a lecture accompanied by animated medical footage), **Love On Leave** (1940), and **The People At No. 19** (1949), a grim 18-minute drama in which a pregnant wife discovers she has contracted syphilis after a sexual dalliance.

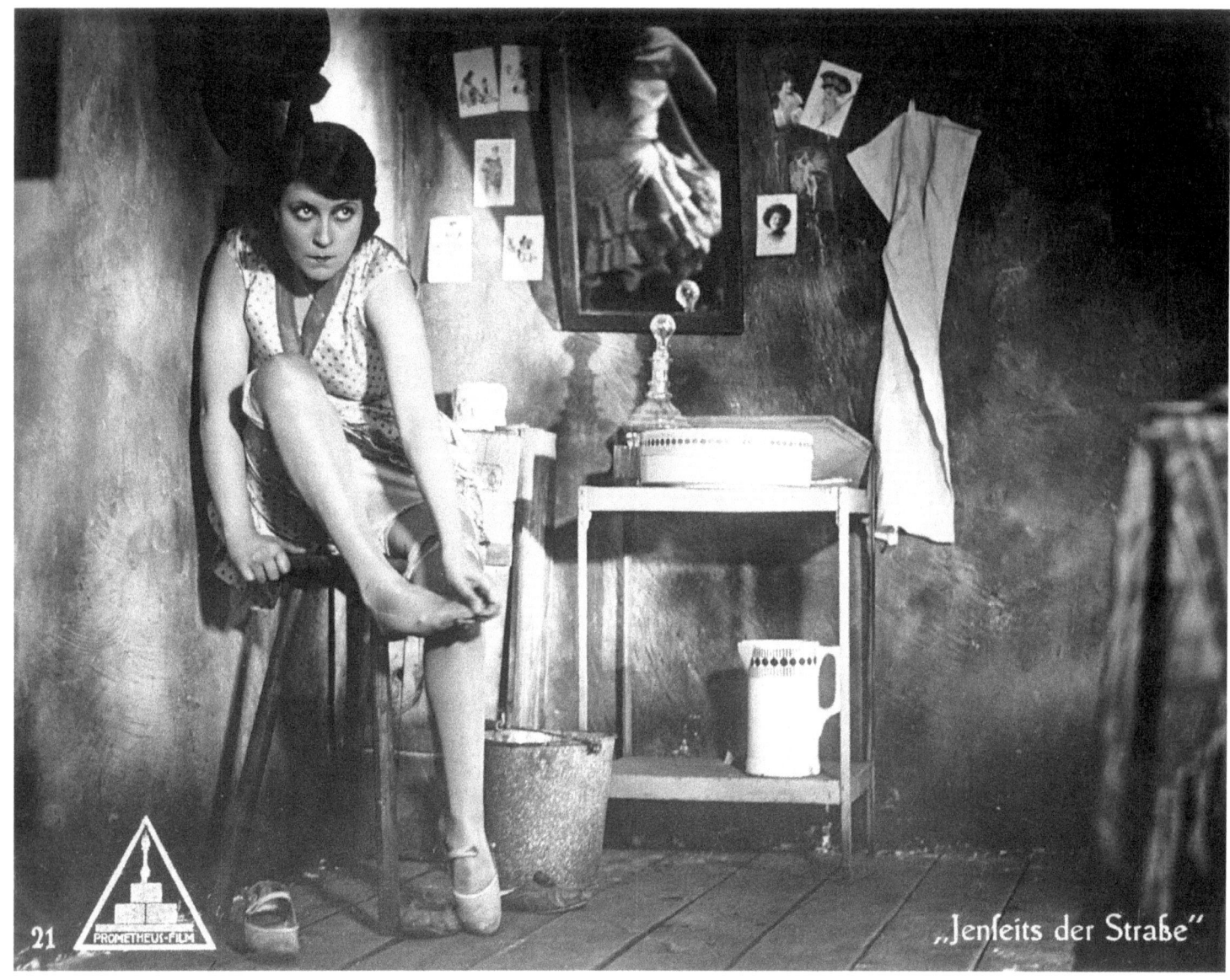

JENSEITS DER STRASSE– PRODUCTION PHOTOGRAPH.

JENSEITS DER STRASSE
("Beyond The Street"; Leo Mittler, 1929: Germany)

A key film in the Neue Sachlichkeit film genre, a form of ultra-realist cinema with its roots in Socialism and the woes of the working-class, as seen in such 1925 films as Pabst's **Die Freudlose Gasse** and Gerhard Lamprecht's **Die Verrufenen** ("Scum"). Lamprecht's quest for social realism peaked with **Unter Der Laterne** ("Beneath The Lantern", 1928), using non-actors in a dingy night-world of prostitution and proletarian drinking dives, and climaxing with suicide by train. Leo Mittler's **Jenseits Der Strasse**, set in Hamburg, depicts an equally desperate underworld of poverty and crime where lost souls prey on each other without remorse. When a beggar finds a pearl necklace, he is stalked by a prostitute who covets the jewels, and who seduces the beggar's young room-mate to steal them for her. After a struggle, the old beggar drowns; his corpse is later dredged from the water, still clutching the necklace which is revealed to be a worthless fake. The heartless whore ditches the youth, and is last seen homing in on fresh prey – a wealthy, obscenely obese society "gentleman" whom she will no doubt rob, perhaps infect with syphilis, perhaps even murder.

UNTER DER LATERNE– PRODUCTION PHOTOGRAPH (*OPPOSITE TOP*); **DIE VERRUFENEN** – PRODUCTION PHOTOGRAPH (*OPPOSITE BOTTOM*).

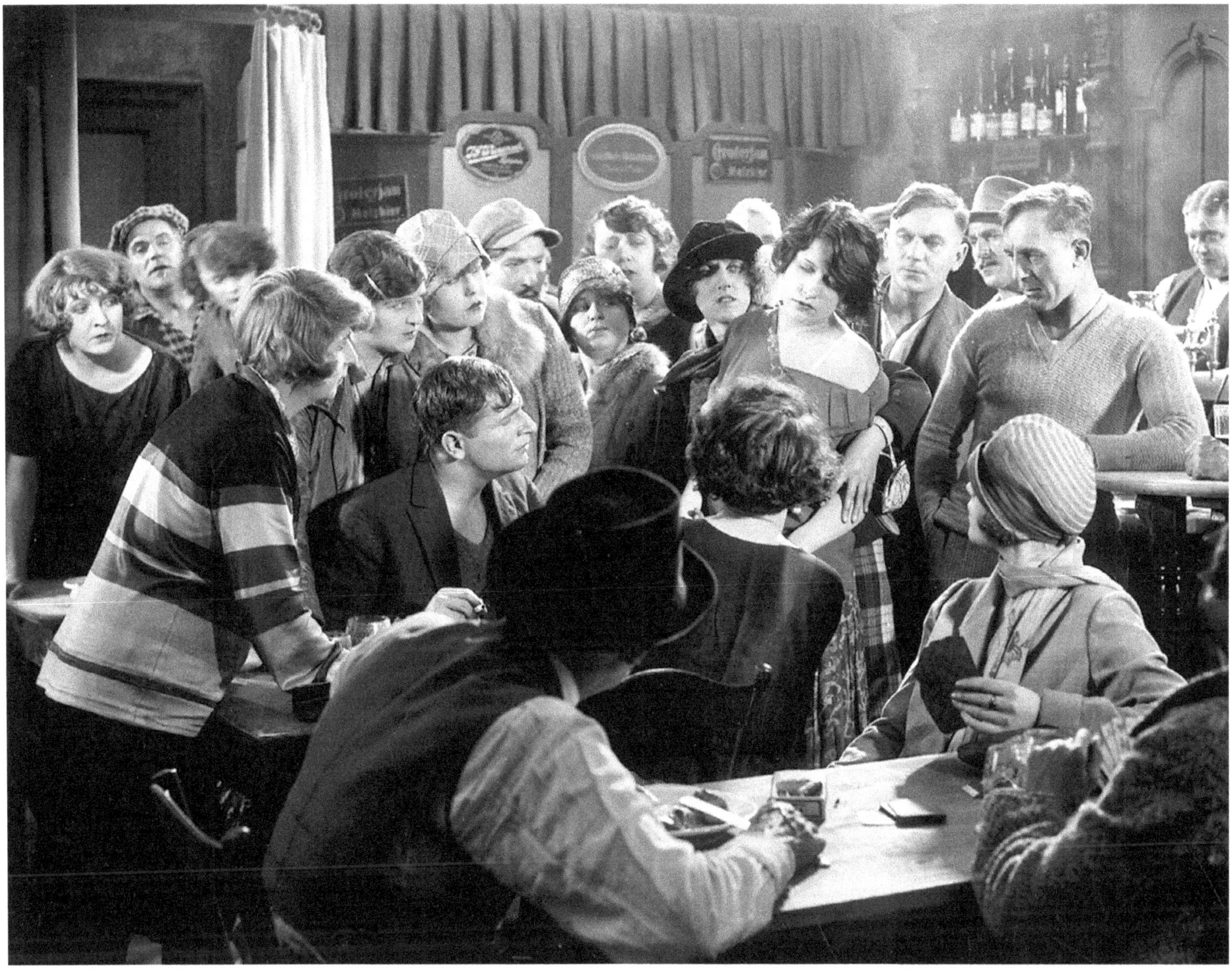

Beerdigungs-Institut
Gustav Erdmann
Teilzahl

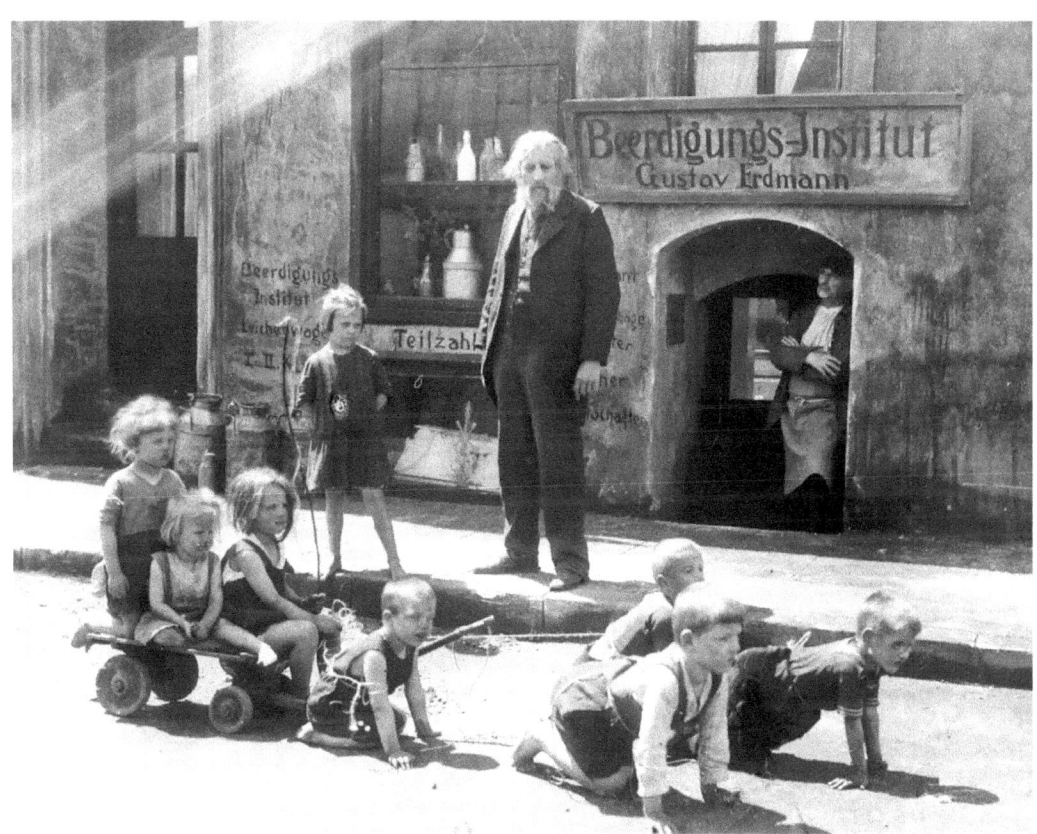

KING OF THE KONGO – PRODUCTION PHOTOGRAPH, FROM PRINTED LOBBY CARD.

KING OF THE KONGO
(Richard Thorpe, 1929: USA)

The last noteworthy 1920s serials with a jungle setting included Mascot's 10-chapter **King Of The Kongo**, said to be the first serial shot with partial sound, and featuring Boris Karloff as a character named Scarface Macklin, plus one of the earliest ape impersonations essayed by stuntman/actor Joe Bonomo, who would often double for Charles Gemora.[1] Produced by Mascot, **King Of The Kongo** was shot on an impressive ruined temple set, and augmented by additional stock footage. The temple is guarded by a hulking gorilla, and a kind of giant mutant lizard is also featured (possibly meant to be a dinosaur). The serial's chapters were: **Into The Unknown; Terrors Of The Jungle; Temple Of Beasts; Gorilla Warfare; Danger In The Dark; Man Of Mystery; The Fatal Moment; Sentenced To Death; Desperate Choices;** and **Jungle Justice**. Boris Karloff's next serial appearance was as a murderous Arab sheikh in Mascot's 12-chapter **King Of The Wild** (1931),[2] set in North Africa; as well as portraying Arabs as villainous scum and native blacks as gibbering primitives, this mystery-crime thriller featured a weird, ape-like creature named Bimi (played by English bit-part actor Arthur McLaglen). It was among the very first wave of all-sound serials – as was Universal's **Danger Island** (1931),[3] another jungle mystery set in Africa. Filmed in twelve chapters, **Danger Island** revolves around the control of a radium mine, and includes a monster orangutan as well as voodoo-style black magic rituals.

1. As the demand for monster-gorillas in all types of movies steadily increased, other regular gorilla-suit wearers would include Fred Humes, Jack Leonard, Clarence Morehouse, Ray Corrigan, Emil van Horn, Art Miles, and Steve Calvert.

2. The twelve chapters of King Of The Wild were: Man Eaters; Tiger Of Destiny; The Avenging Horde; Secret Of The Volcano; Pit Of Peril; Creeping Doom; Sealed Lips; Jaws Of The Jungle; Door Of Dread; Leopard's Lair; The Fire Of The Gods; and Jungle Justice. Richard Thorpe directed.

3. The twelve chapters of Danger Island were: The Coast Of Peril; Death Rides The Storm; Demons Of The Pool; Devil Worshippers; Mutiny; The Cat Creeps; The Drums Of Doom; Human Sacrifice; The Devil Bird; Captured For Sacrifice; The Lion's Lair; and Fire God's Vengeance. Ray Taylor directed.

KING OF THE WILD – PRODUCTION PHOTOGRAPH (*TOP RIGHT*) AND PRODUCTION PHOTOGRAPH FROM LOBBY CARD (*OVERLEAF*).

DANGER ISLAND – PRODUCTION PHOTOGRAPH (*RIGHT*).

KUBI NO ZA
("Decapitation Zone"; Masahiro Makino, 1929: Japan)

Masahiro Makino, son of *jidai-geki* master Shozo Makino, was an actor in such fast-moving swordfight films as Sadae Takami's **Ronin Jigoku** ("Masterless Samurai In Hell", 1926) before erupting onto the Japanese film scene as director with a series of *samurai* pictures designed to take the genre to a new level of action, violence and nihilism. Using a stock company rather than individual stars, Makino concentrated on derelict, poverty-stricken settings and frenzied combat scenes to convey his vision of the *samurai* as a doomed outsider. Such a figure, falsely accused of a crime and condemned to be beheaded, is the protagonist of **Kubi No Za**. Makino first scored a great sensation in 1928, with the opening film of his 56-reel **Ronin-Gai** ("Street Of Masterless Samurai") trilogy, which was ranked at the very top of artistic successes by *Kinema Jumpo* magazine. Makino followed this with **Sozen-ji Baba** ("Sozen Temple Riding-Grounds", also 1928), a violent film version of the classic *kabuki* play *Katakiuchi Sozen-ji Baba* ("Slaughter-Vengeance At Sozen Temple Riding-Grounds"). Other striking examples of the new *jidai-geki* from that year were Seika Shiwa's **Nazo No Ningyo-Shi** ("Puppeteer Of Mystery"), featuring an incredible multiple sword battle conveyed by a precipitous, completely mobile camera and rapid edits, and Daisuke Ito's big-budget **Zanjin Zanbaken** ("Sword For Butchering Horses And Humans"), with its pitched cavalry battle between one faction all on white horses and the other all on black. 1929 also saw the release of Makino's first "talkie", **Modori-Bashi** ("Modori Bridge"), a 4-reel reworking of the legend of Watanabe no Tsuna and the cannibal she-demon Ibaraki which was screened with a synchronised gramophone soundtrack – causing unprecedented technical problems for a number of projectionists. When the Makino Film corporation eventually went bankrupt following his father's death, Masahiro joined Nikkatsu, followed by Toho and Toei. He made over 250 films.

ZANJIN ZANBAKEN – ACTOR RYUNOSUKE TSUKIGATA; PRODUCTION PHOTOGRAPH.

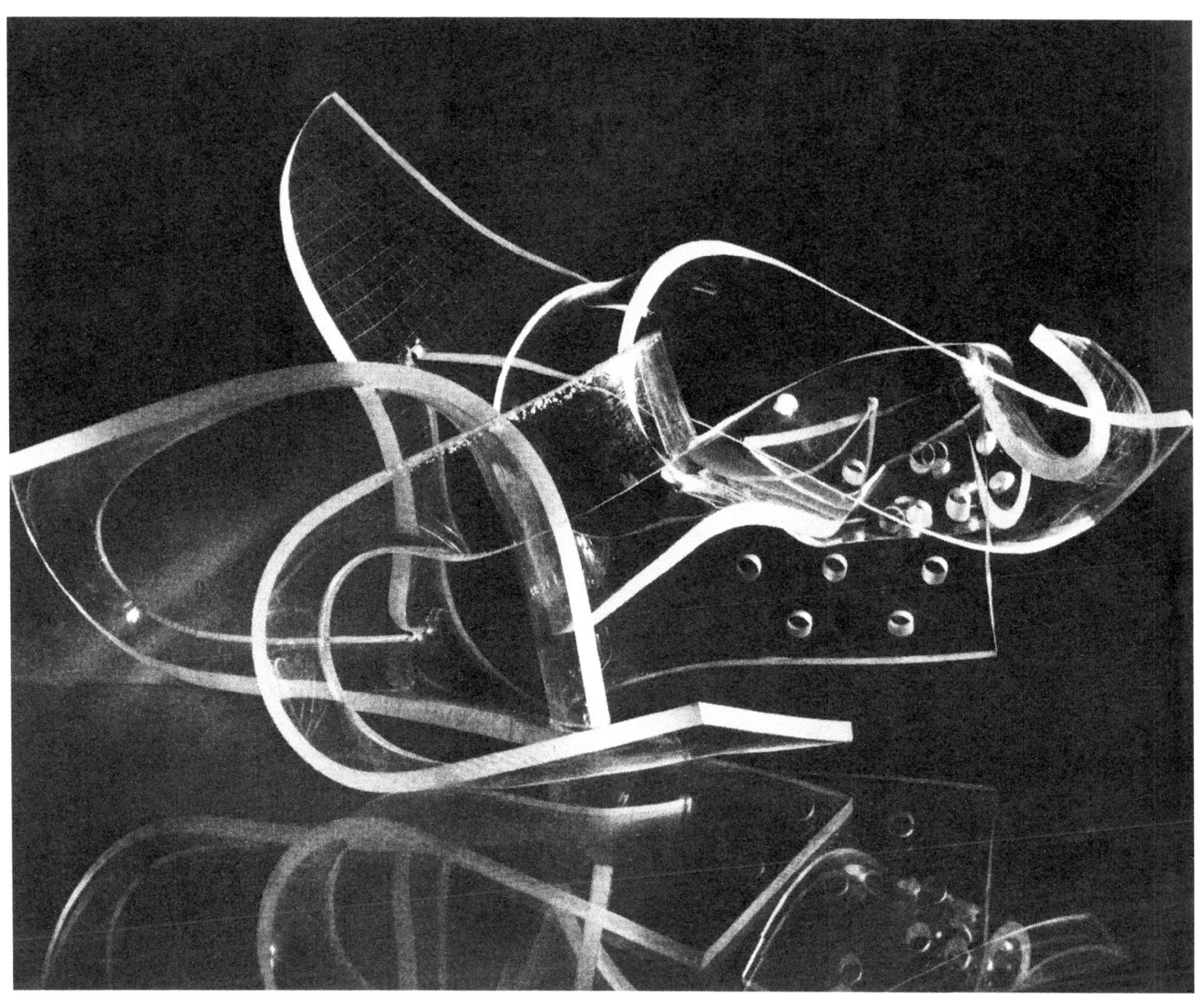

LICHTSPIEL SCHWARZ-WEISS-GRAU – PRODUCTION PHOTOGRAPH.

LICHTSPIEL SCHWARZ-WEISS-GRAU
("Lightplay Black-White-Grey"; Laszlo Moholy-Nagy, 1929: Germany)
This 7-minute experimental film documents the Lichtrequisit Einer Elektrischen Bühne ("Light Machine For An Electric Stage"), László Moholy-Nagy's kinetic sculpture made in Berlin, Germany, in collaboration with Stefan Seboek. Moholy-Nagy actually laid out a complete schema of six films, but only this – actually the last part – was completed. The first five films were intended to show various forms of light, including fire, car headlights, moonlight and prismatic projections; the final part documents Moholy-Nagy's ingenious machine, comprised of discs, mirrors, and rotating spheres which produce an abstract shadowplay for the camera. Moholy-Nagy's more conventional cinematic works of this period include **Berliner Stilleben** ("Berlin Still-Life"), a 9-minute city-film shot between 1926 and 1931; he left Germany when the Nazi Party assumed power in 1933, moving to London where in 1936 he worked on (rejected) design effects for the futuristic H.G. Wells adaptation **Things To Come**.

THE MYSTERIOUS DR. FU MANCHU – PRODUCTION PHOTOGRAPHS.

The MYSTERIOUS DR. FU MANCHU
(Rowland V. Lee, 1929: USA)

The first American interpretation of Sax Rohmer's Fu Manchu, starring Warner Oland as the evil Chinese master-criminal. Fu Manchu's hatred of the "white race" is established by scenes set during the Boxer Rebellion, when his wife and child are killed by soldiers from the occupying forces. Vowing vengeance, he uses hypnotism to turn a young woman into a deadly assassin, and revels in vicious race-hate taunts such as "I hate your detestable white skin" – delivered whilst strangling a woman from behind a curtain. Oland returned as the Oriental devil two more times, in **The Return Of Dr. Fu Manchu** (1930), and **Daughter Of The Dragon** (1931), also starring Anna May Wong. But not until the following year, when Boris Karloff took the role in MGM's **Mask Of Fu Manchu,** would the pulp visions and delirious sadism of Rohmer's original novels be fully expressed on screen.

THE RETURN OF DR. FU MANCHU – PRODUCTION PHOTOGRAPHS (*ABOVE*); DAUGHTER OF THE DRAGON – PRODUCTION PHOTOGRAPHS (*BELOW & OVERLEAF*).

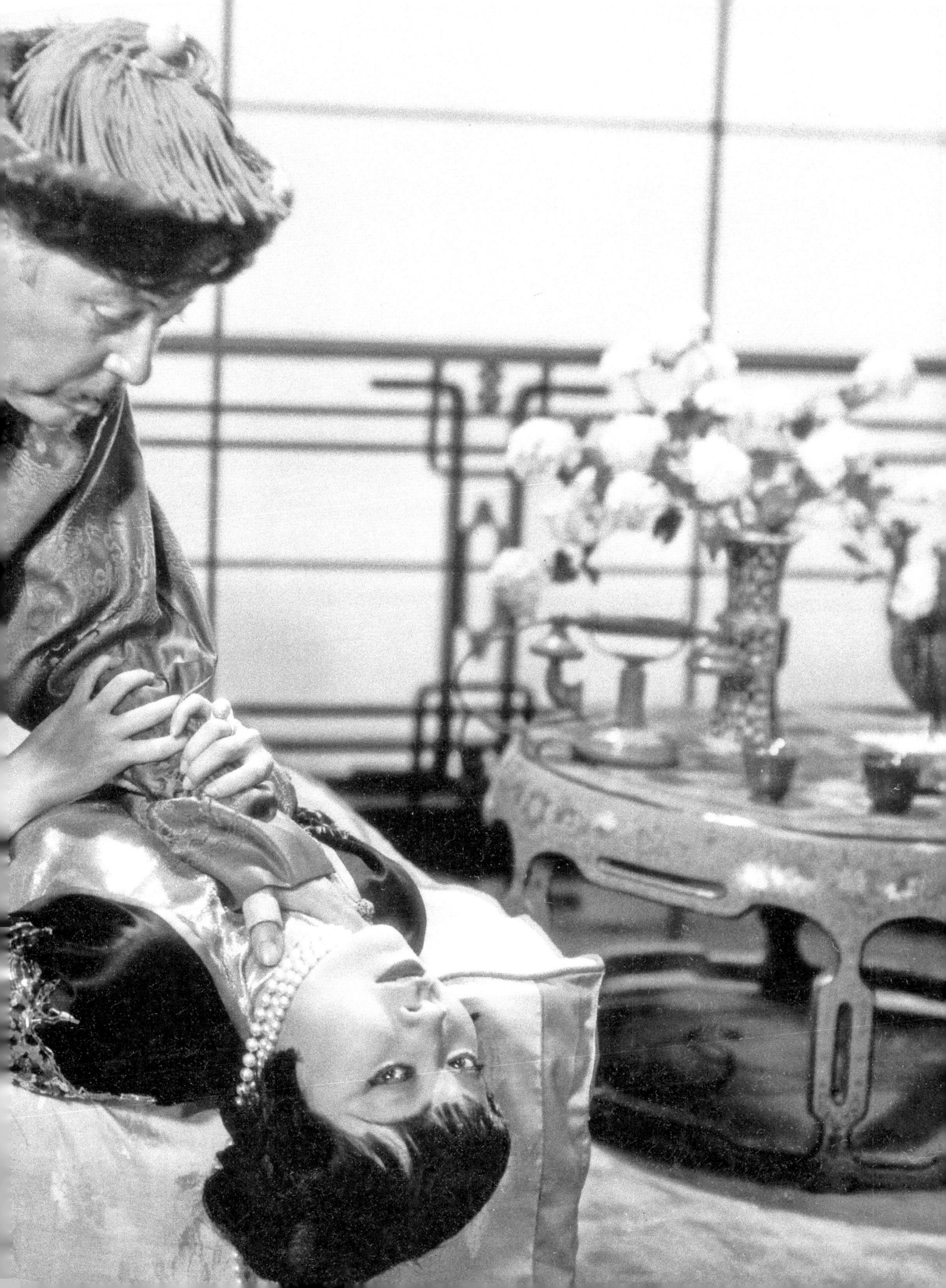

OBLOMOK IMPERII – PRODUCTION PHOTOGRAPHS (ABOVE, BELOW RIGHT & BACKGROUND) AND FILM POSTER (OPPOSITE PAGE).

OBLOMOK IMPERII
("A Fragment Of Empire"; Fridrikh Ermler, 1929: Soviet Union)

A founder member of the Kinoeksperimentalnaia Masterskaia (KEM) collective, Ermler produced his first film **Skarlatina** ("Scarlet Fever"), a short absurdist comedy, in 1924. **Oblomok Imperii**, his key early feature film, is the strange tale of a soldier who was traumatized during WWI, suffers years of amnesia, and suddenly regains his memory in post-revolutionary Moscow. Played by Fedor Nikitin, an actor trained by theatre director Konstantín Stanislávskiy, the ex-soldier experiences a sudden influx of memories shown in a brilliant montage sequence which includes chaotic, shell-shocked images of war such as tanks, machine-guns, cripples, and a crucified Christ-figure wearing a gas-mask. As in Yuliy Rayzman's prison-film **Katorga**, the graphic Expressionism of German artists such as Käthe Kollwitz appears to be influential in the cinematic casting of grotesque and foreboding configurations of human suffering. Like many Soviet films of that period, **Oblomok Imperii** was promoted by a striking Constructivist-style poster by the experimental artists Vladimir and Georgiy Sternberg. Ermler's later films included **Osen** ("The Fall"), an 11-minute experimental study in the unity of images and sound.

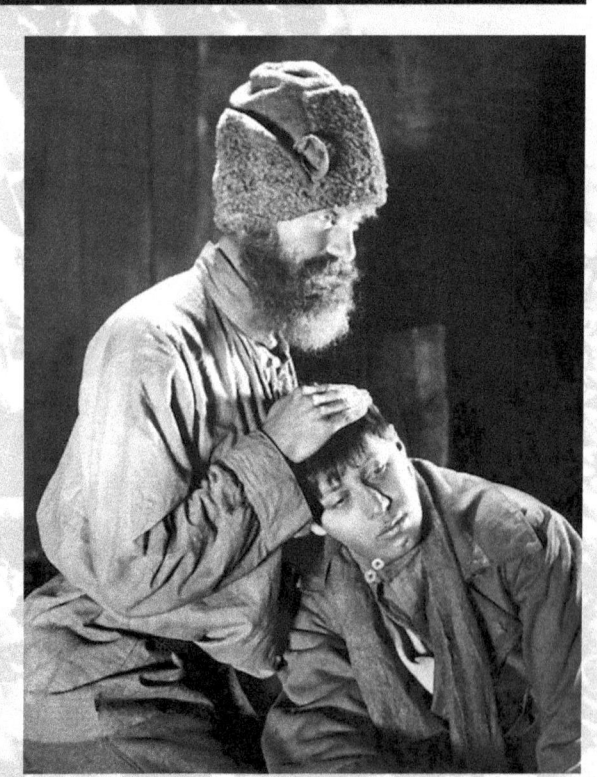

LA PERLE – PRODUCTION PHOTOGRAPH (*ABOVE*).
WITTE VLAM – PRODUCTION PHOTOGRAPH (*BELOW*). USING SOVIET-STYLE MONTAGE EDITING, DEKEUKELEIRE'S 8-MINUTE FILM FOLLOWS A BUTCHER WHO IS HUNTED BY AUTHORITIES AFTER ATTENDING A POLITICAL DEMONSTRATION.

La PERLE
("The Pearl"; Henri d'Ursel, 1929: Belgium)

Written by (and starring) Surrealist Georges Hugnet, whose erotic texts and collages included *Le Feu Au Cul* ("Arse On Fire", 1943) and *La Vie Amoureuse Des Spumifères* ("The Love Life Of The Spumifers", c.1948), **La Perle** is a short, enigmatic fantasy centring on an elusive pearl necklace. Surrrealist elements include shots of a man entering a jewelry shop from a busy street and exiting into countryside, a pair of female cat burglars playing dice in a bathtub, and visual homages to two Surrealist film heroes, Louis Feuillade and Mack Sennett. Voluptuous Euro-vamp Kissa Kouprine (a member of Marcel L'Herbier's stock company) plays the leading jewel thief, clad in a skin-tight bodysuit, a temptress in a waking dream. Other Belgian avant-garde film-makers of this period included Pierre Charbonnier, director of **Ce Soir A Huit Heures** ("Tonight At Eight", 1930); Henri Storck, who with Surrealist artist Felix Labisse made **Pour Vos Beaux Yeux** ("For Your Beautiful Eyes", 1929), a Bataille-inspired phantasy concerning a glass eye; and Charles Dekeukeleire, director of **Impatience** (1928), **Histoire De Détective** ("Detective Story", 1929) and **Witte Vlam** ("White Fire", 1930) – experiments in visual distortion and subjectivity. Dekeukeleire's later **Het Kwade Oog** ("The Evil Eye", 1937) was a mystical evocation of ancient witchcraft and nocturnal terrors, filmed with non-actors in rural Belgium.

PICCADILLY – PRODUCTION PHOTOGRAPH.

PICCADILLY
(E.A. Dupont, 1929: UK)

The outstanding production that resulted from Chinese-American actress Anna May Wong's 1928-30 sojourn in Europe, during which she appeared in a number of films produced or co-produced by British International Pictures.[1] The film's title refers to an area of London notorious for its night-life (the film was released as **Nachtwelt**, meaning "Night-World", in the director's native Germany); Wong plays Shosho, a Chinese dancer who starts as a kitchen-worker in a club but is given the chance to perform on stage. She becomes an overnight sensation, but becomes embroiled in a miscegenous love triangle which eventually costs her her life when she is shot dead. Her killer eventually commits suicide. Director Dupont presents a glittering vision of decadence and sexual taboos, with Wong as the doomed, exotic jewel at its epicentre. Austrian poster art shows the actress dancing bare-breasted, an image which could never be included in the actual film in England, where censorship was among the most oppressive in the world – even a mixed-race kiss between Wong and a male actor was prohibited. Wong returned to a London *milieu* once again in 1934 when, back in Hollywood, she starred in the Paramount production **Limehouse Blues**, set in a docklands slum area notorious for Chinese opium dens, prostitution and crime. The film was also notable for its set decor, which included many items of specially-imported Chinese art.

1. Including the German co-productions **Schmutziges Geld** ("Dirty Money", 1928), **Grosstadtschmetterling** ("Big City Butterfly", 1929) and **Hai Tang** (1929), all directed by Richard Eichberg, in which she also played Asian dancers.

PICCADILLY – PRODUCTION PHOTOGRAPHS.

LIMEHOUSE BLUES – PRODUCTION AND PUBLICITY PHOTOGRAPHS (*THIS PAGE AND OVERLEAF*).

QUEEN OF THE NORTHWOODS – PRODUCTION PHOTOGRAPHS.

QUEEN OF THE NORTHWOODS
(Spencer Gordon Bennet & Thomas Storey, 1929: USA)
One of the last serials from Pathé Exchange, **Queen Of The Northwoods** features a theme of Native Indian "werewolves" driving away white settlers, although the menace is not actually supernatural – an "evil" Indian only dresses in a wolfshead whilst pretending to be the "Wolf Devil". He does, however, appear to have an uncanny control over actual wolves. The serial's ten episodes were: **The Wolf-Devil's Challenge; A Bottomless Grave; Devil Worshippers; Wings Of Death; The Wolf-Devil Strikes; The Leap Of Death; The Flaming Peril; Brand Of The Beast; Trapped By The Fiend;** and **The Den Of Evil**.

LE ROMAN DE RENARD – PRODUCTION PHOTOGRAPH.

L'HORLOGE MAGIQUE ("THE MAGIC CLOCK", STAREWICZ 1928) – PRODUCTION PHOTOGRAPH (*OVERLEAF VERSO*).

DANS LES GRIFFES DE L'ARAIGNÉE – PRODUCTION PHOTOGRAPH (*OVERLEAF RECTO*).

Le ROMAN DE RENARD
("The Story Of Renart"; Wladyslaw Starewicz, 1929-30: France)

Arriving in France in 1920, Lithuanian animator Starewicz almost immediately continued his prolific output of stop-motion films, producing a series of short works of which **Dans Les Griffes De L'Araignée** ("In The Claws Of The Spider", 1925), with its human-faced arachnids, is perhaps the most disturbing. In 1929, Starewicz began work on his first, and only, feature-length animated film, **Le Roman De Renard**. With the assistance of his two daughters, the film was eventually completed after 18 months of painstaking work, utilising human-sized models dressed in suede, velvet and leather. Based on the medieval legend of Renart the fox, the 65-minute film tells the story of how the cruel and crafty Renart habitually mistreats his fellow creatures, until the Lion King finally orders his arrest. Condemned to hang, Renart escapes by promising secret treasures – another trick. The King lays siege to Renart's gothic castle, Maupertuis, but again the fox resists capture. Finally, the King accepts that Renart is a better ally than enemy. With incredibly detailed, flowing stop-motion animation, Starewicz's **Le Roman De Renard** stands as one of the first masterpieces of the puppet cinema. The film was not premiered until 1937, due to the development of its soundtrack. A German version (with funding by the Nazis, who were interested in Starewicz creating an animated adaptation of Goethe) was finally screened in Berlin; a French version was not released until 1941. As a result, it was beaten to release by several other animated features which had actually been made after it; these include Alexandre Ptouchko's 70-minute **Noviy Gullivyer** ("The New Gulliver",

1935) – Swift as Marxist allegory – and the 60-minute **Le Avventure Di Pinocchio** ("The Adventures Of Pinocchio", 1936), directed by Umberto Spano and Raoul Verdini.

SEVEN FOOTPRINTS TO SATAN – PRODUCTION PHOTOGRAPHS (*ABOVE & OPPOSITE TOP*); PUBLICITY PHOTOGRAPH (*OPPOSITE BOTTOM*).

SEVEN FOOTPRINTS TO SATAN
(Benjamin Christensen, 1929: USA)

Although Christensen made the greatest Satanic film of all time, **Häxan**, before relocating to Hollywood in 1924, the "Satan" in **Seven Footprints To Satan** is not the Devil, but a sinister cult leader who revels in infernal regalia. Created by pulp novelist A.E. Merritt, Satan was originally an evil super-villain in the same mould as Sax Rohmer's Fu Manchu – unfortunately, this film version of Merritt's eponymous novel considerably alters the story, and ends in anti-climax. Nevertheless, Christensen does his best with this mandate, creating some magnificent sets – such as Satan's throne room with its huge bat-winged dragons – and manages to include some truly grotesque figures, including a scurrying dwarf (Angelo Rossitto),[1] a dog-faced savant, a facially deformed hag, and a feral, crippled creature known as The Spider (Sheldon Lewis). Charles Gemora also appears, in his customary role as a vicious gorilla, the Beast of Satan. Satan's mansion is a house of sliding panels and secret corridors, of kidnapped and tortured girls, of sinister freaks, of orgiastic devil-worshippers; scenes include a girl being chained and whipped, her legs held fast by the gorilla. The film is finally let down by its tame ending, imposed by the producers, which reveals the whole thing to have been a "prank", a device often used to condescendingly reassure audiences in much the same way as elements of "comic relief" were often jarringly inserted to ruin otherwise potent horror movies.

1. Angelo Rossitto's other main appearance of 1929 was in Warner's **One Stolen Night**, as part of a travelling circus troupe.

SEVEN FOOTPRINTS TO SATAN – PRODUCTION PHOTOGRAPH (*LEFT*).
ONE STOLEN NIGHT – PRODUCTION PHOTOGRAPH (*BELOW*).

The SILENT HOUSE
(Walter Forde, 1929: UK)

A silent mystery-crime film distributed by Butcher's Film Service, **The Silent House** was based on a "yellow peril" stage production by John G. Brandon, in which an evil Mandarin named Chang Fu uses hypnotism to locate hidden bonds. Similar to contemporary US "dark house" mysteries, the film includes such other horrors as a snake-pit, and a suitably hulking Chinese henchman. It was released in Denmark as **Den Gule Doktor** ("The Yellow Doctor"). Some other murder-mysteries from England were **Mystery At The Villa Rose** (1930), **Condemned To Death** (1932), **The Frightened Lady** (1932, from Edgar Wallace), **The Strangler** (1932), **The Scotland Yard Mystery** (1933 – released in the US as **The Living Dead**, in which a pathologist places victims in suspended animation), and **The Shadow** (1933). **Ghost Camera** (1933) was perhaps the most unusual, a mystery-thriller in which photographs of a murder are discovered on a discarded, undeveloped film spool. Also from this period was the 12-chapter mystery-crime serial **Lloyd Of The C.I.D.** (1931), a UK/US co-production filmed in England. Released in the US as **Detective Lloyd**, the serial included SF elements (a death ray) as well as scenes of dark-house horror and a criminal mastermind named The Panther.[1] **The Girl From Scotland Yard** (Paramount, 1937) was a US production with similar themes, involving a female police detective pitted against a deranged anarchist trying to destroy London with a death-ray.

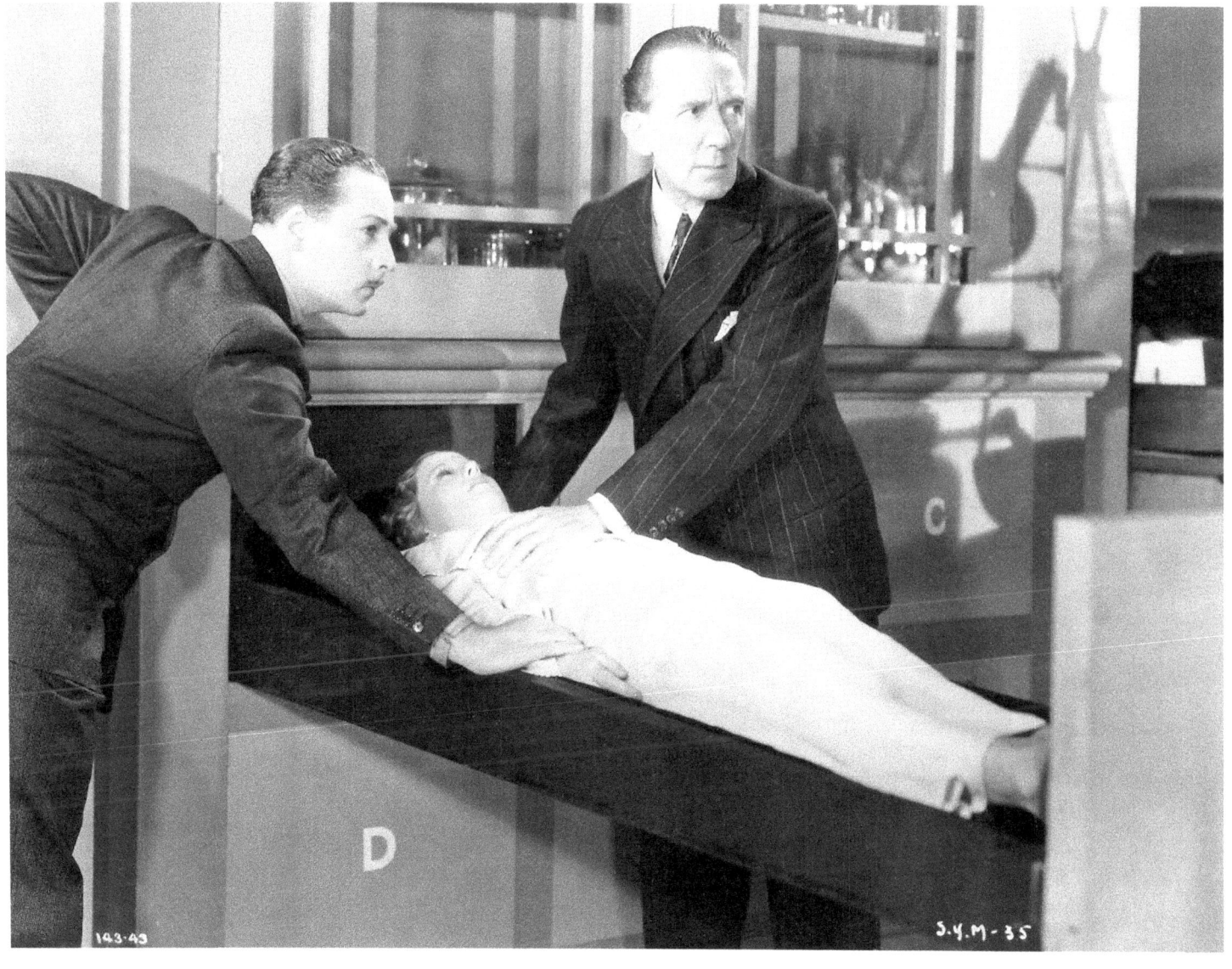

SCOTLAND YARD – PRODUCTION PHOTOGRAPH (*ABOVE*).
THE SCOTLAND YARD MYSTERY – PRODUCTION PHOTOGRAPH (*BELOW*).

1. The twelve chapters of Lloyd Of The C.I.D. were: The Green Spot Murder; The Panther Strikes; The Trap Springs; Tracked By Wireless; The Death Ray; The Poison Dart; The Race With Death; The Panther's Lair; Imprisoned In The North Tower (retitled The Fatal Plunge in the US); The Panther's Cunning; The Panther At Bay; and Heroes Of The Law. It was also released in 1932 as an edited feature-length movie entitled The Green Spot Mystery.

2. One of Hollywood's earliest sound films to involve Scotland Yard was Fox's Scotland Yard (1930), notable as a crime narrative involving identity theft through plastic surgery.

The SKELETON DANCE
(Ub Iwerks, 1929: USA)

First, and still one of the best, of Walt Disney's cartoon series **Silly Symphonies**, which would run until 1939. **The Skeleton Dance** is an inventive, dark, even macabre piece set in a storm-swept graveyard where human bones come to life by night. One of Salvador Dalí's favourite films of all time, which led to his eventual collaboration with Disney on the abortive **Destino**. The dancing skeletons were also used that same year in Disney's **Haunted House**, an Iwerks cartoon featuring the emergent character Mickey Mouse. Iwerks would also reconfigure **The Skeleton Dance** in 1937, creating a Technicolor version entitled **Skeleton Frolic**. Similar scenes can also be found in **Kutsu-Juku Seiklusi** ("Adventures Of Kustu-Juku", 1931), the first animated film to emerge from Estonia. Directed by Voldemar Päts and animated by Elmar Jaanimägi, the 4-minute cartoon emulates its American counterparts by featuring a dog as its lead character.

KUTSU-JUKU SEIKLUSI – ANIMATION FRAME.

SOLE!
("Sun!"; Alesandro Blasetti, 1929: Italy)

One of the last films of the Italian silent era, hailed by many – including Fascist leader Benito Mussolini – as the start of a new national cinema; although some critics dismissed Blasetti's debut as merely an imitation of Soviet propaganda film-making, Mussolini declared it "the dawn of the Fascist film". **Sole!** is based upon the land reclamation of the Pontine Marshes, and depicts an often violent confrontation between swamp-dwellers and the engineers who seek to transform the region into new farmland. The film closes upon an industrial image of a plow turning virgin soil beneath the sun, symbolising the rebirth of Italy itself. The original negative of **Sole!** was reportedly lost or destroyed by the Nazis in 1943; only a single 11-minute reel survives. Blasetti next directed his first sound film, **Nerone** ("Nero", 1930), a satirical revue of ancient Rome and its pyromaniac emperor[1] starring clown actor Ettore Petrolini, best known for his character Fortunello, conceived in 1915. Supposedly part-inspired by American comic-strip *Happy Hooligan*, Fortunello was acclaimed by the Futurists who admired his blend of the mechanical, the grotesque and the absurd. Mario Volpe's **Il Grido Dell'Aquila** ("The Scream Of The Eagle", 1923) is generally considered to be the first Fascist propaganda film; it consists of glorious episodes from WWI and the national war effort, the initial struggles of the Fascist movement, and an exaltation of the country's armed forces. Communism, the enemy of Fascism, is depicted as a snake – staple prey for the eagle's claws. The film was inspired by the march on Rome of October 1922, when tens of thousands of miltants from Mussolini's PNF (Partito Nazionale Fascista)[2] converged on the city threatening armed revolution.

1. The ridiculing of Nero was whispered by some to be a covert mockery of Mussolini and his new dictatorship.
2. The PNF was a 1921 renaming of the PFR (Partito Fascista Rivoluzionario), founded in 1915, following a merger with the PPF (Partito Politico Futurista), founded by F.T. Marinetti in 1918.

NERONE – ETTORE PETROLINI AS FORTUNELLO; PRODUCTION PHOTOGRAPH.

STAMPEDE
(Chaplin Court-Treatt, Stella Court-Treatt & Errol Hinds, 1929: UK)

It seems that almost every developed nation in the 1920s and 30s had its very own husband-and-wife team of ethnographic explorers/film-makers, and England's contribution to this phenomenon were Chaplin and Stella Court-Treatt. Their **Stampede** was the first of three inter-related films released by British Instructional Films (BIF),[1] the other two being **Africa In Flames** (a sound version) and **Stark Nature** (a documentary on the making of the film), both released in 1930. Shot in the Sudan, **Stampede** is actually a fictionalized account of an adopted native boy, Boru, who rises to power. The narrative is intercut with "exotic" sequences directly comparing natives to wild animals, and footage of both male and female specimens running naked. It was doubtless this latter facet which appealed to US roadshow hustler Dwain Esper, who in 1934 cut the film down to its 35-minute essentials, added a prurient warning on the dangers of animal/human miscegeny, and presented it as **Bo-Ru, The Ape Boy**, the tale of a feral child raised by apes. Another notable member of this exotic UK sub-genre was **Nionga** (Stoll Picture Productions, 1925), a "cannibal drama" notable for its sequences of primitive rites and, of course, female nudity. Court-Treatt's Sudanese footage was utilized once more in **Struggle For Life** (1935, also released as **Sudan**), a US concoction released by Bryan Foy who favoured exploitational subjects such as eugenics and nudist camps; a young, bare-breasted Sudanese female graced the title lobby card for **Sudan**, indicating Foy's usual sales angle.

1. BIF was founded in 1919 and became renowned for **Secrets Of Nature**, a long series of single-reel educational films created by a team headed by Percy Smith, an innovator in scientific cinema and time-lapse film experiments. Highlights of the series were close-ups of xeno-horror such as **Battle Of The Ants** (1922).

SUDAN – LOBBY CARD, 1935.

STARK MAD - PRODUCTION PHOTOGRAPHS (ABOVE, OPPOSITE & OVERLEAF).

STARK MAD
(Lloyd Bacon, 1929: USA)

One of many films issued as both silent and with limited sound, **Stark Mad** is one of the first features to showcase ape impersonator Charles Gemora as a sinister, monstrous gorilla (as opposed to the more comic variety which he played in a number of shorts). The film is set in the Mayan jungles of Central America, where a man launches the search for his missing son. Sheltering in an ancient temple, the man and his team discover a secret chamber where a massive gorilla is chained to the floor. This creature is the slave of a crazed hermit, who murdered the man's son. The temple ruins soon become a death maze, with members of the expedition either shot by arrows or abducted by the vicious beast. Lighter moments were doubtless provided by the presence of comic actress Louise Fazenda. With its exotic location and homicidal gorilla, **Stark Mad** is one of several films which prefigured the ultimate monster ape movie, **King Kong**. Another bizarre ape movie of 1929 was the little-known **The Devil Bear,** a Canadian production in which a ship-wrecked gorilla saves his master from various perils, including native Indians who believe the gorilla is some kind of monstrous bear; it is unconfirmed which actor lurked within the animal costume, although the suit is almost certainly one of Gemora's once again.

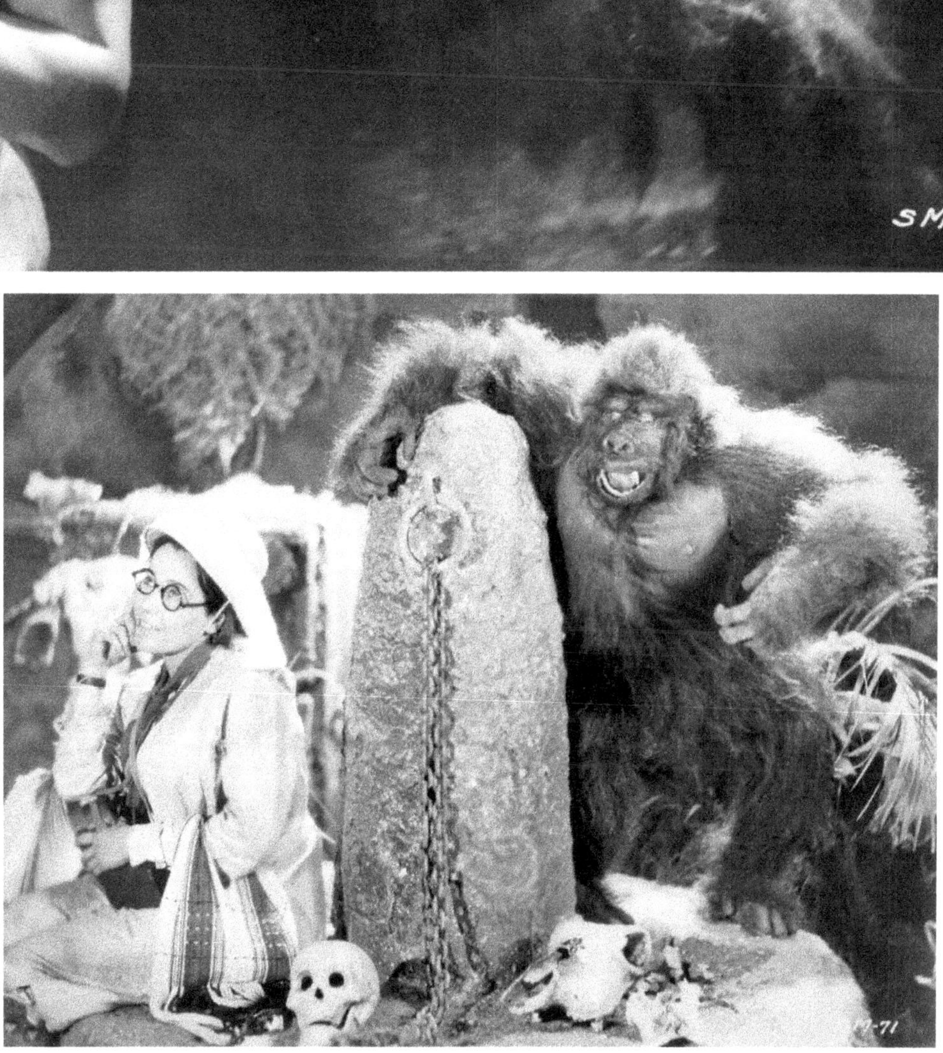

TAGEBUCH EINER VERLORENEN – PRODUCTION PHOTOGRAPHS (*ABOVE & OPPOSITE TOP*).
ASPHALT – BETTY AMANN IN BROOKS MODE; PRODUCTION PHOTOGRAPH (*OPPOSITE BOTTOM*).

TAGEBUCH EINER VERLORENEN
("Diary Of A Lost Girl"; G.W. Pabst, 1929: Germany)

A vivid meditation on female sexuality starring Louise Brooks, already famous for her portrayal of the wanton Lulu in **Die Büchse Der Pandora**, released a few months earlier. In this adaptation of Margarethe Böhme's sensational 1905 novel – first filmed in 1918 by Richard Oswald – she plays Thymian, a young girl seduced and impregnated by an older man; her parents send her away to a reform school for delinquent girls, forced to wear uniforms and short haircuts. Lesbianism and sadism are strongly implied in the school scenes, purveyed by Pabst with gruelling severity; Tymian eventually escapes, but ends up in prostitution. This catalogue of abuse and corruption is finally given a positive ending, but not enough to ruin the preceding peepshow of defiled beauty. The role of a sadistic matron was played by Berlin avant-garde dancer Valeska Gert, whose "grotesque" performances – such as *Die Küpplerin* ("The Procuress"), filmed by Suse Byk in 1925 – comprised radical interpretations of disease, addiction and death. Gert's debut in Berlin was in 1916; her engagements included dancing at cinemas between reels, and later at Dadaist cabarets where her highly individual dances included *Japanischer Groteske* ("Japanese Grotesque"), *Tod* ("Death"), *Hure* ("Whore"), and *Gruss Aus Dem Mumienkeller* ("Greetings From The Mummy's Crypt"). By 1929 she was performing *Tontänze* ("sound dances"), a series of sonic-kinetic experiments; her last film appearance of this period was in Alberto Cavalcanti's short **Pett And Pott** (1934), shot in London for the GPO film unit. The impact of Louise Brooks and her style on Weimar cinema of this period may be clearly seen in Joe May's **Asphalt** (1928-29), a crime film dealing with a young girl (played by German-American actress Betty Amann) who uses her sexuality to escape punishment.

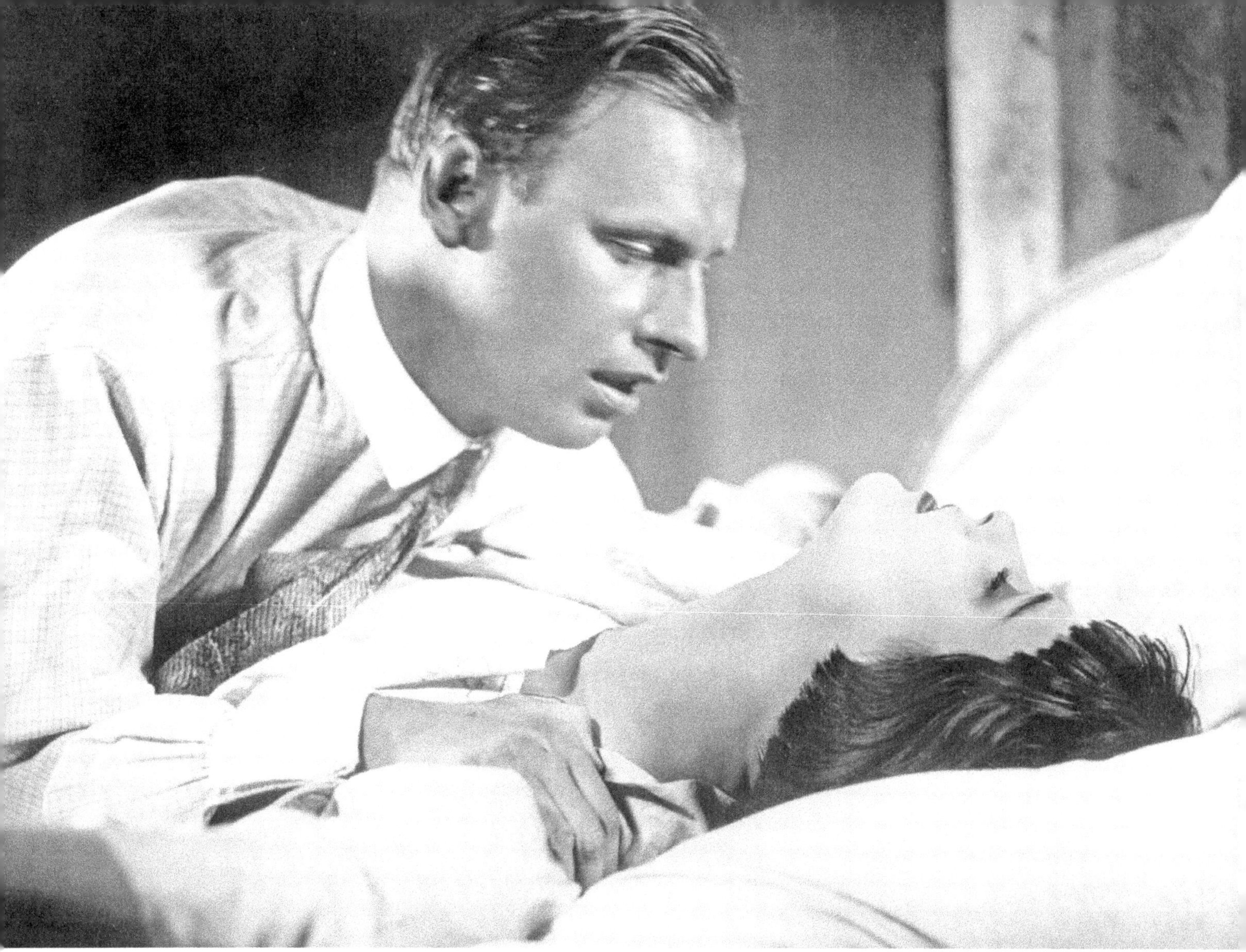

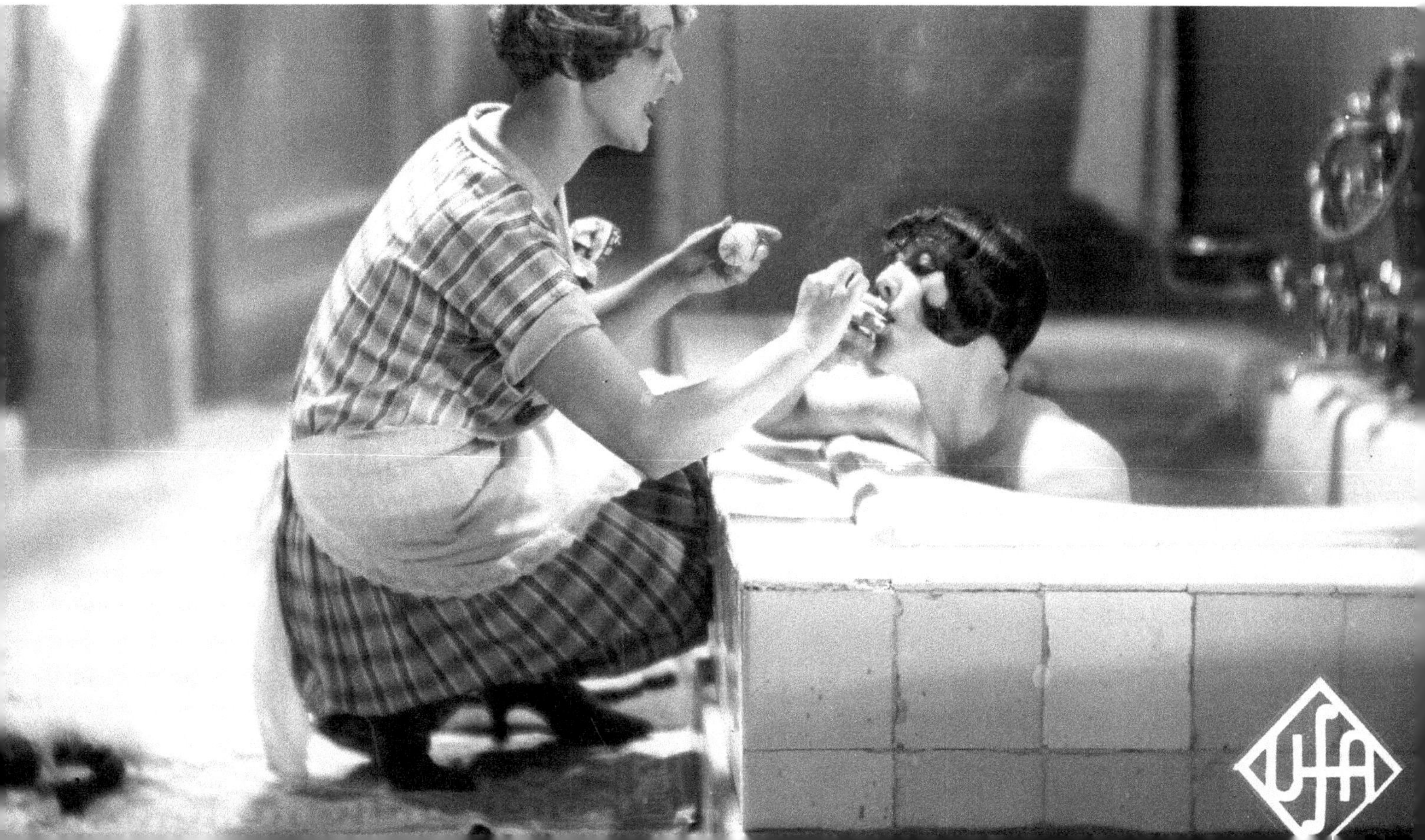

TRADER HORN – PRODUCTION PHOTOGRAPHS.

TRADER HORN
(W.S. Van Dyke, 1929-31: USA)

Produced by MGM, **Trader Horn** was the first fiction feature film shot in Africa (although most of this footage was only used as back-projection). Filming began in 1929, but was extended when it was decided to change the film to a sound production. Framed as an exotic adventure, **Trader Horn** mixes exploitative elements previously seen in certain ethno-documentaries (bare-breasted native women, animals slaughtered on camera) with a narrative concerning the search for a missing white girl in the African jungle. The girl is finally discovered situated as queen of a savage black tribe who apparently revere her as a goddess because of her ivory flesh and blonde tresses, a trope to be found in many such subsequent stories, and dating back to various Selig productions of the 1920s. **Trader Horn** also includes genuine footage of a native bearer being trampled to death by stampeding rhinos, and another crew member was reportedly eaten alive by crocodiles during production (footage not included). The producers were latterly accused of animal cruelty when it emerged that lions were caged and starved before being unleashed on helpless zebras for the benefit of the cameras (scenes reportedly shot in Mexico, where animals were regularly trained for performing in pornographic stag films). Lead actress Edwina Booth, who contracted a debilitating neurological disease during filming, sued MGM and never worked in Hollywood again.

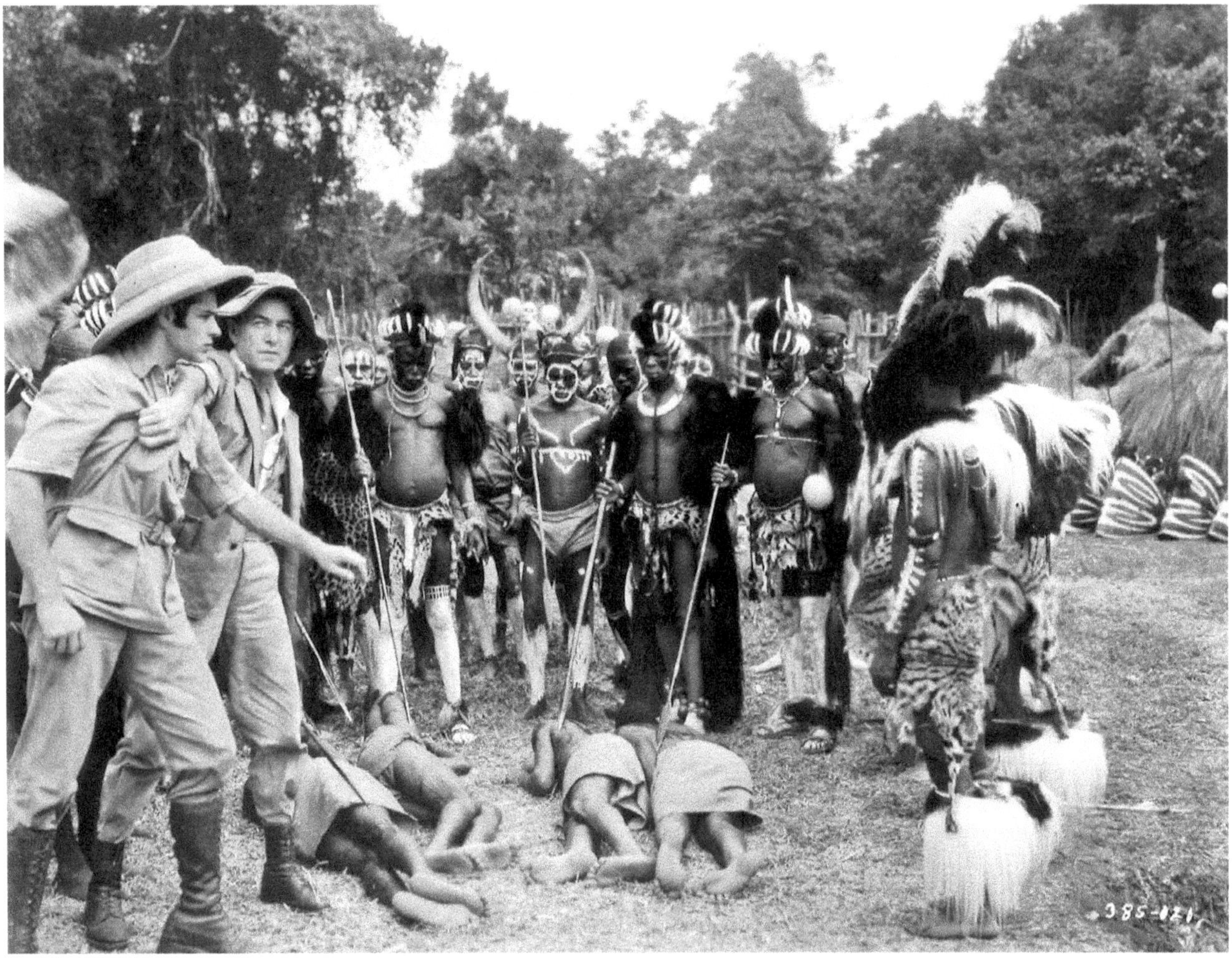
385-121

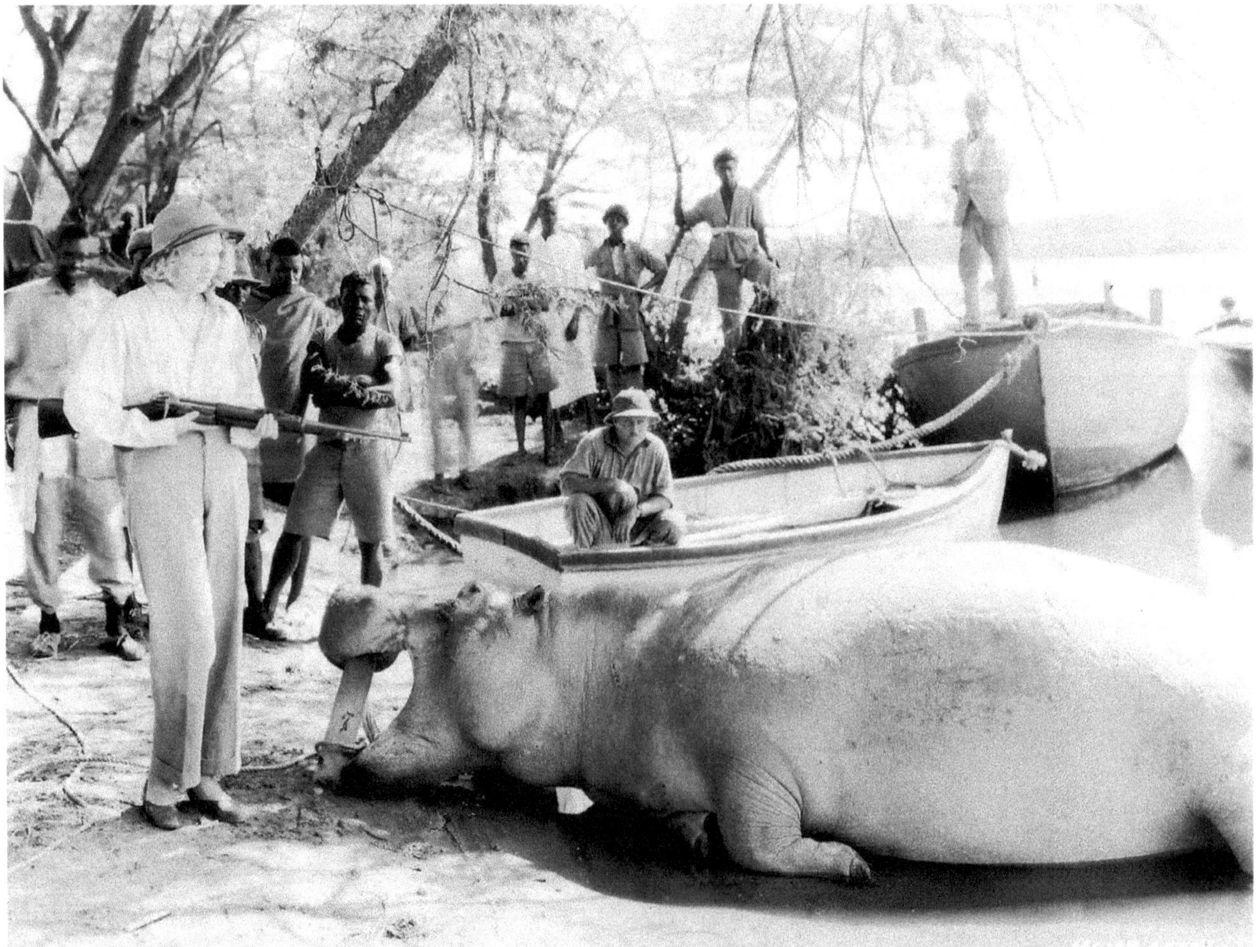

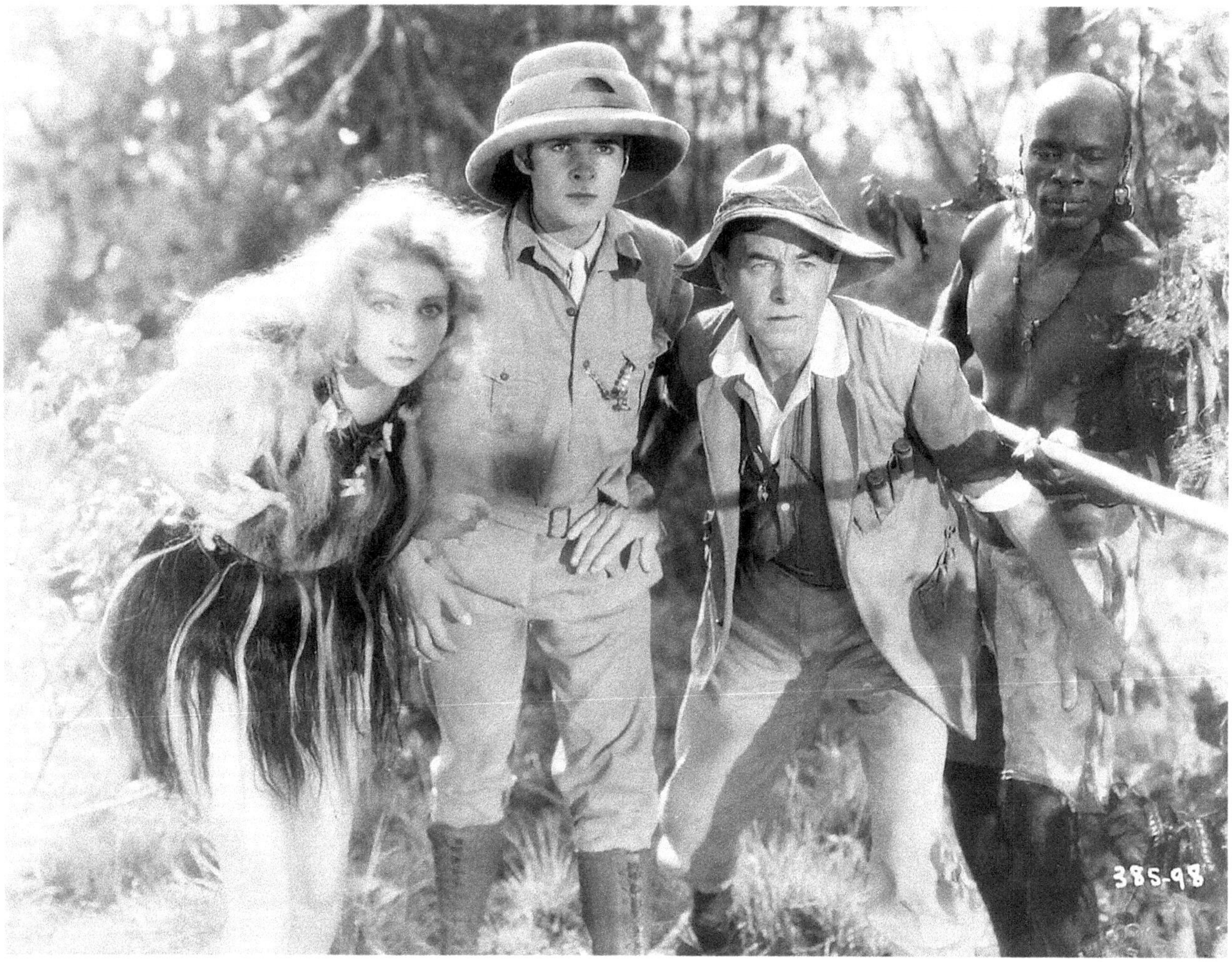
385-98

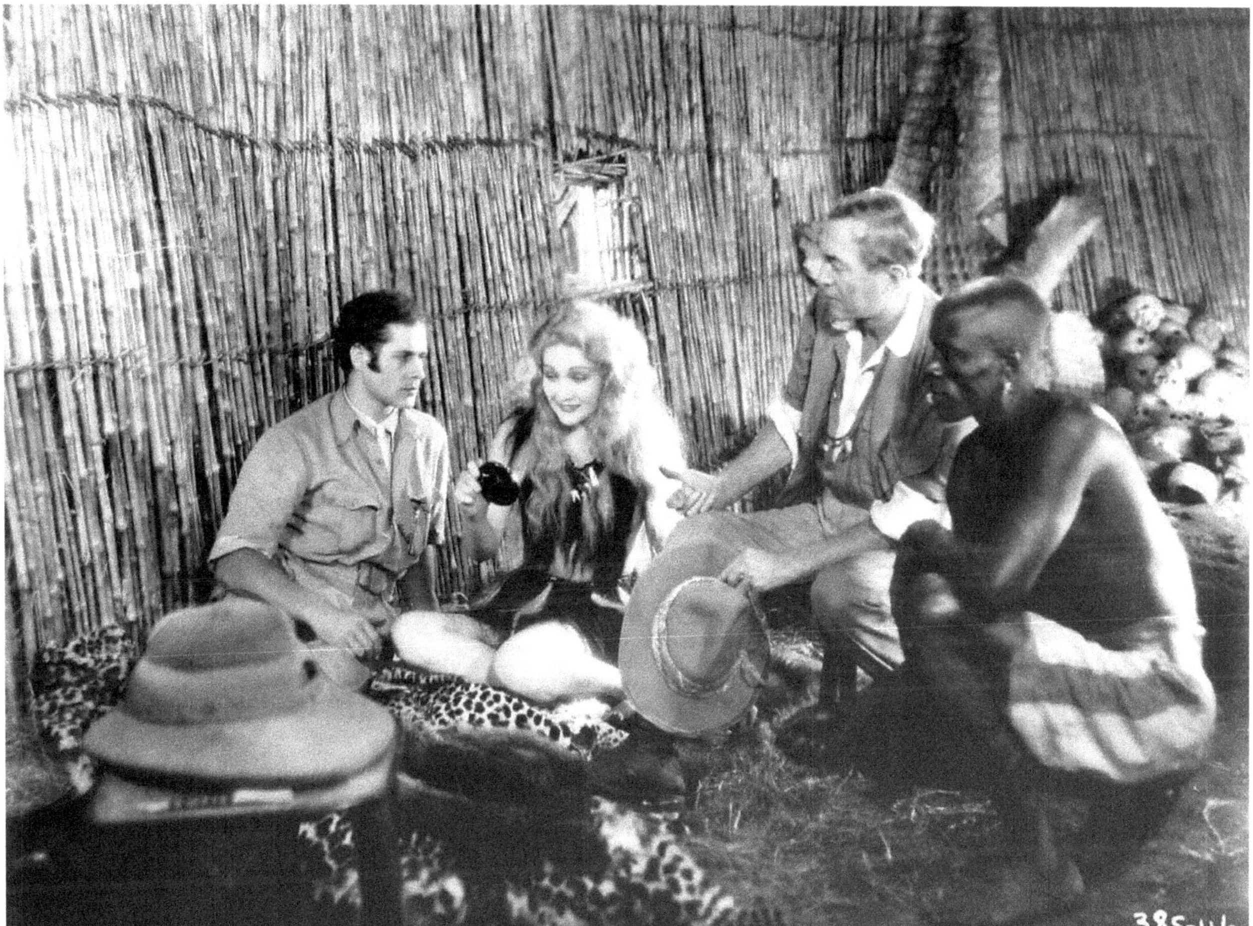
385-116

TUSALAVA
(Len Lye, 1929: UK)

The very first animation by Lye, a pioneer of the art form, presenting organic shapes from the primeval to the complex, and back again. Mutation, synthesis, evolution and abstraction are presented in contrasting aspects, splitting the screen. Influenced both by tribal designs and by notions of "automatic drawing", Lye produced the film from over 4,000 different photographed drawings, or cels. Lye's next animations included **Kaleidoscope** (1935) – sponsored by Churchman Cigarettes – **A Colour Box** (1935), **Birth Of The Robot** (1936) – a promotional film with puppets made for Shell-Mex – **Rainbow Dance** (1936) – an experiment with the Gasparcolor system using stencilled patterns over colourized film of a live dancer – and **Colour Flight** (1938), sponsored by Imperial Airways. **N. Or N.W.** (1937), a live-action film commissioned by the GPO, was shot and edited by Lye in such an extreme and disorienting manner that one sequence was actually censored by the producers. After directing several war propaganda shorts, including the acclaimed sniper docu-drama **Kill Or Be Killed** (1942), Lye moved to New York in 1944, joining the city's avant-garde and collaborating with various painters and film-makers, including Hans Richter. His next animated film, **Color Cry**, was not completed until 1952.

The VOICE FROM THE SKY
(Ben F. Wilson, 1929: USA)

Beginning its release at the very end of 1929, Wilson's 10-chapter SF serial was the first to have a built-in soundtrack (as opposed to recorded discs). The story concerns a masked maniac who, presumably through futuristic devices, has acquired the power to suspend all of Earth's electrical energy and is threatening to rain destruction upon global cities. Secret Services send agents to track him in his desert lair, in conflict with criminals seeking to steal the madman's technology for their own ends. The chapters were: **Doomed**; **The Cave Of Horror**; **The Man From Nowhere**; **Danger Ahead**; **Desperate Deeds**; **Trail Of Vengeance**; **The Scarlet Scourge**; **Trapped By Fate**; **The Pit Of Peril**; and **Hearts Of Steel**. The serial's distribution was limited, due to technical shortcomings. **The Voice From The Sky** may be considered as a sound remake/update of Wilson's 15-chapter silent serial **The Power God** (1925),[1] co-directed with Francis Ford, which also features a scientist who invents a machine to control the atoms of Earth's atmosphere. Wilson and Ford followed **The Power God** with the 10-chapter **Officer 444** (1926),[2] in which a criminal mastermind named The Frog seeks control of a secret formula for chemical weapons which will give him unlimited power. Much of the action takes place in an underground labyrinth of sewers laced with traps and secret chambers, and filled with gibbering lunatics. The part of Officer 444 was Wilson's last serial acting role.

1. The fifteen chapters of **The Power God** were: The Ring Of Fate; Trapped; The Living Dead; Black Shadows; The Death Chamber; House Of Peril; Hands In The Dark; The 59th Second; Perilous Waters; The Bridge Of Doom; Treachery; The Storm's Lash; The Purloined Papers; The Flaming Menace; and The Wages Of Sin.

2. The ten chapters of **Officer 444** were: Flying Squadron; Human Rats; Trapped; Gassed; Missing; The Radio Ray; Death's Shadow; Jaws Of Doom; Underground Trap; and Justice.

WHY BRING THAT UP?
(George Abbott, 1929: USA)

The feature film debut of a famous blackface duo, minstrel act Two Black Crows (Charles Mack and George Moran), who were famous for their watermelon jokes. The Crows starred in two early sound features, the second being **Anybody's War** (1930).[1] By 1933 Moran was replaced; Mack and a new Moran moved into shorts, appearing in seven comedies supervised by Al Christie – **As The Crows Fly**, **Two Black Crows In Africa**, **A Pair Of Socks**, **Hot Hoofs**, **Blue Blackbirds**,[2] **Farmers' Fatal Folly**, and **The Freeze Out** (which ends with the duo in Hell) – before Mack was killed in a car wreck in early 1934. Meanwhile, RKO released Melville W. Brown's **Check And Double-Check** (1930), the first and only film vehicle for Amos'n'Andy, a popular pair of comedic negro radio characters created and voiced by white actors Freeman Gosden and Charles Correll from 1928 onwards; for the film, the actors

WHY BRING THAT UP? – PRODUCTION PHOTOGRAPH (*OPPOSITE TOP*); ANYBODY'S WAR – PRODUCTION PHOTOGRAPH (*OPPOSITE BOTTOM*).
CHECK AND DOUBLE-CHECK – PRODUCTION PHOTOGRAPH (*OVERLEAF VERSO TOP*).
SLIM TIMBLIN – PUBLICITY PHOTOGRAPH (*OVERLEAF VERSO BOTTOM*).
MAMMY – AL JOLSON PUBLICITY PHOTOGRAPH (*OVERLEAF RECTO*).

TAXI
FRESHAIR TAXICAB Co.
OF
AMERICA
INCORPULATED

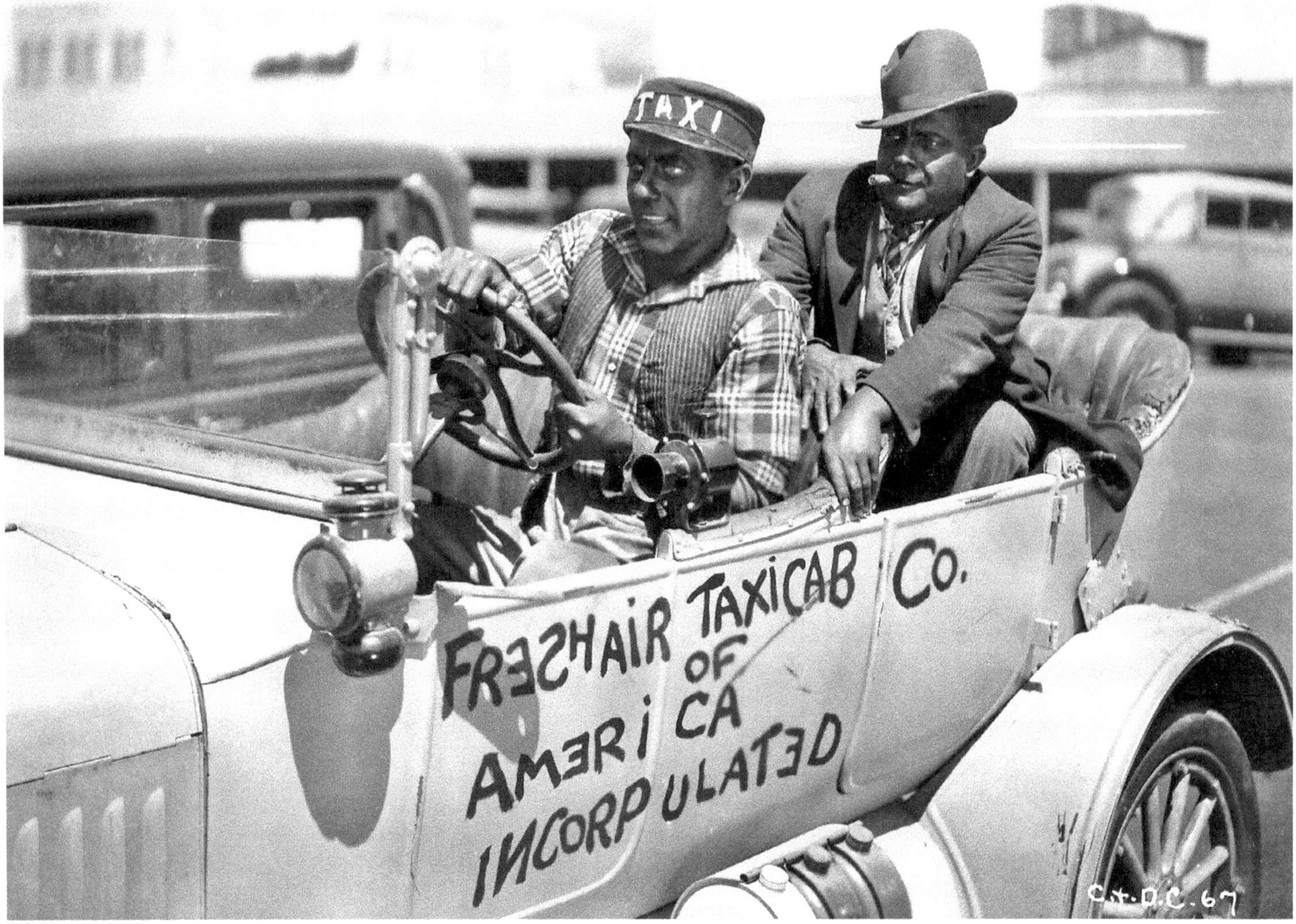

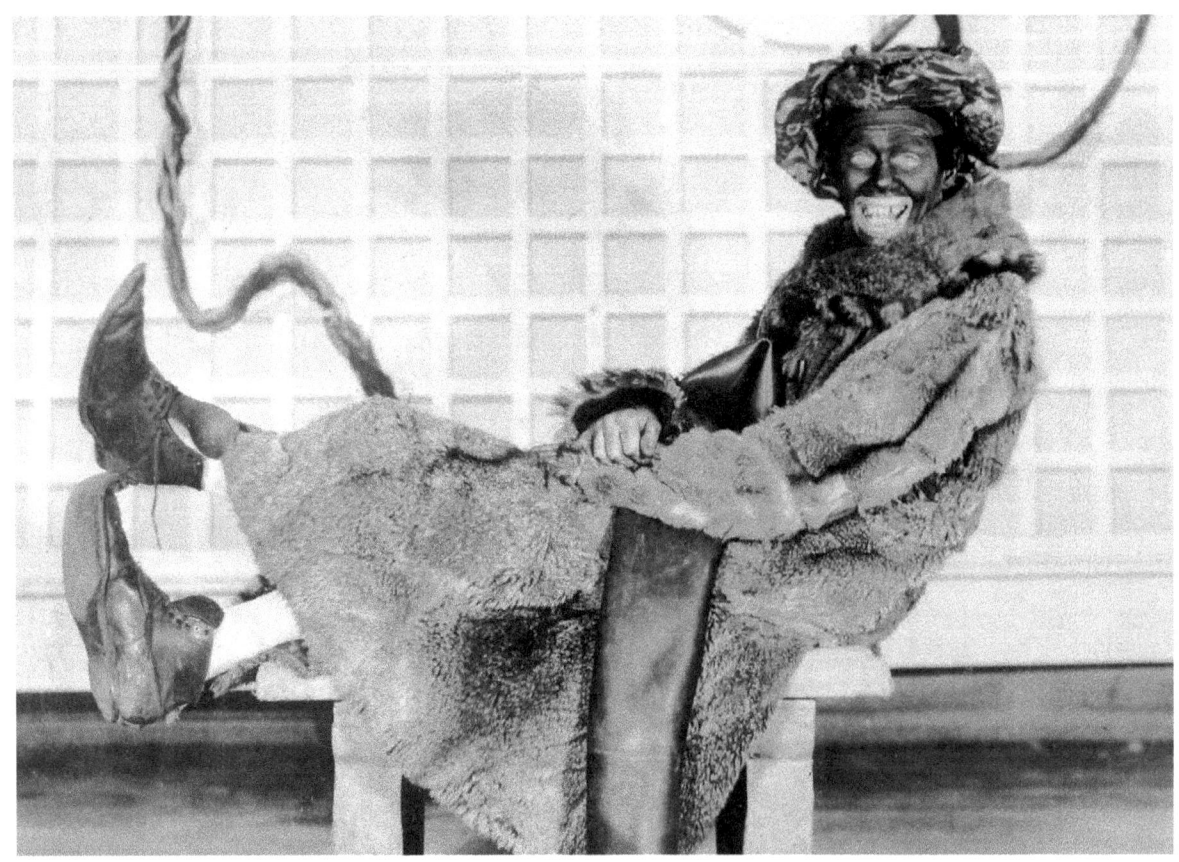

performed in blackface. Not long after its release, the duo came under fire for their "crude, repetitious, and moronic" depiction of black stereotypes, indicating that many listeners had failed to realise that Amos'n'Andy were white imposters. In 1934 Van Beuren released a pair of Amos'n'Andy cartoons, **The Rasslin' Match** and **The Lion Tamer**. Another blackface performer of this period was Slim Timblin, who wore a coonskin coat for his stage act and can be seen in the short Vitaphone comedy **Revival Day** (1930); but at the most visible end of this blackface craze was singer Al Jolson, whose **Mammy** (Warners, 1930) recreated his early years as a performer in a travelling minstel show.

1. Their final feature, **Hypnotized** (1932), was a Mack Sennett production which included a number of circus show-freaks, including midget Topsy McGee (from the Williams troupe), midget Billy Platt, and giant Ed Wolff, who later played a robot-monster in the Bela Lugosi serial **The Phantom Creeps**. Sennett was in the car-wreck which killed Charles Mack, but escaped relatively unscathed.

2. A "trick house" narrative which was remade by Jules White in 1940 as **The Spook Speaks**, one of several short Columbia comedies starring an ageing Buster Keaton.

HYPNOTIZED – PRODUCTION PHOTOGRAPH.

XUE CHEN

("Blood Stains"; Zhang Yunhe, 1929: Taiwan)

The first Taiwanese martials arts feature, and one of only a few films made by an indigenous director during the island's period of Japanese occupation. Produced by Baida Film productions, a company formed in 1929 to shoot cine-theatrical *rensa-geki* loops, **Xue Chen** was reportedly a popular release. The Japanese-Taiwanese co-production **Qixing Dong Ditu** ("Map Of Seven-Star Cave", 1933) was another martial arts film, with detective elements, but such films were rare amid the prevailing exhibition programmes of imported Chinese *wuxia* and locally-produced Japanese "national policy" instructional reels. Chinese films were finally banned in 1937, with Japan's invasion of Shanghai. Japan's rule of Taiwan (then known as Formosa) had begun in 1895, after their victory in the first Sino-Japanese war. Initial Taiwanese resistance was crushed during several months of fighting, although guerilla bands continued to attack the invaders up until 1902 – an insurrection depicted in such early Japanese films as M Pate's **Taiwan Tobatsu-Tai No Yushi** ("Warriors Of The Taiwan Annihilation Squad", 1910).

YOMA KIDAN

("Strange Monster Story"; Tetsuroku Hoshi, 1929: Japan)

From Shochiku, **Yoma Kidan** was an uncredited interpretation of Oscar Wilde's novel *The Picture Of Dorian Gray*, with added elements of black magic. A young man is granted eternal youth by a swamp-witch, but in order for the spell to keep working he must rape and butcher women by night, absorbing their vital essence. Finally he discovers his portrait, hideously disfigured, and blasts it with a gun; blood explodes from his own chest as he expires. A similar theme was explored in Shochiku's later **Shiranui Wakashu** ("Phosphorescent Fire Of Youth", 1937), in which an artist stays young by painting with the blood of the girls he cuts up; he eventually commits suicide by stabbing his self-portrait. Director of photography on **Yoma Kidan** was Eiji Tsuburaya, whose other collaborations with director Hoshi include **Furisode Kaji** ("The Burning Kimono", 1928), a psychological ghost story of death, disease and revenants. Another horror-tinged film from 1929 was Ozawa Eiga's **Hannin Hanju** ("Half Man, Half Beast"), in which a one-eyed man swears revenge against an actress who toyed with him and then discarded him. The actress falls pregnant, and gives birth to a hideous one-eyed baby; the sight of this human monster drives her mad, and she kills herself. In Toa's **Tojin Komori-Den** ("Chinese Bat Legend", 1929), two brothers seek revenge after their father was killed by a man with a bat tattoo, but are faced with a shape-shifting monster. Japanese films of this period were still silent, and the country would be one of the last in the world to fully adapt to the sonic revolution which, by the end of 1929, was poised to change cinema forever.

HANNIN HANJU – PRODUCTION PHOTOGRAPH (*OPPOSITE*).
TOJIN KOMORI-DEN – PRODUCTION PHOTOGRAPH (*OVERLEAF*).

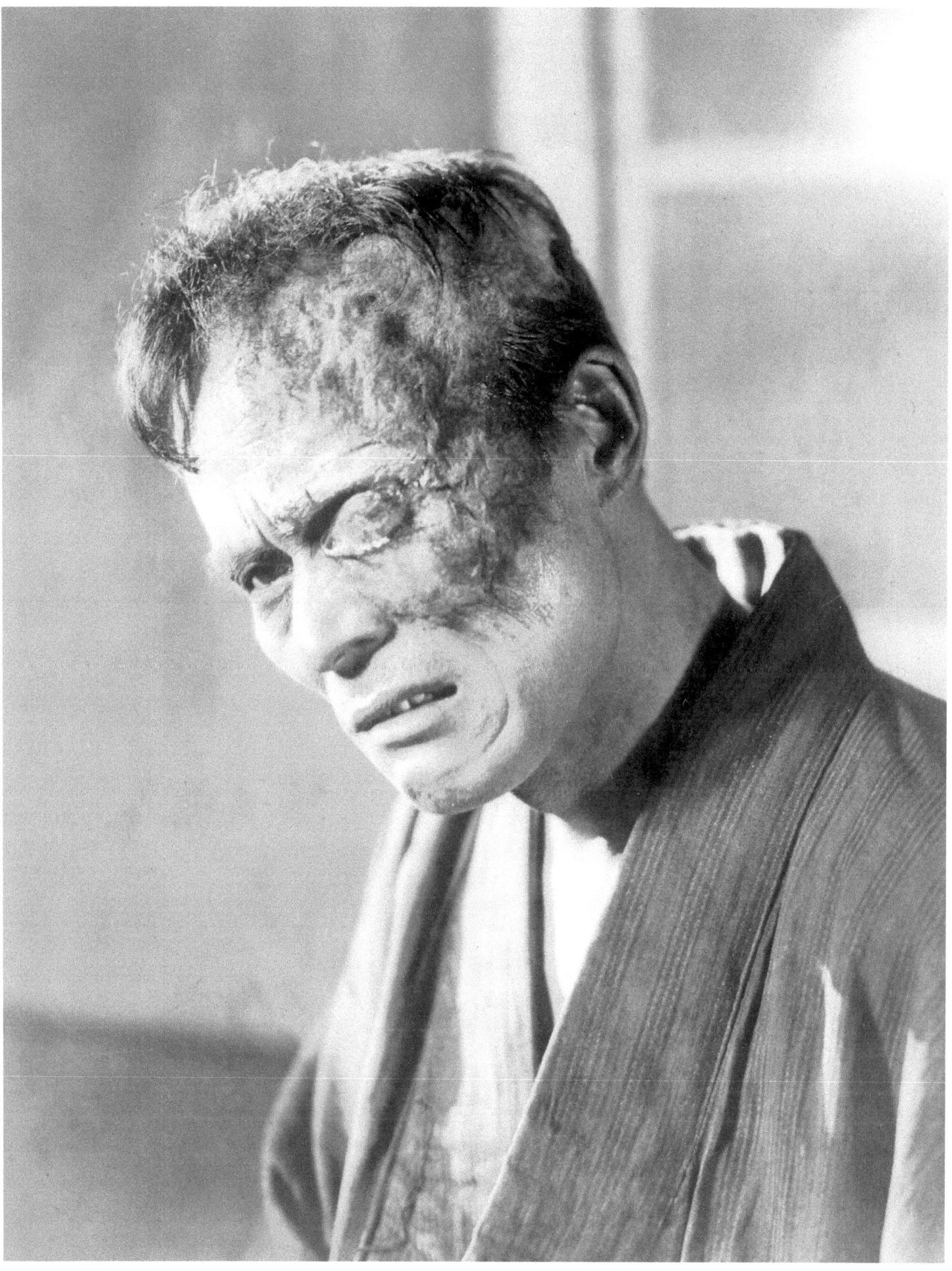

INDEX
OF FILM TITLES

Title	Page
THE ABDUCTION (1928)	18
AN AFFAIR AT THE RIVER (1925)	80
AFRICA IN FLAMES (1930)	172
L'ÂGE D'OR (1930)	92
ALFRED HITCHCOCK PRESENTS (1955-62)	139
ALIBI (1929)	**98, 99**
ALL QUIET ON THE WESTERN FRONT (1929-30)	100
THE ALTAR OF THE FLAMING GOD (1929)	73
AM ABEND (c.1910)	58
AMBUSHED (1923)	48
ANY EVENING AFTER WORK (1930)	139
ANYBODY'S WAR (1930)	184, **185**
THE APE (1928)	40
THE APE MAN (1929)	**129**
ARRESTED! DEFYING THE CENSORS (c.1925-26)	43
THE ARSON TRAIL (1929)	129
AS THE CROW FLIES (1933)	184
ASPHALT (1929)	178, **179**
THE ASSASSIN STRIKES (1929)	129
AT THE LION'S MERCY (1927)	73
ATLANTIC (1929)	105
AUTOPORTRAIT OU CE QUI MANQUE À NOUS TOUS (1930)	24
THE AVENGING CONSCIENCE (1914)	77
THE AVENGING HORDE (1931)	143
LE AVVENTURE DI PINOCCHIO (1936)	163
BABES IN TOYLAND (1934)	82
BACON GRABBERS (1929)	102
BACK FROM DEATH (1929)	129
BARE FACTS (c.1926-27)	43
BARE IN BEAR SKIN (c.1926-27)	43
THE BARGAIN OF FEAR (1927)	48
THE BARKER (1928)	67, **68**
THE BARRAGE (1928)	18
BATTLE OF THE ANTS (1922)	173
BATTLE OF THE STRONG (1931)	48
THE BATTLE STARTS (1925)	80
BATTLING BABES (c.1925-26)	43
BATTLING FOR HER LIFE (1927)	73
BE MY KING (1928)	8
BEARCAT RUNS WILD (c.1930)	41
BEDROOM FOLLIES (c.1928-29)	43
BEDROOM SECRETS (1928-29)	43
BEHIND THE CLOCK (1928)	18
BELIEVE IT OR DON'T (1934)	83
BELLAMY BAITS A TRAP (1925)	80
LA BELLE ET LA BÊTE (c.1932)	58
BERLINER STILLEBEN (1926-31)	147
THE BETRAYAL (1923)	48
BETTY'S BATH (c.1928)	41
BICEPS ET BIJOUX (1929)	24
BIG BUSINESS (1929)	**102**
BIRTH (1930)	134
BIRTH OF THE ROBOT (1936)	184
THE BIRTH OF WHITE AUSTRALIA (1928)	12
THE BLACK BOOK (1929)	129
BLACK BOTTOM BEAUTIES (c.1926-27)	43
THE BLACK DAM (1929)	129
BLACK SHADOWS (1923)	29, 31
BLACK SHADOWS (1925)	184
BLACK WATERS (1929)	104
BLACKMAIL (1929)	**104**
DER BLAUE ENGEL (1929-30)	106
THE BLUE ANGEL (1929-30)	106
BLUE BLACKBIRDS (1933)	184
BLUTENDES DEUTSCHLAND (1933)	108
BLUTMAI 1929 (1929)	53, 108
BO-RU, THE APE BOY (1934)	173
A BOTTOMLESS GRAVE (1929)	160
BRAND OF THE BEAST (1929)	160
THE BRIDGE (1929)	108
THE BRIDGE OF DOOM (1925)	184
THE BROADWAY MELODY (1929)	134
BROKEN JADE (1928)	17
BRONENOSETS POTYOMKIN (1925)	53, 92
BROTHER AGAINST BROTHER (1927)	48
BRUTALITÉS FEMININES (c.1930)	58
DIE BÜCHSE DER PANDORA (1929)	108, 109, 110
THE BULLDOGGER (1923)	48
BURIED ALIVE (1928)	48
DAS CABINET DES DR. CALIGARI (1919)	24, 77
THE CALL OF THE JUNGLE (1928)	70
CALL OF THE JUNGLE (1929)	73
THE CANARY MURDER CASE (1928)	108, **111**
CANNIBAL ISLAND (1956)	29
CANYON OF CALAMITY (1931)	48
THE CAPTURE (1928)	80
THE CARNIVAL MYSTERY (1932)	68
CAPTURED FOR SACRIFICE (1931)	143
THE CAT AND THE CANARY (1927)	55
THE CAT CREEPS (1931)	143
THE CAVE OF HORROR (1929)	184
CE SOIR A HUIT HEURES (1930)	154
THE CHARLATAN (1929)	120, **124**
CHECK AND DOUBLE-CHECK (1930)	184, **186**
CHELOVEK S KINOAPPARATOM (1929)	112, 113, 114, 115
UN CHIEN ANDALOU (1929)	102, 116, 117, 118-119
CHIKEMURI KOJINYAMA (1929)	12, 13
CHIKEMURI TAKADANOBABA (1928)	12
CHIKEMURI TAKADANOBABA (1937)	14
CHILD BRIDE (1938)	134
CHILDBIRTH WITH CAESARIAN OPERATION (1938)	134
CHINA SLAVER (1929)	17
CHINATOWN CHARLIE (1928)	18
THE CHINATOWN MYSTERY (1928)	16, **17**
THE CHINATOWN MYSTERY (1928-II)	17
CHINATOWN NIGHTS (1929)	17
CHINESE LOVE LIFE (c.1925)	18
CHINKORO HEIHEI TAMATEBAKO (1936)	58
CHOKON (1926)	**12**
CHUJI TABI NIKKI (1927)	12, 13, 43
LA CHUTE DE LA MAISON USHER (1928)	20, 21, 24
THE CLAWS OF DEATH (1928)	80
CLEO THE HAREM QUEEN (c.1925-26)	43
THE CLUE OF THE NEW PIN (1929)	104
THE CLUTCHING CLAW (1928)	17
THE CLUTCHING CLAW (1928-II)	48
COCAINE FIENDS (1935)	59
THE COAST OF PERIL (1931)	143
CODE OF THE CARNIVAL (1932)	68
THE CODE OF THE UNDERWORLD (1928)	63
COLOR CRY (1952)	184
A COLOUR BOX (1935)	184
COLOUR FLIGHT (1938)	184
THE COMET (1910)	134
CONDEMNED TO DEATH (1929)	73
CONDEMNED TO DEATH (1932)	171
THE CONVICT STRIKES (1929)	129
LA COQUILLE ET LE CLERGYMAN (1928)	22, 23
CORRIDA (1929)	23
THE COTTAGE IN THE WOODS (1925)	80
COURSE LANDAISE (1937)	24
CREEPING DOOM (1931)	143
THE CRIME CRAFT (1928)	18
THE CRIMSON CIRCLE (1929)	104
THE CROOKED HOUSE (1928)	24
CROSS FIRE (1928)	80
CURIOSA (c.1932)	58
THE DAGGER THAT FAILED (1940)	80
DANGER AHEAD (1929)	184
DANGER IN THE DARK (1929)	142
DANGER ISLAND (1931)	142, **143**
THE DANGER SIGN (1929)	129
THE DANGER TRAIL (1928)	18
DANS LES GRIFFES DE L'ARAIGNÉE (1925)	161, **163**
DARKENED ROOMS (1929)	**120**
DAUGHTER OF THE DRAGON (1931)	148, 149, 150-151
THE DEADLY PERIL (1929)	73
THE DEATH CHAMBER (1925)	184

Title	Page
THE DEATH RAIL (1929)	129
THE DEATH RAY (1931)	171
DEATH RIDES THE STORM (1931)	143
THE DEATH SHELL (1928)	18
THE DEATH TRAP (1927)	73
THE DEATH TRAP (1928)	80
DEATH'S SHADOW (1926)	184
DEATH'S SPECTER (1923)	48
THE DECEIVING MICROPHONE (1940)	80
DECOYED (1928)	80
DEFERRED PAYMENT (1929)	139
DEIN SCHICKSAL (1927-28)	64
DELA I LUDI (1932)	126
DEMONS OF THE POOL (1931)	143
THE DEN OF EVIL (1929)	160
THE DEPTH OF DANGER (1928)	17
DESERT NYMPHS (c.1928)	41
A DESPERATE CHANCE (1928)	18
DESPERATE CHOICES (1929)	142
DESPERATE DEEDS (1929)	184
DESTINO (1946)	172
DETECTIVE LLOYD (1931)	171
THE DEVIL BEAR (1929)	174
THE DEVIL BIRD (1931)	143
THE DEVIL DOGS (1940)	80
DEVIL WORSHIPPERS (1929)	160
DEVIL WORSHIPPERS (1931)	143
THE DEVIL'S DICE (1928)	17
THE DEVIL'S DICTOGRAPH (1940)	80
DIRTY WORK (1933)	33
DISASTER (1928)	80
THE DISASTROUS RESCUE (1928)	80
DIVISION (1928)	44
DIZZY DISHES (1930)	131
DÖDSSKEPPET (1929)	104
DOKTOR GIFT (1929)	54
THE DOME DOCTOR (1925)	83
DON JUAN (1926)	80
DOOMED (1928)	48
DOOMED (1929)	184
DOOR OF DREAD (1931)	143
DOUBLE WHOOPEE (1929)	102, 103
DR. PYCKLE AND MR. PRYDE (1925)	33, 35
THE DREAD PROFESSOR (1928)	80
DRUMS OF DOOM (1931)	48
THE DRUMS OF DOOM (1931-II)	143
EAGLE OR VULTURE? (1932)	68
THE EAGLE STRIKES (1932)	68
THE EAGLE'S WINGS (1932)	68
EHON MUSHA-SHUGYO (1928)	43
EISBRECHER KRASSIN (1928)	62
THE ELEPHANT AVENGER (1927)	73
THE ELEPHANT'S REVENGE (1927)	73
EMPTY SADDLES (1931)	48
END OF HOPE (1940)	80
THE END OF THE TRAIL (1928)	48
THE ENEMY OF TARZAN (1928)	70
THE ENEMY WITHIN (1928)	80
ENTR'ACTE (1924)	92
ENTUZIAZM (SIMFONIYA DONBASSA) (1929)	126, 127
ERIK LE MYSTÉRIEUX (1929)	54
ERIK THE GREAT (1928)	54
EROICHE GESTA DELL'ARTIDE (1928)	62
EROTIK (1929)	127
EROTIKON (1929)	127
1. MAI – WELTFEIERTAG DER ARBEITERKLASSE (1929)	108
DIE ERSTÜRMUNG VON LA SARRAZ (1929)	134
THE ERUPTION OF MOUNT MAYON VOLCANO (c.1929)	130
L'ÉTOILE DE MER (1928)	23, 24
EVE'S LEAVES (1930)	43
THE EXPERIMENT (1928)	24
EXTASE (1932)	127
THE FACE AT THE WINDOW (1940)	80
FACE TO FACE (1923)	48
FACING DEATH (1928)	70
THE FALL OF THE HOUSE OF USHER (1928)	24
THE FALSE MESSAGE (1927)	48
FAN DENG GUI YING (1930)	139
FANTÔMAS (1932)	54
FARMER'S FATAL FOLLY (1933)	184
FAST AND FURIOUS (1924)	83
THE FATAL HOUR (1929)	129
THE FATAL MOMENT (1929)	142
THE FATAL NAME (1931)	48
THE FATAL PLUNGE (1931)	171
FATAL SECRET (1931)	48
THE FATAL SHOT (1928)	48
THE FATAL SPARK (1940)	80
THE FEAST OF VENGEANCE (1927)	73
FEED 'EM AND WEEP (1928)	25
FESSÉES À L'ÉCOLE (c.1930)	58
THE FIERY PIT (1928)	70
THE 59TH SECOND (1925)	184
A FIGHT FOR LIFE (1927)	48
LE FIN DU MONDE (1929)	128
FINIS TERRAE (1929)	21
THE FINISHING TOUCH (1928)	7, 33
THE FIRE DETECTIVE (1929)	129
FIRE GOD'S VENGEANCE (1931)	143
THE FIRE OF THE GODS (1931)	143
THE FLAGELLANTES (c.1929)	130
THE FLAME OF LOVE (1929)	129
FLAMES OF HATE (1928)	70
FLAMES OF VENGEANCE (1923)	48
THE FLAMING ARROW (1940)	80
FLAMING ARROWS (1931)	48
THE FLAMING IDOL (1928)	63
THE FLAMING MENACE (1925)	184
THE FLAMING PERIL (1929)	160
THE FLAMING TRAP (1929)	129
FLIGHT OF WERPER (1929)	73
FLYING SQUADRON (1926)	18
FOILING THE RUSTLERS (1923)	48
A FÖLD HALÁLA (1933)	128
FOLLOW THRU (1930)	131
FORBIDDEN FRUIT (1926-27)	43
FOX MOVIETONE FOLLIES OF 1929 (1929)	130
THE FRAME-UP (1923)	48
FRAMED (1928)	80
FRAU IM MOND (1929)	132-133
FRAUENNOT-FRAUENGLÜCK (1929)	134
FREAKS (1931)	67, 68, 89
THE FREEZE OUT (1933)	184
FREIE FAHRT (1928)	64
DER FREMDE MIT DER TEUFELSMASKE (1920)	53
FRENCH DRESSING (c.1928-29)	43
DIE FREUDLOSE GASSE (1925)	140
THE FRIGHTENED LADY (1932)	171
THE FROG (1937)	80
FROM HEADQUARTERS (1929)	92
FUKKO TEITO SHINFONI (1929)	112
FURISODE KAJI (1928)	188
A FUTURE VENUS (c.1928)	41
GALLOPING FURY (1928)	17
GARR CASTLE IS ROBBED (1940)	80
THE GAS ATTACK (1928)	80
THE GAS CHAMBER (1928)	18
GASSED (1926)	184
GAUMONT GRAPHIC (1910-32)	84
GEROI DOMNY (1928)	60
GESCHLECHT IN FESSELN. DIE SEXUALNOT DER STRAFGEFNGENEN (1928)	26
GHOST CAMERA (1933)	171
THE GHOST CITY (1923)	44, 45
THE GHOST OF BELLAMY CASTLE (1925)	80
THE GHOST OF THE RANCHO (1918)	44
THE GHOST RIDES (1931)	48
GHOST VALLEY (1932)	44, 49

Title	Page
THE GIANT APE STRIKES (1927)	73
GIFTGAS (1929)	53
THE GIRL FROM SCOTLAND YARD (1937)	171
THE GIRL WHO DARED (1928)	63
GLORIFYING THE AMERICAN GIRL (1929)	134, **135**
THE GODLESS GIRL (1928)	**26, 27, 28**
GOGO KARA ASA MADE (1929)	112
GOING GA-GA (1928)	25
GOOFY BIRDS (1928)	82, **83**
GORILLA WARFARE (1929)	142
THE GORILLA'S BRIDE (1927)	73
GOW THE HEAD-HUNTER (1928)	**29, 30**
GOW THE KILLER (1933)	29
THE GREAT ARCTIC SEAL HUNT (1928)	32
THE GREAT GABBO (1929)	**238**
A GREAT TRAGEDY (1927)	73
THE GREEN ARCHER (1925)	79
THE GREEN ARCHER (1940)	79
THE GREEN ARCHER EXPOSED (1940)	79
THE GREEN SPOT MURDER (1931)	171
THE GREEN SPOT MYSTERY (1932)	171
THE GREEN TERROR (1919)	79
GRETCHEN UND FAUST (c.1928)	58
IL GRIDO DELL'AQUILA (1923)	172
GRIPPED BY THE DEATH VICE (1927)	73
GROSSTADTSCHMETTERLING (1929)	155
DEN GULE DOKTOR (1929)	171
HABEAS CORPUS (1928)	**33**
HAI TANG (1929)	155
HALLO! AFRIKA FORUDE! (1929)	**8, 9**
HANDS IN THE DARK (1925)	184
HANDS UP (1928)	48
HANNIN HANJU (1929)	187, **189**
THE HATCHET MAN (1932)	18, **19**
THE HATE SHIP (1929)	104
HAUNTED GOLD (1932)	44, **50**
THE HAUNTED HOUSE (1928)	**36, 37, 38–39**
HAUNTED HOUSE (1929)	172
HAUNTED RANGE (1926)	44
THE HAWK'S NEST (1928)	18, **19**
HÄXAN (1921-22)	164
HEARTS OF STEEL (1929)	184
HEI YI GUAI REN (1929)	139
HET HEKSENLIED (1928)	40
HELL'S ANGELS (1927-1930)	102
HELL'S BELLS (1929)	**138**
HELL'S FIRE (1934)	**139**
HEROES OF THE LAW (1931)	171
HEXENLIED (1909)	40
DAS HEXENLIED (1919)	40
HICKMAN THE FOX (1928)	40
HIDDEN ENEMIES (1928)	79
THE HIDDEN HAND (1929)	129
THE HIDDEN TREASURE (1928)	44
HIPS, HIPS, HOORAY! (1933)	25
HISTOIRE DE DÉTECTIVE (1929)	154
HOLLYWOOD PLAYTHINGS (1930)	59
THE HOLLYWOOD REVUE OF 1929 (1929)	89
HOLLYWOOD SAND WITCHES (c.1928)	41
HOLLYWOOD SCANDALS (c.1925-26)	43
HONG XIA (1929)	95
HOODOO RANCH (1926)	44
HOP OFF (1928)	82
L'HORLOGE MAGIQUE (1928)	**162**
HORO ZANMAI (1928)	43
HORROR IN THE DARK (1931)	48
HOT HOOFS (1933)	184
HOUSE OF FEAR (1939)	55
HOUSE OF HATE (1931)	48
THE HOUSE OF HORROR (1928)	36, 37
HOUSE OF PERIL (1925)	184
THE HOUSE OF PERIL (1928)	79
THE HOUSE OF TERROR (1928)	44
HUANGJIANG NU XIA (1930)	52
HUMAN RATS (1926)	184
A HUMAN SACRIFICE (1929)	73
HUMAN SACRIFICE (1931)	143
HUN SHI MO WANG (1929)	139
HUO SHAO BAI HUA TAI (1929)	**52**
HUO SHAO HONG LIAN SI (1928-31)	**52**
HUO SHAO QI XING LOU (1929)	52
HURLED THROUGH SPACE (1928)	48
HYPNOTIZED (1932)	**188**
THE IDOL: A PHANTASY (c.1928)	41
IM ANFANG WAR DAS WORT... (1928)	64
IM SCHATTEN DER MASCHINE (1928)	53
IMPATIENCE (1928)	154
IMPRISONED IN THE NORTH TOWER (1931)	171
IN QUEST OF THE GOLDEN PRINCE (1924)	29
IN THE ENEMY'S HANDS (1928)	80
IN THE ENEMY'S STRONGHOLD (1925)	80
IN THE PHANTOM'S DEN (1928)	63
INTO THE LION'S JAWS (1927)	73
INTO THE UNKNOWN (1929)	142
THE INVISIBLE ENEMY (1931)	48
THE INVISIBLE HAND (1928)	17
THE IRRESPONSIBLES (1929)	139
ISLAND OF LOST SOULS (1932)	82
IT'S A BIRD (1930)	83
IZIASHNAYA ZHIZN (1932)	126
THE JAIL DELIVERY (1928)	80
JAWS OF DEATH (1928)	70
THE JAWS OF DEATH (1929)	73
JAWS OF DOOM (1926)	184
JAWS OF THE JUNGLE (1931)	143
JAZZ BABIES (c.1928)	41
JENSEITS DER STRASSE (1929)	**140**
THE JEWELS OF OPAR (1929)	73
JIU LONG SHAN (1930)	52
JUNGLE JUSTICE (1929)	142
JUNGLE JUSTICE (1931)	143
THE JUNGLE KING (1927)	73
JUNGLE TRAILS (1927)	73
THE JUNGLE TRAITOR (1928)	70
JUSTICE (1926)	184
K.S.E. – KOMSOMOL SHEF ELEKTRIFIKATSII (1932)	126
KALEIDOSCOPE (1935)	184
KATORGA (1928)	152
THE KID FROM BORNEO (1933)	8
KID SPEED (1924)	33
KILL OR BE KILLED (1942)	184
KING COWBOY (1928)	44, **48**
KING KONG (1932)	29, **174**
THE KING OF THE JUNGLE (1927)	71, **73**
KING OF THE KONGO (1929)	**142**
KING OF THE WILD (1931)	142, **143, 144–145**
KLOSTERGEHEIMNISSE (c.1912)	58
KOBUTORI (1929)	58
KONG GU YUAN SHENG (1930)	139
KONGO (1932)	89
KONVEYYER SMERT (1932)	**60, 61**
KUBI NO ZA (1929)	146
KUNISADA CHUJI (1924)	43
KUNISADA CHUJI (1933)	43
DIE KÜPPLERIN (1925)	178
KURAMA TENGU (1928)	43
KURAMA TENGU: IMON KAKUBEIJISHI (1927)	43
KURAMA TENGU: KYOFU JIDAI (1928)	43
KUTSU-JUKU SEIKLUSI (1931)	**172**
HET KWADE OOG (1937)	154
LADIES' NIGHT IN A TURKISH BATH (c.1928-29)	43
THE LAST MOMENT (1927)	**54**
THE LAST PERFORMANCE (1928-29)	**54**
THE LAST STAND (1927)	48
THE LAST WARNING (1928)	**55**
THE LAW WINS (1928)	63
LEAGUE OF THE LAWLESS (1931)	48
THE LEAP OF DEATH (1929)	**160**

Title	Page
THE LEOPARD'S LAIR (1928)	70
LEOPARD'S LAIR (1931)	143
THE LEOPARDS' ATTACK (1927)	73
LEPROSY (c.1929)	130
LICHTSPIEL SCHWARZ-WEISS-GRAU (1929)	147
DAS LIED VOM LEBEN (1931)	134
A LIFE AT STAKE (1928)	80
THE LIGHTNING WARRIOR (1931)	44, 48, 49
LIKVIDATSIYA PRORYVA NA ZAVODE «MANOMETR» (1931)	60
LIMEHOUSE BLUES (1934)	157, 158-159
THE LION TAMER (1934)	188
THE LION'S LAIR (1931)	143
THE LION'S LEAP (1928)	70
THE LIVING DEAD (1925)	184
THE LIVING DEAD (1933/35)	171
LLOYD OF THE C.I.D. (1931)	171
LOOP OF DEATH (1929)	73
THE LOST EMPIRE (1929)	29
LOST IN THE JUNGLE (1928)	70
LOT IN SODOM (1933)	24
THE LOVE CRY (1928)	70
LOVE ON LEAVE (1940)	139
LULU (1980)	108
THE LURE OF THE SERPENT (c.1926-27)	43
THE MAELSTROM (1923)	48
MAMBA (1929)	89, 91
MAMMY (1930)	187, 188
THE MAN FROM NOWHERE (1929)	184
THE MAN OF A MILLION VOICES (1932)	68
THE MAN OF MYSTERY (1929)	129
MAN OF MYSTERY (1929)	142
MAN TO MAN (1923)	48
THE MAN WHO KNEW (1931)	48
THE MAN WHO KNEW (1932)	68
THE MAN WHO LAUGHS (1928)	56, 57
THE MAN WITHOUT A FACE (1928)	17, 18
MAN EATERS (1931)	143
MANOMETR-1 (1930)	60
MANOMETR-2 (1931)	60
THE MARK OF CRIME (1928)	18
MARK OF THE FROG (1928)	80
THE MASK OF FU MANCHU (1932)	108, 148
DER MASKIERTE SCHRECKEN (1921)	53
THE MASTER STRIKES (1928)	18
MELODIE DES HERZENS (1929)	105
MENACE OF THE PAST (1929)	129
MESSE NOIRE (c.1928)	58
METROPOLIS (1925-26)	104, 132
MIDNIGHT AND NOSES (1925)	33
THE MIDNIGHT INTRUDER (1923)	48
A MIDNIGHT MAID (c.1928-29)	43
THE MIDNIGHT WARNING (1925)	80
MIRROR OF TREACHERY (1940)	80
MISSING (1926)	184
MISSING MEN (1928)	44
IL MISTERO DELL'ARTIDE (1930)	62
A MODERN VENUS (c.1928-29)	43
MODORI-BASHI (1929)	146
LE MOINE (c.1920)	58
MOMOTARO (1918)	58
MOOSE HUNTING IN NEWFOUNDLAND (1905)	32
MOR VRAN (1930)	21
MOROCCO (1930)	106, 107
LA MORT DE LA TERRE (1933)	128
MUTINY (1931)	143
MUTTER KRAUSENS FAHRT INS GLÜCK (1929)	53
LES MYSTÈRES DU CHÂTEAU DE DÉ (1929)	23, 24
LES MYSTÈRES DU COUVENT (c.1928)	58
THE MYSTERIOUS DR. FU MANCHU (1929)	148
THE MYSTERIOUS THIRTEEN (1928)	17
A MYSTERIOUS VISITOR (1928)	18
MYSTERY AT THE VILLA ROSE (1930)	171
THE MYSTERY MILL (1929)	129
THE MYSTERY OF LOST RANCH (1925)	44, 49
THE MYSTERY RIDER (1928)	44, 45, 48
THE MYSTERY ROOM (1928)	63
THE MYSTERY SHIP (1925)	80
N. OR N.W. (1937)	184
NACHTWELT (1929)	155
THE NAKED TRUTH (c.1928-29)	43
NAZO NO NINGYO-SHI (1928)	146
THE NECKLACE OF TREACHERY (1940)	80
NERONE (1930)	172
NIHON-ICHI MOMOTARO (1928)	58
NIONGA (1925)	173
NO ESCAPE (1927)	73
NOTICIARIO DE CINE CLUB (1930)	53
NOVIY GULLIVYER (1935)	163
OBLOMOK IMPERII (1929)	152, 153
ODINNADTSATYI (1928)	53
OFFICER 444 (1926)	184
ON FLAMING WATERS (1929)	129
ON THE SPOT (1932)	68
ON THE STORM KING ROAD (1925)	80
ON TRIAL (1928)	80, 81
ONE STOLEN NIGHT (1929)	164, 170
ONE WAS TAKEN (1929)	84
ONE-EYED MONSTERS (1927)	73
OOKA SEIDAN SUZUKAWA GENJURO (1928)	14
OOKA SEIDAN SUZUKAWA GENJURO (1928-II)	14
OPIUM (1928)	58
L'OR DES MERS (1931)	21
THE ORDEAL OF FIRE (1931)	48
ORIENTAL FANTASY (c.1928-29)	43
OSEN (1939)	152
OUR GANG (1922-38)	8
OUT OF THE NIGHT (1928)	44
OUT OF THE SHADOWS (1929)	129
THE PACE THAT KILLS (1928)	59
THE PACE THAT KILLS (1935)	59
PAID (1930)	28
A PAIR OF SOCKS (1933)	184
PAINTED FACES (1931)	48
A PAIR OF TIGHTS (1929)	25
THE PANTHER AT BAY (1931)	171
THE PANTHER STRIKES (1931)	171
THE PANTHER'S CUNNING (1931)	171
THE PANTHER'S LAIR (1931)	171
PARIS AFTER DARK (1934)	128
PAT UND PATACHON ALS KANNIBALEN (1929)	8
PATHÉ GAZETTE (1918-45)	84
PAWNS OF EVIL (1928)	44
PAYING THE PENALTY (1928)	80
LE PAYSAN ET LA NONNE (c.1920)	58
PEARLS AND SAVAGES (1921)	29
THE PENALTY (1928)	80
THE PEOPLE AT NO. 19 (1949)	139
A PERILOUS MISSION (1928)	18
PERILOUS PATHS (1928)	70
PERILOUS TRAILS (1928)	44
PERILOUS WATERS (1925)	184
PERILS OF THE JUNGLE (1927)	71, 73, 76
LA PERLE (1929)	154
PERWOJE MAJA W BERLINE (1929)	108
PESN O GEROYAKH (1931)	127
PESN O METALLE (1928)	60
PETE ROLEUM AND HIS COUSINS (1939)	83
PETT AND POTT (1934)	178
THE PHANTOM (1928)	63
PHANTOM CITY (1928)	44, 46-47
THE PHANTOM CREEPS (1939)	188
THE PHANTOM OF THE OPERA (1925)	139
THE PHANTOM OF THE WEST (1931)	44, 48, 50
THE PHANTOM'S TRAP (1928)	63
PICCADILLY (1929)	155, 156
PIKK DÁMA (1921)	54
PINHOLES (1932)	68
THE PIT OF DARKNESS (1929)	129

Title	Page
THE PIT OF PERIL (1929)	184
PIT OF PERIL (1931)	143
PODVIG VO LDAKH (1928)	62
THE POISON DART (1931)	171
POLICE REPORTER (1928)	63
POLIZEIBERICHT ÜBERFALL (1928)	64
POUR VOS BEAUX YEUX (1929)	154
THE POWER GOD (1925)	184
PRATER (1929)	112
PRICE OF SILENCE (1931)	48
THE PRIMROSE PATH (1931)	59
PRISON BARS BECKON (1940)	80
PRISONER OF THE APES (1929)	73
PRISONERS IN THE SKY (1928)	18
LE PROFESSEUR (c.1930)	58
PRORYV NA ZAVODE (1930)	60
THE PURLOINED PAPERS (1925)	184
PUTTING PANTS ON PHILIP (1927)	33, 35
PUTYOVKA V ZHIZN (1929)	126
PYATILETKA: PLAN VELIKIH RABOT (1929)	126
QIONG YA JIAO GONG (1933)	65
QIXING DONG DITU (1933)	188
QUEEN KELLY (1928)	138
THE QUEEN OF SIN (c.1928-29)	43
QUEEN OF THE NORTHWOODS (1929)	160
THE QUEST FOR THE STEGOSAUR (c.1928)	24
A RACE WITH DEATH (1928)	80
THE RACE WITH DEATH (1931)	171
THE RADIO RAY (1926)	184
RAINBOW DANCE (1936)	184
RANCHO NOTORIOUS (1952)	106
THE RASSLIN' MATCH (1934)	188
THE RECKONING (1928)	70
RED HOT MAMMA (c.1925-26)	43
RED SHADOWS (1931)	48
RETFAERDIGHEDENS TRIUMF (1931)	63
THE RETURN OF DR. FU MANCHU (1930)	148, 149
THE RETURN OF THE FROG (1939)	80
RETURN OF THE TERROR (1934)	80
REVENGE (1928)	44
REVIVAL DAY (1930)	188
THE RING OF FATE (1925)	184
THE ROAD AGENT (1927)	48
THE ROAD OF HEALTH (1938)	139
THE ROAD OF PERIL (1928)	18
THE ROAD TO OPAR (1929)	73
RODINA ZOVYOT (1936)	126
ROGUE'S ROUNDUP (1931)	48
LE ROMAN DE RENARD (1929-30)	161
ROMANCE SENTIMENTALE (1929)	134
RONIN JIGOKU (1926)	146
RONIN-GAI (1928)	146
DER ROTE KREIS (1928)	104, 105
SÃO PAULO, SINFONIA DA METRÓPOLE (1929)	112
SAY AH-H! (1928)	82
SCARED STIFF (1926)	33
THE SCARLET EMPRESS (1934)	106
THE SCARLET SCOURGE (1929)	184
DAS SCHIFF DER VERLORENEN MENSCHEN (1929)	97
SCHMUTZIGES GELD (1928)	155
SCHWARZE MESSE (c.1928)	58
SCOTLAND YARD (1930)	171
THE SCOTLAND YARD MYSTERY (1933)	171
SEAL HUNTING IN NEWFOUNDLAND (1912)	32
SEALED LIPS (1931)	143
THE SECOND HUNDRED YEARS (1927)	33, 34, 35
THE SECRET MISSION (1928)	18
SECRET OF THE CAVE (1931)	48
THE SECRET OF THE VAULT (1929)	129
SECRET OF THE VOLCANO (1931)	143
SECRET PASSAGE (1928)	44
THE SECRET PASSAGE (1940)	80
THE SECRET TUBE (1928)	63
SECRETS OF NATURE (1922-33)	173
SENTENCED TO DEATH (1929)	142
SEVEN FOOTPRINTS TO SATAN (1929)	36, 164-169, 170
THE SHADOW (1933)	171
THE SHADOW OF THE EAGLE (1932)	68
THE SHADOW UNMASKED (1932)	68
SHANGHAI EXPRESS (1932)	106, 107
THE SHANGHAI GESTURE (1941)	106
SHANHKAYSKIY DOKUMENT (1928)	65
SHINPAN OOKA SEIDAN (1928)	14
SHINPAN OOKA SEIDAN (1928-II)	14
SHINPAN OOKA SEIDAN (1928-III)	14, 15
SHINPEN TANGE SAZEN: YOTO-HEN (1938)	14
SHIRANUI WAKASHU (1937)	188
A SHOT IN THE NIGHT (1929)	129
SIDE SHOW (1931)	67
THE SIDESHOW (1928)	66, 67
THE SIGN OF THE VAMPIRE (c.1928)	24
THE SILENT HOUSE (1929)	171
SILK STOCKING BRIGADE (c.1928-29)	43
SILLY SYMPHONIES (1929-39)	138, 172
SILVER VALLEY (1927)	44, 49
A SIMPLE SAP (1928)	83
SIRENS OF THE SEA (c.1928)	41
SKARLATINA (1924)	152
THE SKELETON DANCE (1929)	172
SKELETON FROLIC (1937)	172
THE SKY CLEARS (1928)	18
SKYSCRAPER SYMPHONY (1929)	112
A SLEEPLESS NIGHT (1940)	83
THE SLINKING DEMONS (1927)	73
THE SMOKE CLEARS AWAY (1925)	80
SOLE! (1929)	172
SOMNAMBOL (1927-28)	120
SOZEN-JI BABA (1928)	146
LE SPECTRE VERT (1930)	120, 122-123
SPOOK RANCH (1925)	44
THE SPOOK SPEAKS (1940)	188
THE SPY (1929)	108
STAIRWAY OF DOOM (1931)	48
STALKING AND SHOOTING CARIBOU IN NEWFOUNDLAND (1907)	32
STALNOY PUT (1929)	60
THE STAMPEDE (1928)	48
STAMPEDE (1929)	172
STARK MAD (1929)	174, 175, 176-177
STARK NATURE (1930)	172
STEKLYANNYY GLAZ (1928)	59
THE STING OF DEATH (1927)	73
THE STOLEN GOLD (1923)	48
THE STORM BREAKS (1928)	18
THE STORM'S LASH (1925)	184
THE STRANGLER (1932)	171
THE STRIPED TERROR (1927)	73
STRUGGLE FOR LIFE (1935)	173
SUDAN (1935)	173
SUGAR DADDIES (1927)	33, 34
SWEENEY TODD (1928)	69
SWEET SIXTEEN (c.1926-27)	43
SWIRLING WATERS (1928)	44
TAGEBUCH EINER VERLORENEN (1918)	178
TAGEBUCH EINER VERLORENEN (1929)	178, 179
TAIWAN TOBATSU-TAI NO YUSHI (1910)	188
TAKO NO HONE (1927)	58
TALL STORY COMEDIES (1934)	83
TALONS OF THE NIGHT (1923)	48
TANTOR THE TERROR (1929)	73
TARZAN AND THE GOLDEN LION (1927)	73
TARZAN THE MIGHTY (1928)	70, 71, 72
TARZAN THE TERRIBLE (1929)	71
TARZAN THE TIGER (1929)	70, 71, 73, 74-75
TARZAN'S RAGE (1929)	73
TARZAN'S TRIUMPH (1929)	73
THE TELEPHONE CIPHER (1932)	68
THE TELLTALE HEART (1928)	77
TEMPLE OF BEASTS (1929)	142

Title	Page
TEN NIGHTS IN A BAR ROOM (1931)	59
THE TERRIBLE PEOPLE (1928)	80
THE TERROR (1928)	36, **78-79**
THE TERROR (1938)	80, **81**
THE TERROR OF TARZAN (1928)	70
TERRORS (1930)	24
TERRORS OF THE JUNGLE (1929)	142
A TEST FOR LOVE (1937)	139
THAT SCHOOLGIRL COMPLEXION (c.1928-29)	43
THERE IT IS (1928)	82
A THIEF IN THE DARK (1928)	120, **125**
A THIEF IN THE NIGHT (1928)	70
THINGS TO COME (1936)	147
THE THIRTEENTH CHAIR (1929)	120, **121**
THE THIRTEENTH HOUR (1928)	17
THE THUNDERING HERD (1923)	48
THE TIGER MEN (1927)	73
TIGER OF DESTINY (1931)	143
THE TIGER'S CLAW (1928)	18
THE TIGER'S DEN (1927)	73
THE TIGER'S MARK (1928)	18
THE TIGER'S SHADOW (1928)	17, **18**
DIE TODESZECHE (1930)	53
TOJIN KOMORI-DEN (1929)	188, **190-191**
TOKAIDO KOSHIN-KYOKU TANUKI TAIJI (1929)	43
TONGUES OF FLAME (1928)	44
TRACKED BY WIRELESS (1931)	171
TRADER HORN (1929-31)	179, 180, **182**, **183**
A TRAGEDY OF SPEED!! (1920)	**84**
THE TRAIL OF BLOOD (1927)	73
TRAIL OF VENGEANCE (1929)	184
TRAITOR'S HOUR (1931)	48
THE TRANSFORMED ISLE: BARBARISM TO CHRISTIANITY (1924)	32
THE TRAP SPRINGS (1931)	171
TRAPPED (1925)	184
TRAPPED (1926)	184
TRAPPED (1927)	48
TRAPPED (1928)	48
TRAPPED BY FATE (1929)	184
TRAPPED BY THE FIEND (1929)	160
TREACHERY (1925)	184
TRIAL FOR MARRIAGE (1936)	139
13 DNEY. DELO PROMPARTII (1930)	126
TRIPLE VENGEANCE (1928)	80
TSUKI NO MIYA NO OJOSAMA (1934)	58
TURKSIB (1929)	60
TUSALAVA (1929)	184
TWO BLACK CROWS IN AFRICA (1933)	184
UMON ICHIBAN TEGARA NANBAN YUREI (1929)	43
UMS TÄGLICHE BROT (1929)	53
UNDERGROUND TRAP (1926)	184
UNDERVERDENENS MYSTISKE HERSKER (1931)	63
THE UNHOLY NIGHT 1929)	120, **124**
THE UNKNOWN (1927)	67
UNMASKED (1928)	18
UNMASKED (1928-II)	48
UNMASKED (1929)	120
UNTER DER LATERNE (1928)	140, **141**
UNTITLED [DAKAR-DJIBOUTI MISSION] (1931-33)	92
UNVEILED (c.1928-29)	43
URASHIMA TARO (1931)	58
VANISHING JEWELS (1940)	80
THE VANISHING RIDER (1927)	44, 48, **51**
VÄSTFRONTEN 1918 (1930)	101
VENGEANCE (1927)	48
THE VENGEANCE OF LA (1929)	73
DIE VERRUFENEN (1925)	140, **141**
VIERGES ET DEMI-VIERGES (c.1930)	58
THE VIKING (1930)	32
THE VIRGIN OF BAGDAD (c.1928-29)	43
THE VOICE FROM THE SKY (1929)	184
THE WAGES OF SIN (1925)	184
THE WALKING DEAD (1936)	40
WAS WIR WOLLEN – WAS WIR NICHT WOLLEN (1928)	53
THE WATER TRAP (1923)	48
THE WATERS OF DEATH (1927)	48
WEST OF ZANZIBAR (1928)	85, 86, 87, **88**, 89
WESTFRONT 1918 (1930)	100, **101**
THE WHARF RAT (1928)	63
WHAT GIRLS DO WHEN ALONE (1928-29)	43
WHEEL OF DESTINY (1927)	67
WHEN THIEVES FALL OUT (1932)	68
WHERE EAST IS EAST (1929)	89, **90**
WHILE LONDON SLEEPS (1926)	48, **51**
WHITE CARGO (1929)	89, **91**
WHITE GORILLA (1945)	71
WHITE SHADOWS IN THE SOUTH SEAS (1928)	**92**
WHITE ZOMBIE (1932)	92
WHOOPEE! (1930)	134, **136**
WHOOZIT (1928)	82
WHY BRING THAT UP? (1929)	184, **185**
WHY GIRLS WALK HOME (c.1929)	41
WHY SAILORS GO WRONG (1928)	8, **9**
WILD BABIES (1932)	8, **10-11**
WILD OYSTERS (1941)	83
THE WIND (1928)	**93**, **94**
WINGS OF DEATH (1929)	160
THE WINGS OF FURY (1927)	48
WITTE VLAM (1930)	**154**
THE WOLF MAN (1931)	48
THE WOLF-DEVIL STRIKES (1929)	160
THE WOLF-DEVIL'S CHALLENGE (1929)	160
THE WOOD NYMPH (c.1928)	41
THE WRECK (1928)	17
WRONG AGAIN (1928)	102, **103**
WU NU FUCHOU (1928)	95
THE X-RAY GOWN (c.1928-29)	43
XUE CHEN (1929)	188
YEBAN GESHENG (1937)	139
YOMA KIDAN (1929)	185
YOU CAN'T WIN (1928)	63
YOU'LL BE SORRY (1928)	82
ZANJIN ZANBAKEN (1928)	**146**
ZEITBERICHT – ZEITGESCHICHTE (1928)	53
ZEITPROBLEME. WIE DER ARBEITER WOHNT (1930)	53
ZEMLYA ZHAZHDET (1930-31)	126
ZOKU BANKA JIGOKU (1928)	43
LA ZONE (1928)	95
ZVENIGORA (1927)	53
ZWISCHEN VIERZEHN UND SIEBZEHN (1929)	134

PHOTO CREDITS

The authors and publishers wish to acknowledge the institutions and/or individuals who provided images for this book and the series as a whole, as follows: MOMA; Margaret Herrick Library; USC; Eastman House; Library of Congress; UCLA; BFI; Cineteca Nacional; UNAM; China Film Archives; National Film Archive of Japan; Kawakita Memorial Library; Cinématheque Française; Deutsche Kinemathek; Národní Filmový Archiv; Nemzeti Filmintézet; Filmoteca Española; Cineteca Nazionale; Wien Film Museum; Wien Theater Museum; Deutsche Film Institut; Archivio Fotografico; and DFI. Any omission will be corrected in future printings. No image may be copied or reused without appropriate consent. With special thanks to Nero-Film AG (Berlin) for **Die Büchse Der Pandora**.

THE COMPLETE 15-VOLUME SERIES (1872-1949)

www.ingramcontent.com/pod-product-compliance
Lightning Source LLC
Chambersburg PA
CBHW051310110526
44590CB00031B/4364